Data-Driven Marketing

Data-Driven Marketing

The *15* Metrics Everyone in Marketing Should Know

Mark Jeffery   Kellogg School of Management

WILEY

John Wiley & Sons, Inc.

Published by John Wiley & Sons, Inc., Hoboken, New Jersey.
Published simultaneously in Canada.

For general information on our other products and services or for technical support, please contact our Customer Care Department within the United States at (800) 762-2974, outside the United States at (317) 572-3993 or fax (317) 572-4002.

Wiley also publishes its books in a variety of electronic formats. Some content that appears in print may not be available in electronic books. For more information about Wiley products, visit our web site at www.wiley.com.

Library of Congress Cataloging-in-Publication Data:
Jeffery, Mark, 1965-
  Data-driven marketing : the 15 metrics everyone in marketing should know / Mark Jeffery.
    p. cm.
  ISBN 978-0-470-50454-3 (cloth)
  1. Marketing research. 2. Marketing–Mathematical models. 3. Marketing–Case studies.
  I. Title.
  HF5415.2.J44 2010
  658.8'3—dc22

                                                                      2009035908

Printed in the United States of America.

12

To Ann, Anthony, and Mateo.

CONTENTS

DOWNLOADABLE ROMI RESOURCES

ACKNOWLEDGMENTS

There are many people who have helped in my journey to write this book. First, I want to thank Richard Narramore, my editor at John Wiley & Sons, Inc., for his guidance and constructive input on the drafts of the manuscript. I also want to thank Mohan Sawhney, director of the Center for Research on Technology and Innovation (CRTI), for his support and early input on the research; and Dipak Jain, dean of the Kellogg School, 2001–2009, for enabling a significant sample for the research and for his guidance. The research was in collaboration with Saurabh Mishrah and Alex Krasnikov, as post-doctoral researchers at CRTI. They are now both professors, and I am incredibly appreciative of their effort. The research discussed in Chapters 1 and 11 was partially funded by Teradata, and I want to thank Mary Gros for her continual enthusiasm.

Many executives contributed their experience through my interviews, and I have quoted them throughout. I want to particularly thank Rob Griffin for his in-depth feedback and input on the Internet search marketing in Chapter 7; David Schrader for providing the DIRECTV, NAB, and Ping case studies in Chapter 9; and Richard Winter for his deep insights and contribution to the architecture discussion in Chapter 10. Thanks also to Mike Collins and Nina Rotello for their detailed proofreading and feedback on the manuscript, and to Rob Komorous-King for the excellent graphics throughout. Finally, this book would not have been possible without my wife, Ann—thanks for your understanding and support!

INTRODUCTION

In October 2008, a few months after the fall of Bear Stearns and the start of the financial meltdown, I had a meeting with a Fortune 500 chief marketing officer (CMO). I was invited to talk about marketing metrics but I wanted to understand the real challenge, so I asked: "What is keeping you up at night?"

"Well, if you really want to know, I talked with the chairman yesterday and he wants to cut my budget by 36 percent. I thought it was a joke, but today I realize the chairman is serious."

At 8:00 A.M. the next morning I received a call on my cell: "Mark, I have a meeting with the chairman at 2:00 P.M. today and need your help."

These are the most difficult economic times in more than two decades, and this CMO is not alone. Marketers are struggling to justify their budgets and are constantly being asked to do more with less. Marketing is frequently viewed with skepticism by nonmarketing business executives and when times are tough is often one of the first budget cuts. For marketing managers the challenge of providing concrete results is amplified since branding and awareness are "fuzzy" and are not directly related to sales revenues.

My research of 252 firms, capturing $53 billion of annual marketing spending, shows that many marketers struggle with marketing measurement; 55 percent of the marketing executives surveyed reported that their staff does not understand essential marketing metrics, and more than 80 percent of organizations do not use data-driven marketing. These gaps can be overcome, without a major investment in time and resources, by focusing on measuring the right metrics in the right way.

This book is intended for anyone in marketing who wants to significantly improve his or her marketing performance and justify marketing spending, and for nonmarketing managers who want to drive real results from marketing. Instead of listing the 50 or 100 metrics applicable to marketing, I focus on the 15 that are really important. I show how to actually use these metrics to quantify the value of marketing and radically improve marketing performance. My research also shows how firms that master data-driven marketing have significantly better financial performance relative to competitors. The approach of focusing on just 15 metrics has the benefit that you can easily master and apply the principles. I give detailed examples for both large and small organizations, and free downloadable Excel spreadsheet templates complement all the quantitative examples.

The book is divided into three sections: Part I: Essentials, Part II: 15 Metrics to Radically Improve Marketing Performance, and Part III: The Next Level. The book takes a systematic and pragmatic approach toward articulating data-driven marketing and marketing measurement principles, but after Chapter 3 can be read in any order. Part I: Essentials consists of three chapters. The first chapter discusses the marketing divide, that a few firms "get" data-driven marketing and many do not, and introduces the 15 essential metrics. Chapter 2 answers the question "Where do I start?" and discusses strategies to overcome the five roadblocks. Chapter 3 provides a systematic framework for strategic marketing measurement using the 10 classical metrics.

The 15 metrics are expanded upon in detail in Part II, and the interested reader can jump directly to the metrics of interest. The Internet is increasingly an essential component of all marketing campaigns, and 5 of the 15 metrics are devoted to this important medium. Chapter 7 is an in-depth discussion of Internet marketing and the five new-age metrics—you can jump to this chapter at any time. If you are rusty on financial concepts, I suggest reading the finance for marketers discussion in Chapter 5 before tackling financial return on marketing investment (ROMI) and customer lifetime value (CLTV) in Chapter 6.

Part III of the book focuses on advanced topics. I give strategies to take the data-driven marketing principles and metrics of the previous chapters to the next level. These four chapters discuss agile marketing, analytic and event-driven marketing, data-driven marketing infrastructure, essential marketing processes to drive performance and the Creative X-factor. This book is not a textbook; however, it can act as a good supplement in a course on data-driven marketing. A short appendix is provided with resources for instructors interested in using this book and related case studies in the classroom.

My hope is that this book will provide you with deep insights into how marketing delivers value and how to use the 15 essential metrics for marketing as levers to strategically drive performance in your organization.

—Mark Jeffery
Evanston, IL

Essentials

The Marketing Divide

Why 80 Percent of Companies Don't Make Data-Driven Marketing Decisions—And Those Who Do Are the Leaders

A senior marketing manager in a Fortune 100 company once told me: "Every week I have to go to a gun fight, the senior executive leadership meeting, and I am tired of going to this gunfight carrying only a knife." His frustration was the result of having no concrete data to answer hard questions about the value of marketing activities in his division. We are living in difficult times, and marketing measurement and data-driven marketing are becoming increasingly important. Now more than ever, managers need to justify their marketing spending, show the value that they create for the business, and radically improve their marketing performance.

Why is data-driven marketing so difficult for many organizations? There are many reasons, ranging from "we don't know how" to the challenge that branding and awareness marketing activities are fuzzy and don't directly impact sales revenues in a short time period. The challenge is compounded by the exponential growth of data. International Data Corporation (IDC) estimates that data storage is growing at 60 percent per year, which suggests the volume of stored data is doubling approximately every 20 months. These vast amounts of data are overwhelming and marketers struggle, with limited time and resources, to measure the efficacy of what they do.

A few marketers and organizations, however, have mastered data-driven marketing principles and marketing metrics. Invariably, these individuals are heroes within their firms, are promoted faster, and rise to more senior positions. As we will see, organizations that embrace marketing metrics and create a data-driven marketing culture have a competitive advantage that results in significantly better financial performance than that of their competitors.

A few years ago, I asked Barry Judge, now senior vice president and chief marketing officer (CMO) of Best Buy, who Best Buy's primary competitor was. He said Wal-Mart. Not so surprising since Wal-Mart is the world's largest retail channel; and with its amazingly efficient supply chain and economy of scale, driving price and margins to the bare minimum, the company has radically changed the global retail landscape. However, I thought he was going to say Circuit City, so I asked why he did not.

"They just don't get it," he told me.

Circuit City's marketing strategy was to constantly run sales. This drew customers into stores and drove sales revenues. But since the advent of Wal-Mart, margins in retail are thin, so running sales actually loses money for the business; that is, it has a negative profitability. The result, as Judge put it, is a "death spiral," where continual sales are needed to drive revenues that continuously lose money.

Of course, the Circuit City story is now history; the firm went bankrupt and liquidated in January 2009. A similar story has played out across mid-tier retail in the United States over the last two decades: Marshall Field's in Chicago and John Wanamaker, the venerable Philadelphia retailer, for example, are now consolidated, along with hundreds of other well-known regional retailers that were unable to compete profitably. These stores now fly the Macy's flag.

But Best Buy is different. Sure, a significant amount of the marketing budget is spent on demand generation marketing—this is marketing designed to get customers into the stores. However, Best Buy spends more money on branding, customer relationship management, and infrastructure to support data-driven marketing compared with competitors. Best Buy also keeps score: measuring the results of marketing initiatives in a feedback loop of adaptive learning to optimize its marketing.

Best Buy marketers analyze customer purchasing characteristics and demographics on a store-by-store basis. For example, they identified one segment in certain geographies, which they called "Jills." This segment is a "soccer mom" who may well be working but is also running the family. She also makes the primary electronics purchasing decisions for the household. Based on these data, Best Buy customized the marketing for specific stores where there are a significant number of Jills in the surrounding population. The marketing included large in-store banner advertising of moms with kids using electronics, direct-mail advertising, and changing up the product mix to appeal to Jills. The resulting sales lift (percentage change) in these stores was then measured before and after the marketing activities.

This example illustrates the marketing divide: a few firms "get" marketing, and many do not. The result is that firms that get marketing have a competitive advantage, and those that do not often struggle, gradually losing market share and/or profitability, to end up eaten by competitors or to go out of business.

In collaboration with Saurabh Mishrah and Alex Krasnikov, I have surveyed 252 firms capturing $53 billion of annual marketing spending on marketing performance management and return on marketing investment (ROMI) best practices. The research demonstrates the existence of a divide between market leaders and laggards. A few statistics from the research highlight the gaps in stark contrast:

- Fifty-three percent of organizations do not use forecasts of campaign ROMI, net present value (NPV), customer lifetime value (CLTV), and/or other performance metrics. (See Chapter 5 for the essential financial metrics and Chapter 6 for CLTV. Free downloadable templates accompany all financial metric examples.)
- Fifty-seven percent do not use business cases to evaluate marketing campaigns for funding. (For best practices, examples, and templates, see Chapters 5 and 9.)

- Sixty-one percent do not have a defined and documented process to screen, evaluate, and prioritize marketing campaigns. (For best practices and examples, see Chapters 3 and 11.)
- Sixty-nine percent do not use experiments contrasting the impact of pilot marketing campaigns with a control group. (For best practices and examples, see Chapters 2 and 3.)
- Seventy-three percent do not use scorecards rating each campaign relative to key business objectives prior to a funding decision. (For best practices and examples, see Chapter 3.)

I was shocked by these findings, since they suggest that the majority of marketing organizations do not have professional processes in place to manage marketing and that most do not use marketing metrics in their day-to-day marketing activities. After all, if there is no business case or ROMI defined prior to campaign funding, how can you measure success after the fact? The divide is even more pronounced when we look at marketing organizations' use of data:

- Fifty-seven percent do not use a centralized database to track and analyze their marketing campaigns (see Chapters 2, 6, 9, and 10).
- Seventy percent do not use an enterprise data warehouse (EDW) to track customer interactions with the firm and with marketing campaigns (see Chapters 8 through 10).
- Seventy-one percent do not use an EDW and analytics to guide marketing campaign selection (see Chapters 2, 6, 8 through 10).
- Eighty percent do not use an integrated data source to guide automated event-driven marketing (see Chapters 8 through 10).
- Eighty-two percent never track and monitor marketing campaigns and assets using automated software such as marketing resource management (MRM) (see Chapter 11).

The vast majority of organizations therefore do not use centralized data to manage and optimize their marketing. The leaders, however, are on the other side of the divide and are the smaller percentage of firms, less than 20 percent, that actually do data-driven marketing and use metrics for measurement in their day-to-day marketing activities. As we will see later, these firms have significantly better financial and market performance relative to competitors.

Why is there a marketing divide, and why is it so hard for organizations to do data-driven marketing? These statistics are symptoms of why data-driven marketing and marketing measurement are so difficult for many organizations: the internal processes do not support a culture of measurement, and they also do not have an infrastructure to support data-driven marketing and marketing metrics. But beyond these high-level processes, my experience is that most marketers are overwhelmed with data and do not know where to start in terms of measuring the right things to drive real results. Furthermore, 55 percent of managers report that their staff does not understand metrics such as NPV and CLTV. (Financial metrics such as NPV are discussed in Chapter 5, and Chapter 6 is all about CLTV.)

Don't be discouraged if your organization is one of the 80 percent that does not use data-driven marketing and/or you are not familiar with these metrics—this book is about the simple secrets of the leaders. The goal of this book is to give you transparent metrics, tools, examples, and a road map to actually do data-driven marketing and apply marketing metrics in your organization.

The 15 Essential Marketing Metrics

When I first started executive training at Microsoft in 2003, some Microsoft marketers suggested that what they needed was a "killer app" (software application) for ROMI. What was funny to me is that Microsoft makes the killer app: it is called Microsoft Excel. The spreadsheet is an incredibly powerful tool.

In this book, I focus on relatively simple, but effective, metrics and frameworks for marketing measurement and data-driven marketing, and Excel is a great tool to get started. More advanced tools and techniques exist for linking marketing to sales. These techniques are indeed useful; regression, for example, is often used by packaged goods firms to correlate marketing spending with revenues. However, these methods have significant limitations, including the need for large, clean data sets, which often are not available to most companies. The approach of this book is therefore to focus on a framework for marketing measurement, balanced scorecards with the few key metrics that point to value, and approaches for analysis that are relatively straightforward to implement. (As a side note, regression definitely has its uses. In Chapter 9, I discuss how Meredith Publishing uses regression to figure out what product a customer might buy next, and I compare regression analysis with other data-mining methods such as decision trees for EarthLink customer retention marketing.)

To get started, there is a lot you can do with Excel, and I provide downloadable spreadsheet templates for all of the quantitative examples in this book. For ongoing data-driven marketing, you will most likely want to automate the process, and especially if you have a large customer base, you will need marketing infrastructure, including a database and more sophisticated analysis tools. Approaching this journey is the focus of the next chapter, "Where Do You Start?" and Chapter 10 answers the question "What's it going to take?" in detail for infrastructure.

My perspective is to concentrate on as few metrics as possible that capture the most value for marketing. In summary, the 15 essential metrics for marketing I define are:

1. Brand awareness
2. Test-drive
3. Churn
4. Customer satisfaction (CSAT)
5. Take rate
6. Profit
7. Net present value (NPV)
8. Internal rate of return (IRR)
9. Payback
10. Customer lifetime value (CLTV)
11. Cost per click (CPC)
12. Transaction conversion rate (TCR)
13. Return on ad dollars spent (ROA)
14. Bounce rate
15. Word of mouth (WOM) (social media reach)

Again, don't worry if you are not familiar with some or all of these metrics. They are explained in detail with examples in Chapters 3 through 7.

The first 10 metrics are what I call the classical marketing metrics. Metrics numbered 1 through 5 are the essential nonfinancial metrics discussed in Chapters 3 and 4: these metrics define the efficacy of branding, customer loyalty, comparative marketing activities, and marketing campaign performance. Metrics numbered 6 through 9 are the essential financial metrics every marketer should know. Note that return on investment (ROI) is *not* one of these metrics—we will discuss why in Chapter 5. Rounding out the top 10 is CLTV, the essential financial metric for customer value–based decision making; Chapter 6 is entirely devoted to this metric.

Over 100 years ago, John Wanamaker said the famous line: "Half the money I spend on marketing is wasted—the problem is I don't know which half." More recently, a CMO told me: "Half the money I spend on marketing is wasted, but today I know which half: TV advertising." His comment reflects the rise of the new media for marketing, the network (both Internet and cell phone), and the ability to track marketing activities in this medium like never before.

Of the 15 essential metrics, the last 5, metrics numbered 11 through 15, are what I call the "new age marketing metrics": search engine marketing effectiveness is captured by metrics numbered 11 through 13. Bounce rate, metric #14, is the key metric to understand how good your web site is, and the new frontier of social media marketing is captured by metric #15, word of mouth. Chapter 7 covers these metrics in detail with lots of examples. Feel free to jump to Chapter 7 at any time—it is an in-depth discussion of Internet marketing best practices. However, throughout the following chapters, I give multiple examples of how to use the Internet to radically improve marketing performance. Let's start the journey with a few general case examples of data-driven marketing and how to use marketing metrics in practice.

Case Examples

So what do you do if you are a small company with a small customer base? The answer is that you can purchase lists that are targeted. A few years ago, I received a postcard mailer at my house. On the front was a picture of a nice golf course with the slogan: "Mark, A Special Invitation." What caught my eye was that it was specifically for me.

Wow, I felt special. Of course, we all know the scenario—we sort our mail into piles: bills in one, letters from Mom in another, and junk in the third. The junk mail is summarily tossed in the trash. Hence, traditional direct mail is incredibly expensive, due to the high printing and mailing costs, and is often ineffective since customers don't look at it. However, the postcard I received was different.

First, somehow they knew I like golf, possibly surmised from my purchasing history, and second, it was addressed to me, Mark. The customization and targeting meant that I put the card on one side—it did not go directly in the trash. There are then good odds I will look at the back. The back was particularly interesting. There was a custom web uniform resource locator (URL): www.companyname.com/Mark.Jeffery. Realize that anyone who types in the URL and clicks return can be tracked and followed up with a phone call as a lead, even if he or she doesn't complete the web form to provide more information.

Figure 1.1 is a similar example for the 2008 Porsche Turbo Cabriolet new product launch. A stamped "raw" metal plate was delivered to existing Turbo Cab owners to coincide with the press announcement of the new product launch. The mailing provided personalized log-in credentials and encouraged visits to the web site with: "The raw Porsche 911 Turbo Cabriolet awaits your color selection." On the web site, the customers chose their favorite color and ordered a personalized Turbo Cab poster.

Figure 1.1 Porsche Turbo Cabriolet new product launch integrated direct-mail marketing. A letter with a customized stamped "raw" metal plate encouraged customers to visit the web site and order a customized poster with "their" new car color.

Source: Adapted from Porsche Cars North America Marketing.

The design of the campaign, integrated with the Internet web site, enabled end-to-end tracking. There were 2,700 unique log-ins with an average session time of almost 15 minutes, and 5,670 posters were ordered. Interestingly, there was also a significant WOM component, with nearly 500 send-to-a-friend invitations. (See essential metric #15—WOM, in Chapter 7.) The campaign overall had a 30 percent response rate, and 38 percent of Turbo Cab buyers during this period received the mailer.

The response rate and time on site is truly amazing given the high cost of the product ($130,000) and target demographic: busy executives, lawyers, and doctors. But what's great about this example is that the direct-mail marketing was designed for measurement and was integrated with the Web, enabling the capture of customer response data and identifying potential leads.

Customization and data-driven marketing can have a significant and measurable performance impact for both small and large firms. Large organizations clearly have an advantage in terms of size and resources, but few truly leverage this advantage in their marketing. As another example, let's look at a large Fortune 500 business-to-business (B2B) company.

The DuPont Tyvek® brand is well known in the United States. The reason for the product's success has to do with both the innovative properties of the material and DuPont's marketing of the innovation.[1] Tyvek has unique properties that liquid water cannot pass through, but water vapor can, and it is extremely durable. Tyvek today is used in packaging, protective apparel, envelopes, covers, graphics, and home construction.

Tyvek's permeability makes it extremely useful in the construction market, where it is used as a building envelope, wrapped around the frame of a building to allow moisture to escape while preventing water/rain from penetrating. This helps mitigate the growth of mold and mildew caused by condensation, protecting homes and buildings from expensive water damage. Figure 1.2 is an example of recent print advertising for DuPont Tyvek.

Data-driven marketing and marketing metrics start with the principle of keeping score for all major marketing activities. In the case of the print advertising in Figure 1.2, this is challenging, since the advertising is designed to brand Tyvek by creating awareness for the product and an emotional attachment that your home is safe with Tyvek. However, in addition to the print marketing, DuPont used the sponsorship of Jeff Gordon in NASCAR.

Figure 1.2 DuPont Tyvek print advertising.
Source: DuPont Marketing, Note 1.

NASCAR, or U.S. stock car racing, is a very interesting sport from a marketing perspective. NASCAR is the number one in-person attended sporting event and the number three most watched sport on TV in the United States: approximately 80 million people regularly watch NASCAR. Combined with Formula 1, auto racing is the number one live event in the world. The viewership demographic for NASCAR also tracks the U.S. population well, with income and age closely matched to the U.S. population. DuPont sponsors Jeff Gordon, who has won the NASCAR championship—the race for the cup—four times, and according to an ESPN sports poll is the eighth most recognized sports figure in the United States.

For the Tyvek Home Wrap product, the activation campaign included painting Jeff Gordon's number 24 car with a Tyvek "TV panel" on the back for a 2006 race in Kansas, and TV advertising blanketed the Kansas area during the race to build consumer awareness. The primary focus of the campaign, however, was on three sets of B2B customers for the Tyvek product: retailers, builders, and specialists in construction.

Figure 1.3 is an example of the print poster marketing for Tyvek Home Wrap sent to building distributors throughout the United States.

Figure 1.3 Tyvek Home Wrap activation poster.
Source: DuPont Marketing, Note 1.

The offer was for an "ultimate race weekend" luxury box for the race and opportunity to actually meet Jeff Gordon. Awards went to the top 24 retailers across the country who sold the most DuPont products, the top 24 builders who bought the most DuPont products, and the top 24 specialists who signed up the most new and existing retailers.

The results of the campaign were impressive: 438 retailers signed on, 202 new and 236 existing, and there was a 186 percent sales increase during the promotional period, as measured by pallets of Tyvek shipped. Most important from a data-driven marketing perspective was that DuPont kept score. They measured pre- and post-campaign sales; which resulted in a significant ROMI.

A weakness of the marketing measurement was that the impact of the brand and awareness component of the marketing was not captured particularly well. Anecdotal evidence suggests a significant brand component, however. Figure 1.4 is the Tyvek logo that is visible on all new construction that uses the Home Wrap product. The following was posted on the www.NASCAR.com blog:

> My favorite NASCAR memory includes our favorite driver, Jeff Gordon, and my son, Logan. When Logan was two, we would drive by new housing developments and he would tell us which houses were Jeff Gordon's. We didn't put it together for a couple of months, but every time we would walk by or drive by a new housing development Jeff Gordon almost always had a house there. Finally, we realized our two-year-old was matching the DuPont Logo from Jeff Gordon's

Figure 1.4 The Tyvek Home Wrap branding visible for several weeks on all new construction using the product.

Source: DuPont Marketing, Note 1.

racecar with the DuPont House Wrap logo (Tyvek) on the new homes. Kudos to DuPont for its brand.

We will discuss branding and awareness marketing metrics and measurement in more detail in Chapters 3 and 4. For now, the takeaway is that the Tyvek Home Wrap campaign primary objectives were designed to be measured; DuPont marketing was keeping score, and the pre-post change in number of pallets shipped justified future marketing investments.

As a next example, let's look at Sears's direct-mail marketing. Sears is a venerable retailer that in recent years has fallen on hard times and as a result was taken over by Edward (Eddie) Lampert in 2004; Lampert previously bought bankrupt Kmart for cents on the dollar. In the United States, Sears started by creating one of the first product catalogs at the turn of the century and enabled settlers on the frontier in the United States to have access to the same products as those living in the major eastern cities. These products could be ordered at the frontier store and the order sent by telegraph back east; the product would arrive in "real time" several weeks later by steam locomotive.

In 2001,[2] Sears's annual revenues were more than $30 billion, and its financial challenges stemmed primarily from changing consumer preference toward big-box specialty retailers located in the suburbs. I remember receiving the Sears "phone book" catalog at home when I was a child and sitting excitedly as I picked out my Christmas wish list. Today, the phone book catalog is replaced by the much smaller color mailer, approximately 20 pages, that is a newspaper insert or is direct mailed. The following example is for the 2001 Sears mailers that were direct mailed with the objective of getting customers to come to the stores. This example is for a very large marketing budget and involves analysis of a large amount of data, which many readers may not have access to. But it is a great example, and I give examples of how to get started with a small amount of data and a limited budget in the next chapter.

The original marketing consisted of direct mailing more than 250 million catalogs per year, targeting 14 to 18 million customers spread over 18 separate mailings. These mailers generated incremental sales of $900 million per year. The existing campaign targeted the top 40 percent of customer households, based on recency, frequency, and monetary value. There was also limited geographic versioning. That is, the southern United States, such as Florida, got a different mailer from Chicago, in the Midwest, since the weather is very different in these two geographies. However, everyone in the Midwest received the same mailer, as did everyone in the South.

Clearly, the mailer was driving significant sales revenues, but what was the profitability of this marketing? If we assume the mailer cost $1, order of magnitude, to print and mail, then the marketing is costing approximately $250 million per year. These mailers were driving incremental revenues of $900 million. The marketing cost was therefore approximately 25 percent of these revenues. But we know the margins for retail in the United States are very thin, due to competition from Wal-Mart, and are approximately 10 percent or less, again order of magnitude. What does this mean? It means that this marketing initiative, while driving significant sales revenues, was losing more than $100 million per year!

The marketing management team realized that business as usual, the standard marketing, was helping to dig a hole for Sears. The solution was to segment the market and target the direct-mail marketing. Market segmentation, of course, is a very old idea. Segmentation 20-plus years ago was very difficult, with limited data and only primitive computers, so marketers typically focused on three segments: high, medium, and low.[3] But, today, data-warehousing technology enables data mining and much more fine-grained segmentation (see Chapter 9).

For this example, Sears used an EDW and analytics to split the targeted customers into 25 distinct segments, based on a robust series of variables, attributes, and purchase characteristics. They then versioned the mailers, based on products and categories relevant to the various groups. Furthermore, they eliminated the strict cutoff that included only the top 40 percent of customers, and instead captured "upsell" opportunities among lower-value customers with upside potential.

What happened? The mailer revenue increased $215 million dollars per year, based on improved targeting and campaign management. That is, Sears took a $900 million marketing initiative and made it into a $1.1 billion initiative. But what I most like about this example are the detailed metrics to quantify the performance improvement of the campaign: there was 1 percent improvement in number of trips generated among customers who received direct mail, 5 percent improvement in average purchase dollars per trip, and 2 percent improvement in gross margin, as "right" product featured captured sales without reliance on "off-price" promotions.

That is, people who receive the mailer come to the store more and, when at the store, buy more. But, better still, there is a very significant improvement in gross margin. This is attributed to what I call the "Ah, that's exactly what I need!" effect: if you show customers you have the product they want when they need it, there is much higher probability they will purchase and you don't have to put the product on sale (see Chapter 9).

The changes in this example are a few percentage points, but when there are a large number of customers and margins are small, the impact is very large. The 2 percent improvement in gross margins has a huge financial impact, for example. In the final analysis, the catalog targeting project alone had an NPV exceeding $40 million. This is an exceptional ROMI for a print direct-mail campaign. (Financial metrics such as NPV are discussed in Chapter 5.)

This section has given four different examples of how to radically improve the performance of marketing. There are many more throughout this book. The summary takeaways are that data-driven marketing in its simplest form is "keeping score," which enables justification of marketing investments. The act of measurement can improve marketing performance by making explicit what is working and what is not and by ensuring that marketing dollars are invested in activities that are measured to be high performing. At the next level, data-driven marketing uses analytics to dramatically improve performance. These techniques can be used by both large and small organizations with dramatic results.

Michael Porter is widely regarded as the father of modern competitive strategy.[4] Porter's works include the famous five forces analysis, which is a framework for defining a firm strategy given competitors and market forces. Porter defines sustainable competitive advantage as the *coordination of activities that are not easily duplicated*. At the highest level, strategic advantage from marketing is created by the coordination of activities that are not easily duplicated, and data-driven marketing and measurement are significant components of those activities.

Marketing Budgets: Key Differences between the Leaders and the Laggards

In order to better understand marketing measurement and data-driven marketing, I conducted a research study entitled "Strategic Marketing ROI: Myth versus Reality." This new study focused on the processes needed to drive marketing performance and ROMI. For the study, we first interviewed senior marketing executives at firms such as Best Buy, Microsoft, Continental Airlines, HP, Dell, Lowe's, and many other firms. These interviews helped focus the research and enabled the team to understand the essential research questions. We then created a survey capturing the best practices identified from the interviews.

Of the 2,000 mailed surveys, we received 254 total responses: 92 percent of the respondents identified their role as CMO, chief executive officer (CEO), or their direct reports. Average corporate revenues in the study were $5 billion and the average marketing budget was $222 million; the research ultimately captured $53 billion of annual marketing spending. The respondents to the survey were primarily large firms, but, as we will see, many of the results are applicable to both large and small marketing organizations.

The first two insights from the research were discussed in the first section of this chapter: the vast majority of marketing organizations do not keep score, and do not leverage data and analytics for marketing. The next insight was how marketing organizations invest their budgets. If you ask CMOs how they spend their budget, you most often hear the percentage spent on TV, print, Internet, direct mail, telemarketing, and so on. But this breakdown is not particularly useful, since it does not tell us what these organizations actually do with their money. That is, what is the intended outcome of the marketing?

The research takes a different approach and asks what the marketing investments are actually intended to do. Specifically, we defined buckets of funding for demand generation marketing, branding and awareness, customer relationships, shaping markets, and infrastructure and capabilities. These buckets are defined as follows:

- *Demand generation marketing.* These are marketing activities to drive revenues in a relatively short time period after the marketing campaign. Examples are sales, coupons, and events.
- *Branding and awareness.* These marketing activities drive awareness and can include sports sponsorship, naming rights to events or properties, and advertising (TV, print, Web, or e-mail) designed specifically for awareness, not to promote an upcoming sale.
- *Customer relationships.* This marketing focuses on creating a personal link to the customer that drives loyalty and engagement. Examples might be thank-you notes after a purchase and loyalty programs such as concierge shopping services.
- *Shaping markets.* These marketing activities are designed to make the market receptive to your products or services, often through independent third-party recommendations. Examples include analyst relationships for B2B firms and social media blogging to influence perception.
- *Infrastructure.* These investments are in technology and training to support the marketing team. Example technology investments include EDW, analytics, and marketing resource management software that supports data-driven marketing.

We then asked the respondents to tell us what percentages of their budgets fell into these categories. Figure 1.5 is the average spending breakdown in these buckets reported by the 254 respondents. Demand generation marketing is marketing intended to drive sales in the near term, and on average 52 percent of marketing spending falls in this category. At the next level up, branding and awareness is 10 percent and customer equity marketing is 12 percent, respectively. Infrastructure and capabilities, the technology and training to support marketing, is 14 percent of spending.

One observation is that approximately 50 percent of marketing budgets go to demand generation marketing activities. Demand generation marketing (such as sales, coupons, or events) is designed to create revenue, and these sales revenues are recorded a short time after the marketing (when the coupon is cashed or the customer visits the store for the sale he or she saw advertised). By definition, if you know the sales

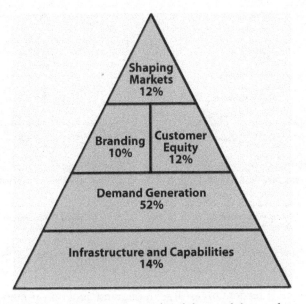

Figure 1.5 Average percentage breakdown of the marketing
investment portfolio.

revenue from the marketing and the cost of the marketing, you can use
financial metrics to quantify the marketing performance. This is an
important insight: *financial metrics can be used to quantify approximately
50 percent of marketing activities.*

At the beginning of this chapter, we started by discussing a marketing divide between firms that "get" marketing and those that do not.
Figure 1.6 is the marketing investment portfolio mix for the top and
bottom 25 percent performers. Figure 1.6 illustrates the marketing
divide in stark contrast.

First, note that the low performers invest 4 percent less than the
average on marketing overall, and the high performers invest 20 percent
more than the average on marketing. Furthermore, low performers spend
more on demand generation marketing. How much more? They spend
10 percent more of their marketing budgets, meaning the low performers
invest 58 percent versus 48 percent for the high performers. Also note that
the high performers invest more in branding and customer equity—a total
of 27 percent for the high performers versus 18.5 percent for the low
performers. Finally, notice that the high performers spend significantly
more on marketing infrastructure—16 percent for high performers versus
10 percent for the laggards.[5] Taken together, these data validate the

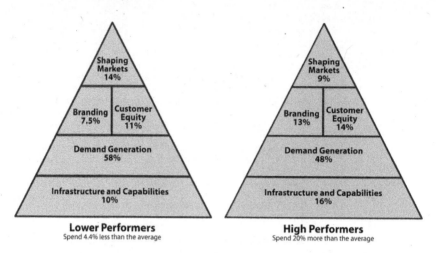

Figure 1.6 Research data to support the marketing divide.

hypothesis that leaders invest less in demand generation marketing, on a percentage budget basis, and more in branding and customer equity. The leaders also spend more on infrastructure to support data-driven marketing.

In summary, the research shows that the marketing divide is real and that there is a significant difference between leaders and laggards: the leaders spend less on demand generation marketing and more on branding and customer equity and on infrastructure to support data-driven marketing. Chapter 11 delves into the research in more detail, and as we will see, the leaders have processes in place to optimize marketing management. As a result of these processes and their different marketing spending, the leaders have significantly better sales growth and financial performance compared with the laggards'. It may come as no surprise that the key marketing processes of the leaders include using metrics to keep score and using data-driven marketing (see Chapter 11).

Using Marketing Metrics to Weather Difficult Economic Times

In dark economic times, a natural reaction of senior business leaders is to aggressively cut costs. However, choosing a hatchet rather than a scalpel can have significant impacts on both short-term and long-term firm performance. Even though marketing may seem like an easy cost-cutting target due to the difficulty with which its returns are quantified, it is important to note that there is a significant link between market-leading firms' investment in marketing and their performance during and following a recession.

Research shows that a better strategy is to *increase* marketing spending. In a study of U.S. recessions, McGraw-Hill Research analyzed 600 companies covering 16 different Standard Industrial Classification (SIC) industries from 1980 to 1985.[6] The results showed that firms that maintained or increased their advertising expenditures during the 1981 to 1982 recession averaged significantly higher sales growth, both during the recession and for the following three years, than firms that eliminated or reduced advertising spend. By 1985, sales of companies that took an aggressive advertising approach during the recession had risen 256 percent over those that failed to keep up or increase their advertising spending.

Paradoxically, market-leading firms actively invest in marketing during an economic downturn. In analysis of the 1990 to 1991 recession, Penton Research Services and Coopers & Lybrand, in conjunction with Business Science International,[7] found that better-performing businesses focused on a strong marketing program, enabling them to solidify their customer base, take business away from less aggressive competitors, and position themselves for future growth during the recovery.

Examples across industries include:

- In the 2001 technology industry recession, Intel invested $2 billion in new chip manufacturing facilities and aggressively marketed new dual-core technology in order to grab market share from competitor AMD.

- In 2008, three years into a recession in construction, Johnson Controls rolled out a new ad campaign continuing its "Ingenuity Welcome" effort. The campaign, which included significant print and online advertising, demonstrates Johnson Controls' efforts to build energy-efficient environments for customers.

- Hanley Wood, one of the most successful B2B publishers of the last decade, is facing challenging times. Hanley Wood CEO, Frank Anton, admits his company is getting "hammered" by the downturn, but says the company is continuing to invest aggressively in digital, event, and magazine marketing.[8]

- Other examples include Revlon and Philip Morris in the 1970s' recession—they both increased advertising to gain market share. In the first quarter of 2009, Procter & Gamble, PepsiCo, Verizon, and NewsCorp Media all increased their ad spending at the peak of the global financial meltdown and recession.

Spending on marketing to drive performance is not limited to times of recession. As we discuss throughout this book, real results happen in good times and bad when you invest in marketing and apply data-driven marketing principles.

The First Step: Defining the Data-Driven Marketing Strategy

We have discussed how sustainable competitive advantage is created by the coordination of activities that are not easily duplicated, and there is a marketing divide between leaders and laggards. One might conclude that leaping the marketing divide is an impossible task, since the leaders have capabilities that are not easy to duplicate. I argue, though, that the leaders follow a similar pattern and have a small set of capabilities that are providing them substantial performance gains in marketing. Understanding and implementing these capabilities can give your organization a similar advantage; the trick is to focus on the right things.

As a first step, it is useful to have a framework for developing a data-driven marketing strategy. The framework in Figure 1.7 starts with defining the strategy and objectives and then collecting relevant data (see Chapters 2, 3, 6, 9, and 10 for detailed examples).

The ability to "know yourself" before starting the journey is both simple and profound. Research has shown that the data warehousing projects that fail do so most often failed because management did not have a plan for what to do with the data once they were collected. That is, data were collected from across the enterprise at great expense in terms of time and money, and then the team could not figure out what to do with them. This "data dilemma" should be faced up front, and the strategic plan should be figured out before funding the larger project to build the database.

Throughout this book, I share stories of how organizations defined their data-driven marketing vision and strategy and their journey through execution. Specifically for the first two steps in the framework shown in Figure 1.7, the next chapter, and Chapter 6 give examples of how to define your strategy and collect customer data. Chapter 10 is all about data-driven marketing infrastructure and answers the questions

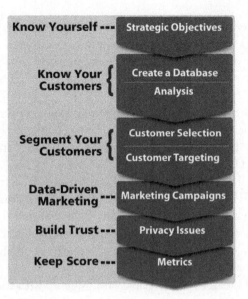

Figure 1.7 A framework for data-driven marketing strategy.

Source: Adapted from Russell Winer, "A framework for customer relationship management," *California Management Review,* 2001.

"What data do you need?" and "What's it going to take?" for small, medium, and large customer bases.

Working with managers, I often find that there is a misconception that you have to have all of the data before moving to the next step in Figure 1.7. This is absolutely not the case. The idea is to figure out which data are important using the 80/20 rule: ask what is the 20 percent of data that will give 80 percent of the value? Then think through how to get these data first. In a large company, these data are most likely in two or three of the existing siloed data marts (small databases). Small companies may not have access to large amounts of data. But, again, ask the questions—what data do you have, or could collect/purchase, that will potentially deliver the highest value? I share examples of how to do this from Royal Bank of Canada and Continental Airlines in Chapter 2.

The next step is analysis to understand your customers. As a first cut, I encourage using Excel if the data set is for several thousand customers. For millions of customers, you will most likely need more industrial-strength tools (see Chapters 6, 8, 9, and 10). The approach often involves fine-grained segmentation, which then leads ultimately to customer targeting and data-driven marketing activities. The Sears examples given earlier in this chapter followed this pattern: data collection and analysis that led to insight on customer characteristics, then targeting and direct mail data-driven marketing. Chapters 6 and 9 discuss how to do segmentation and targeting analysis through real examples.

In the framework in Figure 1.7, privacy issues are near the bottom. One can argue that this should be a first consideration. There is no question that privacy is very important and there are a variety of international laws to protect personal privacy. In 2004, METRO, the large German-based food retailer, stopped using radio frequency identification (RFID) tags on products for electronic checkout due to fear of individuals' personal information being compromised. Privacy laws in different geographies should, of course, be observed, but in the United States at least, a person's information is as cheap to obtain as the cost of a T-shirt.

What do I mean by this? People often sign up with their address and contact information for in-store promotions that give a free gift of a hat or T-shirt, or drop their contact information into a jar at a chance to win a free lunch. In the United States, the vast majority of us have a grocery store card in our wallet. Why? To get discounts at the grocery store, of course.

Note that there is a crystal-clear value proposition to the grocery store "loyalty card" that everyone who uses the card accepts: you provide your household detailed shopping data to the store and in return get discounts. Hence, collecting customer data (business-to-consumer [B2C] or B2B) requires a clear value proposition—what's in it for me, the customer or B2B partner. There is also an implicit contract that the data will be protected and not shared without permission. This contract is essential to build trust with the customer. It should be formally stated in your corporate privacy policy and easily accessed on your web site and marketing to collect data. We discuss data collection in the B2B context in the next chapter.

The framework in Figure 1.7 concludes with metrics to "keep score," and this is the primary focus of this book. I believe that if you can measure marketing, you can control it and radically improve performance. The next chapter answers the question "Where do you start?" and provides strategies for overcoming the five major obstacles to data-driven marketing. Chapter 3 gives a framework for marketing measurement focusing on the 10 classical marketing metrics. The complete 15 essential metrics are then expanded upon in detail in Part II.

In 1974, bar code scanners were introduced in retail, and for the first time this enabled the tracking of individual consumer product purchases at the point of sale. This technological innovation spawned "marketing science," the idea that marketers could quantify marketing using analytic principles. Today, the Internet and cell phone networks are enabling the next leap in data collection of customer interactions with marketing. I tell my MBA students that now is the best and most exciting time to be in marketing. The new data-driven approaches and infrastructure to collect customer data are truly changing the marketing game, and there is incredible opportunity for those who can act upon the new insights the data provides.

Chapter Insights

- A marketing divide exists between organizations that do data-driven marketing and use marketing metrics and those that do not.
- The 15 essential metrics quantify the vast majority of marketing activities.
- Research shows that firms that "keep score" for marketing have significantly better financial and market performance compared with those that do not.
- Higher-performing firms spend more on branding, customer equity, and technology for data-driven marketing and spend less money on demand generation marketing.
- Sustainable competitive advantage from marketing is derived from the coordination of activities that are not easily duplicated.
- There is a framework for developing a data-driven marketing strategy; you don't need 100 percent of the data to get started.

CHAPTER 2

Where Do You Start?

Overcoming the Five Obstacles to Data-Driven Marketing

I am not a marketer by training. My introduction to marketing started when Kellogg received fairly large contracts for worldwide executive training in marketing for three major Fortune 100 companies. I was "volunteered," since I had written the chapter on return on investment (ROI) in the Wiley *Internet Encyclopedia*[1] and had completed a study of 179 Fortune 1000 firms on best practices for technology investment and management.[2] Technology and marketing were becoming intimately related, and I was asked to apply my experience to marketing.

There were quite a few sleepless nights leading up to those first executive sessions, since I was teaching a subject I did not know to an audience of experts. It was trial by fire, but I found that if I talked about data-driven marketing and marketing metrics, we were all in the same boat; very few participants really knew how to do data-driven market-ing, and all were struggling with how to get started.

I realized that most marketing managers have a fairly good handle on what they are doing right now from an activity perspective, but only a few can articulate what data-driven marketing might look like. I also found that there were consistent roadblocks that were holding marketers and organizations back from adopting data-driven marketing principles.

So why is marketing measurement and data-driven marketing so difficult? I have asked this question of many groups of marketing managers and executives. Following are the answers that I often hear grouped into five major categories:

Obstacle 1: Getting Started

- We don't know how.
- We don't have the right metrics.
- The problem is not too little data; quite the opposite—we have lots of data, but none of the data are useful.
- We don't know where to start.

Obstacle 2: Causality

- There are too many confounding factors; overlapping campaigns make defining cause and effect impossible.
- There is a time delay between the marketing campaign and customer action.
- Awareness campaigns do not directly result in sales, but our chief financial officer (CFO) wants to see the financial ROI.

Obstacle 3: Lack of Data

- We are a business-to-business (B2B) company and sell indirectly. As a result, we don't know who our customers are.
- We can't collect customer data due to privacy issues.

Obstacle 4: Resources and Tools

- We don't have the time and/or it cost too much.
- We don't have the tools and/or systems to support data-driven marketing.
- We are marketers and can't communicate with information technology (IT) people.
- IT builds systems, but they are not the resources and tools we need.

Obstacle 5: People and Change

- We don't measure because we don't want accountability.
- Our incentives are all for marketing activity, not results.
- We do not have a culture of measurement.
- We don't have the skills for data-driven marketing.
- Our organization is resistant to new ideas, such as data-driven marketing.
- Marketing is creative: imposing metrics and process will kill creativity and innovation.

This chapter focuses on answering the question "Where do I start?" and provides strategies for how to overcome these five obstacles.

Overcome Obstacle 1: Getting Started—Focus on Collecting the Right Data and Create Momentum by Scoring an Easy Win

Royal Bank of Canada (RBC) started the journey toward data-driven marketing by looking internally. Said Cathy Burrows, who led the RBC initiative, "You have to look at what you do today and think, 'How can I do this better, cheaper, faster, and smarter?'" RBC started by looking at the Canadian equivalent of individual retirement account (IRA) contributions, tax-free voluntary retirement investments made once a year.

Each year around IRA contribution time the sales force was given a list by the RBC marketing department. Sales then called the list, which was ordered alphabetically. For each salesperson, the average yield was one to two people accepting the offer from the list of the top 10 candidates for the salesperson to call.

The RBC marketing team built a model to rank and score the list based on propensity to contribute more than $5,000 to an IRA (see Chapter 9 for how to do this). The model involved analyzing more than 1 million customers, for 12 months of data, and scoring them to find the top 250,000 that would potentially contribute.

The size of this data set may seem intimidating, but realize that if you can solve a problem for 10 customers, you can solve it for 1,000 customers; if you can solve the problem for 1,000 customers, you can do it for a million or more. (Note, however, that while the principles are the same for large customer bases, most likely you can't use a personal computer. Chapter 10 answers the question "What's it going to take?" from an infrastructure perspective when you have a large customer base.)

At RBC, collecting the relevant data to do the scoring required a lot of manual legwork and took six months of effort at a cost of approximately $100,000. The output of the initiative was to give each salesperson a new targeted list of the 25 top customers to call. The results were impressive: 8 out of 10 customers called by each salesperson now accepted the offer to set up an IRA.

However, it took time for the sales force to realize the value of the new list. In the first year, only 25 percent of the sales force participated, but by the third year, more than 75 percent were participating. This illustrates how new experiments with data-driven marketing cannot just be pushed down from corporate. Burrows told me: "I wanted the salespeople to say, 'Damn, that list was good,' and drive adoption from the bottom up. The small IRA marketing initiative was the starting point. This win enabled us to build the business case and gain executive sponsorship for the much bigger $4 million marketing initiative."

The point is that you don't need 100 percent of the data and a multimillion-dollar infrastructure to get started. The key is to focus on collecting the right data. Ask what are the 20 percent of data that will give 80 percent of impact? Start there. Then show the quick win in order to get executive support and secure funding for the next stage.

As a second example, Figure 2.1 is a picture of three stores of the Walgreens pharmacy chain on a map. Walgreens is a $59 billion annual revenue pharmacy company with 6,850 stores throughout the United States. This geospatial picture shows dots that are the customers and where they live and are coded by shape depending on which of the three Walgreens stores they shop. The "diamond" customers shop at Store 1; the "square" customers, at Store 2; and the "star" customers, at Store 3.

This pharmacy retail chain predominantly markets using flyers in newspapers. The way they pay for the marketing is by zip code, denoted by the dashed line, for example, in the picture. Mike Feldner, the marketing manager who first created these pictures, noticed something interesting: the circle on the picture is two miles in radius, and after looking at many pictures throughout the United States, he noticed that there are no dots (customers) for a store more than two miles from the

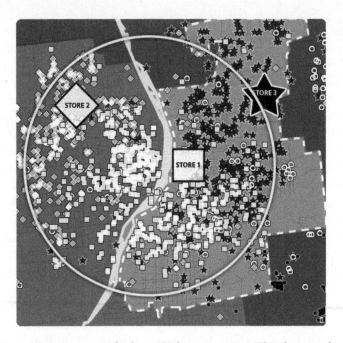

Figure 2.1 A map with three Walgreens stores. The dots on the
pictures are where the customers live. The customers are
coded depending on where they shop.

Source: Adapted from original data by Walgreens Marketing.

store. He concluded that in the United States, if you live more than two
miles from a pharmacy store, you probably don't shop there.

At that time, Walgreens treated each U.S. locale equally; allocating
equal dollar amounts for newspaper advertising in each zip code across
the United States. But the data show that if there is no store within
two miles of the zip code, customers do not shop at the store. Based on
these data, Walgreens ultimately stopped spending advertising dollars
in all zip codes without a store within two miles of the zip code. As you
might guess, the impact to sales revenues was exactly zero. The impact
to marketing, however, was a cost saving of more than $5 million, for a
total cost of collecting the data and creating the plots of approximately
$200,000.

This multimillion-dollar saving in marketing did not require a lot of
money, and the analysis was done on a personal computer (PC).
Walgreens already had the ESRI map and graphing software (www
.ESRI.com) to manage its store locations. Feldner's innovation was to

add in Walgreens' newspaper marketing spending. Feldner told me, "We started with simple Excel spreadsheets that contained the advertising circulation distributions by zip code. It was not hard to get the advertising data into the software and to create maps with the store and customer locations—we did it all on a PC."

The bigger challenge, however, was in changing Walgreens' business process to use data-driven marketing insights. Feldner said to me, "When we first started, we made too many changes too quickly and did not do a good job communicating what we were doing." As a result, the Store Operations area was uncomfortable with the changes to how the advertising dollars were spent, and within a few weeks the changes were rolled back to marketing as usual.

"I realized we had to start small," Feldner told me. "I found a Store Operations VP and district manager who were willing to try things. I remember flying with my advertising counterpart to meet with them. We showed them the pictures, and they could see that it did not make sense to spend $80,000 in advertising in a zip code five miles from the store that was generating, at most, $20,000 in sales. With five examples, we cut $300,000 off the bat and showed the approach really worked." Given this win, they then set up a process to review the marketing spending with each district manager throughout the United States. The Store Operations group came around pretty quickly when they were shown how to cut their specific marketing budgets and increase profitability. Feldner told me, "The initial failure, and then the success that came from starting over with a small win, was the biggest learning experience of my career."

In the mid-1990s, Continental Airlines was positively the worst airline in the industry, and this was backed up by data; Continental ranked dead last on every conceivable airline metric. The crowning moment was when David Letterman called out the airline in his nightly Top 10 list. At the height of the baseball player's strike in the United States in 1995, the number 10 item on Letterman's tongue-in-cheek list of baseball players' demands was "No team flights on Continental Airlines." This was seen by more than 5 million viewers that night.

Gordon Bethune, CEO of Continental from 1994 until his retirement in 2004, orchestrated an amazing worst-to-first turnaround.[3] He first focused on making Continental clean, safe, and reliable and changed the incentive scheme for employees. Employees received $100/month cash bonus if the planes ran on time. The results were amazing—in one month Continental became the number one on-time airline. Bethune then took his worst-to-first approach to the next level with the goal of becoming first-to-favorite for customers.

Kelly Cook, who worked on the Continental data-driven marketing component of the initiative, told me:

> At Continental, the essential first step was to talk to our customers. Focus groups were a low-cost and relatively quick way for us to test our ideas. We also gained invaluable feedback on what we as a company needed to change and what the priorities should be. We did not have the budget or the resources to integrate all of our data, so we focused on the two databases of the 45 silos that, if we combined the data, gave us the greatest return.

The marketing managers had a hunch that if they sent a letter to high-value customers who had experienced a catastrophic event, defined as lost luggage, a canceled flight, or a major flight delay, good things would happen. They did not have millions of dollars of consolidated infrastructure. They had 45 disconnected databases scattered across the company, and the marketing database had been outsourced to an agency. Their first step was to find the two most important databases: customer flight profitability and service exceptions.

They then designed a marketing campaign that sent a letter within 12 hours of an event and arranged for focus groups of customers who received the letters. The letter was very simple, and said, " . . . you are a valued customer to Continental Airlines and we are sorry. . . . " As part of the experiment, some of the letters had one-pass frequent flyer miles, and others had free passes to the Presidents Club, the executive club lounges in the major airports Continental served.

The focus groups' results that measured the impact of the letters were always the same. In control groups that did not get the letter, one person would explain their story of misery of flight cancellation or lost luggage. Another person would then explain that he or she could top that story and give an even worse account. Before long, the group would degenerate into a hate-fest for Continental Airlines.

Groups that got the letters were completely different. Representative reactions were, "Wow, I had not completed my trip yet, and yet the letter was there when I returned home" and "No company had ever said that they were sorry to me before." Their reaction was completely different. These focus groups provided qualitative evidence that there was a significant customer perception change by sending the letter.

Interestingly, a significant percentage of those customers who received the free passes to the Presidents Club signed up for the club. This made the marketing initiative have a very positive return on marketing investment (ROMI), since the Presidents Club is a high-margin, high-profitability offering for an airline. Later, when the systems were in place to integrate the 45 databases and enable the calculation of true profitability and customer lifetime value (CLTV; see Chapter 6 for the definition and calculation), they found that those who received the letter had an 8 percent improvement in revenues.

The takeaways are that to start the journey toward data-driven marketing, Continental started small and used focus groups and experiments. The early results built momentum for the marketing initiative and helped the line managers secure executive support. Mike Gorman, senior director of customer management at Continental, told me: "Creating the database was hard work. But once we had the capability, we were able to quickly spin off tools for customers and the enterprise that created an enormous amount of value."

Overcome Obstacle 2: Causality—Conduct Small Experiments

Another objection to data-driven marketing I hear frequently is that "there are too many possible causes of anything you measure to identify a single cause and effect; overlapping marketing campaigns makes it impossible to tell what's working and what's not working!" The "answer" in large part is one of taking a systematic and disciplined approach to marketing campaign execution. The idea is conceptually simple: conduct a small experiment, isolating as many variables as possible, to see what works and what does not.

Although the majority of marketers are aware of this approach, my research shows that the vast majority of marketing organizations, almost 70 percent, do not use experiments to pilot test marketing campaigns relative to a control group. Why? The answer is that most marketing organizations' reward systems are based on activity, not results. Addressing this cultural challenge is the focus of overcoming Obstacle 5 at the end of this chapter. For now, let me share some examples of the power of designing marketing experiments.

Harrah's Entertainment is the world's largest casino gaming company, and it routinely design experiments to quantify the impact of its marketing. As one example, it designed an experiment targeting two groups of frequent slot machine players in Jackson, Mississippi. The experiment consisted of a control group, the standard marketing offer, and a test marketing offer, the "Challenger." The control group consisted of the typical offer: a $125 package of a free room, two steak dinners, and $30 in free chips at the casino. As expected, gaming activity for this group was the same as previously.

The Challenger offer consisted of $60 in free casino chips, no hotel room, and no steak dinner. Gaming activity of those who received this new offer was measurably higher than that of the control group in subsequent months. Additional experiments showed the same result in other U.S. geographies. As a result, Harrah's was able to cut the budget for this type of marketing by more than 50 percent and increase the performance of the marketing.

This type of marketing was classified as demand generation marketing in Chapter 1. The marketing activity drives demand in a relatively short time period following the offer, often because the offer expires. Limiting who gets the experimental offer addresses the causality issue and, because it is demand generation marketing, there is a minimal time delay between executing the campaign and obtaining the results of the campaign.

In the previous section, I gave the example for the Walgreens pharmacy chain and how data were used to refocus its newspaper advertising. Following this initial win, the marketing manager started to conduct experiments with different newspaper insert advertising in different zip codes. Using specific zip codes as control groups, measuring pre-post changes of sales through the channels (stores), Feldner was able to optimize the newspaper marketing.

Newspaper marketing is the most traditional marketing medium, dating back hundreds of years, yet this example shows how experimental design combined with new technology (geospatial data) can be used to radically improve performance of marketing in this medium (see Figure 2.1). The use of geospatial customer data is applicable to a broad range of marketing activities. Microsoft, for example, uses similar geospatial data to isolate clusters of piracy networks and then focuses antipiracy marketing on these specific geographies. The idea is that all geographies are not equal, and marketing should focus on the highest-value areas. See Chapter 6 for other examples of value-based marketing.

Another objection related to causality is that there can be a significant time delay between marketing, such as branding, and actual product purchase. An executive once told me with frustration that her chief financial officer (CFO) wanted to see the financial ROI of branding initiatives. Financial metrics work great for demand generation marketing, which has a short time delay between action and reaction of the customer—the customer purchases as a result of the promotion or event, and the purchase can be measured with cash. But financial metrics do not work for awareness marketing designed to build brand, which is often separated in time from the purchase. The CFO was asking for the impossible—financial ROI simply does not work for branding.[4]

If your CFO is expecting a financial ROI for all marketing activities, you may need to sit down and explain to him or her why branding and awareness is important in customer decision making and that different metrics are needed that are leading indicators of purchasing intent. The next chapter provides a framework and examples for marketing measurement linking the 10 classical metrics to major marketing activities. The takeaways are that the problem of identifying a cause and effect can be addressed by (1) using experiments to isolate out impacts and (2) using the appropriate metrics for each different type of marketing activity.

Overcome Obstacle 3: Lack of Data—Strategies for Obtaining Customer Data

Many marketers struggle with too much data, rather than not enough. Collecting and analyzing the right data was the subject of the overcoming Obstacle 1. However, B2B companies have a legitimate data challenge, since these companies do not sell directly to customers. They sell through a channel and do not have direct access to customer transactional data. There are three approaches to overcome this obstacle.

1. Channel Partner Data Sharing

Each morning John Chambers, CEO of $39 billion network infrastructure company Cisco Systems, first opens a can of Diet Coke and then logs on to the·Cisco e-Sales portal. Through this enterprise, web application, he can drill down globally into all sales that occurred the day before, dicing by geography, company that purchased, or products, or tied to a specific sales account manager. This is a neat trick, especially considering that Cisco sells more than 95 percent of its products indirectly through value-added resellers (VARs).

How does Cisco do it? The answer is that it contractually requires VARs to share customer sales data. Most B2B companies find that requesting customer data from the channel partner is met with a firm "no way." The partner refuses on the grounds that the data are its property and the source of its competitive advantage.

Cisco appears to be the exception rather than the rule, requiring channel partners contractually to share data in order to resell their products. Many B2B firms I work with tell me that the relationship (the contract) is already in place and can't be changed. I argue that everything is negotiable. One firm I worked with had a large dealer network and owned 15 percent of the largest dealers: an easy solution for them was to start with the dealers they owned, show the benefit of the data-driven approach, and use this as a motivation for other large dealers to share.

The B2B company must answer the question: "What's in it for my channel partner to share its data?" One carrot is in the fact that B2B companies often spend considerable marketing dollars comarketing with channel partners. Shared data analysis provides deep insights into how to radically improve the performance of this type of marketing. Microsoft, for example, found that original equipment manufacturer (OEM) partners gladly accepted and used the Microsoft-developed comarketing collateral, and in some cases were willing to share customer data to show the efficacy of the marketing.

Note that the B2B firm does not necessarily have to know the name and address of the customer; this could be deleted from the shared data file. What you really need is insight into what products or services the customer purchases, and the ability to act upon these data, perhaps through the channel partner. The approach of "disguising" the customer data can sidestep the channel partner's concern that if the B2B firm has the customer data, it will want to go direct and cut the channel out of the deal.

2. Frequent Drinker Programs

Suntory is one of the largest liquor distillers in Japan and brews a beer called Suntory Malts. The three major brands of beer in Japan are Asahi, Kirin, and Sapporo. Suntory Malts beer is in the third tier of popularity, in terms of sales revenue and brand awareness. In the late 1990s, Suntory did something with the Internet that at the time was particularly innovative: it created a frequent drinker web site.

Suntory sells all of its beer indirectly through beer distributors, bars, restaurants, grocery stores, and vending machines. The idea of the web site was that consumers would come to the web site and input the number of beers they drank, given by codes on the bottles, and in return get points. With the points, customers got to purchase silly hats, bottle tops with their name on it, or the chair that is too uncomfortable to sit in.

What brilliant marketing! At the peak of the campaign, Malts reported 300,000 visitors a month to the web site: these were the high-value customers, the frequent drinkers. And the web site enabled the collection of data for direct marketing of other Suntory products.

I lived in Japan for two years and am intimately familiar with the vast amounts of alcohol consumption in the office parties after work. Japan has a culture of drinking that makes this example work, whereas in the United States it is not politically correct. However, the idea of frequent drinker programs transcends cultures and geographies.

Similar to Suntory, Coca-Cola has used the approach for My Coke Rewards (www.mycokerewards.com). The web site is a loyalty program for frequent Coke-branded product drinkers. Again, users get points for how many Coke drinks they have, and then get rewards such as T-shirts, DVDs, and discounts with the many partners affiliated with the marketing activity. Yes, the customer data are as cheap as a T-shirt! My Coke Rewards enables Coke to have direct access to their "frequent drinkers" and to do direct marketing via e-mail. The portal also serves as a revenue generator for Coke through the paid ads on the site.

The frequent drinker program idea is not limited to beverage manufacturers—let me give you a different B2B example. Microsoft sells almost all of its products indirectly through OEM partners and channels. As a result, except for the largest enterprise customers, it does not know who purchases its software. One market segment that is particularly important to Microsoft is the midmarket business segment. These are medium-sized companies that use Microsoft products, and Microsoft sees this segment as an area for potential future growth.

The challenge, again, is that Microsoft sells indirectly to this segment and as a result does not actually know what the customers purchase. The Microsoft revenue model for midmarket and enterprise businesses is to sell annual software licenses. However, if the customer does not renew the license, uses the product, and then later goes to purchase the upgrade, there is an additional fee for off-license product use.

Microsoft created the midmarket portal, a web site where midsized customers can enter their licenses, and in return Microsoft will ensure that firms optimally manage their licenses. While the exact numbers are proprietary, Microsoft now has a significant fraction of global midmarket companies in its database. The midmarket portal enables Microsoft to provide value to its customers—it provides a service, helping midmarket customers to manage their licenses and save money. In return, Microsoft collects data on the product purchases and can use this information for outbound marketing. As an example, Microsoft does analysis of product preferences to understand the bundles of products customers purchase and what might be a good product offer for a particular customer (see Chapter 9 for the three essential data analysis techniques). As a result of this analysis and targeted marketing, Microsoft saw a more than five times increase in performance of marketing campaigns.

Note that in all of these examples there is a crystal-clear value proposition for customers or resellers to share their data. In the case of the Suntory and My Coke Rewards web sites, the value is the ability to get discounted products and services. In the Microsoft case, it was cost savings due to better software license management. For your business, ask: "What is the value proposition for customers to provide their data?"

3. Use Surveys as a Proxy for Customer Data

The third approach is to use focus groups and surveys for fine-grained segmentation and target marketing. The idea is to capture the demographics, characteristics, and purchasing affinities of your end customers through in-depth market research. You can then create survey-based, data-driven marketing offers targeting these segments, and again test these ideas using focus groups and experiments discussed in detail for overcoming Obstacle 2. This approach is not as effective as analyzing large customer transaction data sets, but it can be a great way to get started if you are a B2B firm and have a major roadblock of obtaining direct customer data. I discuss using surveys and focus groups to overcome the B2B data challenge in more detail in the next chapter.

Professional services firms may charge $20,000 or more to design, conduct, and do data analysis for a focus group session of 10 to 15 participants. You can get started, however, for the cost of a free lunch and a gift for participants to incent them to show up. Invoke Solutions (www.invokesolutions.com) conducts online focus groups. For the cost of an in-person focus group for 10 people, you can potentially gather data from 100 people or more online. In my experience, online works great for consumer products and for testing display advertising. There are some challenges getting a critical mass of users to sign up, however. So your sample might be biased toward frequent Internet users and may not be a good fit for your product or service. I prefer small, in-person focus groups as a first step and Internet focus groups as a next step, if appropriate.

Customer Data Collection Ethical and Legal Issues

Customer data collection can be touchy, and you need to be sure you are following the highest ethical and professional standards. One marketer once told me that her legal department was instructing them to actively delete customer data for fear of liability. The reason for this was that the company did not have a privacy policy in place and the legal department did not understand what marketing intended to do with the customer data. Marketers should clearly communicate the privacy policy both externally and internally and how data will and will not be used.

In some cases, there are laws preventing direct collection of customer data. In the United States, for example, the Health Insurance Portability and Accountability Act (HIPAA) prevents pharmaceutical drug companies from knowing patient prescriptions. These laws should unquestionably be followed; however, there is always an opportunity to add value to customers. For example, when someone is facing an illness, web sites that have information and provide community support groups can be used, in an appropriate way, to provide product information to customers and gain customer feedback and insights.

The theme here is to always add value, not subtract value, from the customer interaction. Answer the question "What's in it for me?" from the customers' perspective. Then treat the data with respect, as an asset for your firm. Guard its security and add value—this is the winning combination that builds the trust of your customers.

Overcome Obstacle 4: Resources and Tools—Build the Infrastructure for Data-Driven Marketing

Marketers are busy people, and a common obstacle is lack of time, resources, or the right tools. A key to making data-driven marketing work, and for the approach to be easy rather than painful, is to design all campaigns in advance so that they are easy to measure. It's actually not that hard.

My experience is that defining the appropriate metrics and how the data will be collected usually takes only a few hours during the campaign planning stage—and at most a day or two for a very large campaign—but lays the essential groundwork for data-driven marketing during the campaign execution. The next chapter is a systematic discussion of how to choose the right metrics for any marketing activity and how to design campaigns for easy measurement. Designing for measurement up front is the proverbial 1 percent that yields the 99 percent of value after the campaign is done: it enables you to quantify the impact of your marketing.

The great thing about data-driven marketing and marketing measurement is that, by definition, they create a business case for future marketing investments so that you can justify increased spending for infrastructure to support data-driven marketing activities.

Infrastructure for Data-Driven Marketing

The laptop computer, combined with Microsoft Excel, is an amazingly powerful tool. For infrastructure, this is all most marketers need to get started on the data-driven marketing journey. I want to manage expectations, though. Microsoft Excel 2003 had a limit of 65,536 rows, or customer records, in a spreadsheet, and Excel 2007 had a limit of 1,048,576 rows by 16,384 columns.[5] This means that if you have a large number of customers, Excel is not going to work as a marketing database, nor should it. You want a single version of the truth, not different duplicate copies of customer data on each marketer's desktop.

Excel is great for analyzing branding and customer satisfaction survey data (Chapter 4), getting started with Internet metrics (Chapter 7), and calculating financial return on marketing investment (ROMI; Chapter 5). You can also get started with marketing campaign scorecards in Excel (Chapter 3), and in Chapter 8 I show how Microsoft tracked a $17 million campaign using near-time weekly data in Excel. So Excel works to get started with the vast majority of metrics in this book. Where Excel does not work is as a direct marketing database (Chapters 1 and 9), for value-based marketing (Chapter 6), and for analytic marketing for a large customer base (Chapter 9).

For these applications, your data requirements will drive the scale of the infrastructure you need. If your data requirements are to analyze a data set of several thousand customers, segment the customers and multiple dimensions, and then design target marketing for these customers, you are good to go with a laptop and software such as Excel or SAS JMP (see Chapter 10 for a detailed example for EarthLink with a downloadable data set and instructions). However, if your goal is to solve the same problem for 50 million customers, segment out the top 1 million using multiple dimensions, and do target marketing for these 1 million, you need industrial-strength infrastructure. Said Richard Winter, an expert in high-performance data warehouse design: "The difference in these requirements is the difference between building a ranch house or the Empire State Building."

Furthermore, if your plan is to do the analysis on a one-time basis, you can start using relatively low-cost systems and do a lot of the data pulling manually. But if the plan is for event-driven marketing, based on current customer purchases and the real-time calculation of their future value, then the infrastructure requirements again increase.

My point is that size of the data set, which comes from the customer base and related interactions of the customer with your firm, and what you plan to do with the data, drives the requirements for the marketing infrastructure. The size of the customer base, as well as the amount of data and how often you want to analyze it, will determine how much money you need for the infrastructure. Chapter 10 discusses these infrastructure trade-offs for different customer base sizes and marketing requirements.

However, I return to the essential theme of this chapter: think big, start small, and scale up fast. The takeaway is that when thinking big, there needs to be a realization that the end goal of a data-driven marketing strategy will ultimately drive the infrastructure requirements and that you need infrastructure to scale fast.

Infrastructure for a Large Firm

A very senior business executive in a Fortune 500 company recently exclaimed to me in a very exasperated tone, "What does it all do?" He was frustrated by the high cost of the data-driven marketing infrastructure technology and the inability of IT to communicate in plain English what it did. Another business manager told me, "IT couldn't explain what they do at a party." Let's first take a look at data-driven marketing infrastructure; I'll define the essential components and provide a conceptual model for how it all works. Then we can discuss how to overcome the hurdle of marketing working collaboratively with IT.

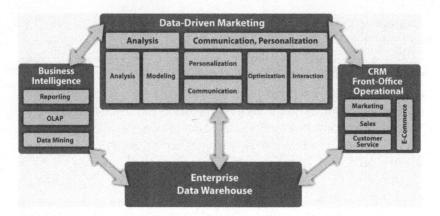

Figure 2.2 Translating data-driven marketing strategy into infrastructure for a large firm.

A large firm with a large customer base requires a corresponding infrastructure, shown in Figure 2.2. Think of Figure 2.2 as the end-state infrastructure that embodies the data-driven marketing strategy. On the right-hand side are systems to collect data from the various touch points of the firm with the customer. These systems are typically called operational customer relationship management (CRM). They collect customer data from the point of sale, call centers, the web site, and customer returns. So, for example, when a customer at Jiffy Lube pulls around to the back of the oil change station, these operational CRM systems collect the license plate data and prompt the service representative to say, "Hi, Mark, it's been 4,000 miles since your last oil change," just as you get out of the car.

Data from each customer visit are tagged and input into the enterprise data warehouse (EDW), shown on the bottom of Figure 2.2. In a large enterprise, the EDW is a very big data store of all customer interactions with the firm, and ideally also includes firm operational and financial data. On the left-hand side of Figure 2.2 are the technical tools needed to mine the EDW and generate reports. Example reports might include weekly updates on district sales numbers, customers who canceled their subscriptions, and so on.

In Figure 2.2, most important is the data-driven marketing on top of the EDW: analytics for segmentation, targeting, and relationship building with customers. For the Jiffy Lube example, the "hello" at the point of sale is an example of personalized interaction marketing and would be facilitated by a program script that takes the license plate data, searches the EDW, pulls the customer record, uses a business rule to figure out what the prompt should be, and finally displays the prompt on the computer screen of the Jiffy Lube technician (see Chapter 6 for another detailed example at RBC).

Analysis and modeling involves using the data-mining tools for targeted marketing. Chapter 9 gives examples of the three essential analysis techniques—propensity modeling, market basket analysis, and decision trees. For example, Meredith, publisher of *Better Homes and Gardens* and many other women's magazines, uses modeling analysis to figure out which product customers are most likely to buy next. Weekly marketing campaigns are accomplished with communication and personalization tools that pull the customer data from the EDW, run the offer prediction model, and then send a customized e-mail to specific customers. See Chapter 9 for the details.

How do you start to build this infrastructure? Start small, with a clearly defined business case, and show the how data-driven marketing enables a better, faster, cheaper, and smarter way to do something your marketing already does. Then build infrastructure incrementally with a business case for each stage. Chapter 10 answers the question "What's it going to take?" for data-driven marketing infrastructure and describes the Harrah's infrastructure story in detail. The Harrah's example shows how it incrementally created a portfolio of value that became a source of strategic advantage in the casino gaming industry.

The Marketing and IT Relationship

I often find tension between marketing and IT in companies. My perspective is that the relationship between marketing and IT should be like going to your doctor. For example, if you hurt your elbow playing tennis, you don't go to the doctor and say, "I want an MRI and a jar full of Vicodin to kill the pain." Rather, you explain your symptoms and the doctor prescribes the solution. Similarly with IT, you have to clearly define the marketing business requirements, the objectives, what you want to do with the data, and so on. IT should then prescribe the solution and is responsible to meet your requirements—they should deliver the system in a reasonable amount of time and to the budget you agreed upon. Marketing is responsible for the business returns of the system, not IT.

For readers who have experienced a life-threatening illness of a family member—a parent, child, or other relative—a natural response is to become an "expert" in the illness. You seek out all the information you can, consult experts for opinions, and become educated on the best practice course of treatment, prognosis, and associated risks. Data-driven marketing infrastructure projects are no different.

As a marketer, you have to become an educated consumer of the technology that supports your data-driven marketing activities. Learn to ask the right questions to ensure that the wheels don't fall off the project and that the system delivers value. Chapter 10 is an in-depth discussion of these issues and will give you the essential knowledge to be an educated partner in the development of data-driven marketing IT. In summary, data-driven marketing technology is too important to leave to the technologists.

Overcome Obstacle 5: People and Change—Create a Data-Driven Marketing Culture

I often hear, "But I am a line manager and have no influence to create change." I find that many people underestimate their potential to influence others. After all, small changes can sometimes have big impacts. In Chapter 8, I share the in-depth case example of Microsoft's Security Guidance campaign. As we will see, just changing the landing page for the impression advertising resulted in a 400 percent improvement in the campaign performance. The takeaway is that small changes can have big impacts.

Realize that you are a culture of one person and change starts with you. I suggest starting with changes that positively impact those around you. For example, the next chapter details how to systematically apply marketing metrics to marketing campaigns and how to create a balanced scorecard for marketing. You can apply these principles to your marketing, train your team on how to use the scorecards, and educate your management on the value of the approach. Results talk, and the scorecards will enable you to keep score for your marketing initiatives.

Of course, creating a data-driven marketing culture requires more than one person. You have to convince others, and the quick win is an essential early step. If you are down the chain of command, this may seem like a daunting task, so I asked executives what they did when they were starting out in the organization.

Kelly Cook explained that when she was at Continental Airlines, she first found out which areas of the business had the data she needed. She then made relationships with the four or five key people in the different functional areas who were like-minded. The result was that she convinced others at her level across the business to work together, and they formed an informal team that worked toward early successes. Convincing the right people requires an understanding of who has the power in your organization. Often, the most powerful people are not the senior executives.

The Trouble with Change Is People

If you are a small firm, given the boss's buy-in and demonstrated results, driving change should be fairly straightforward. However, in a large organization, transforming the culture to data-driven marketing is no easy undertaking. Significant buy-in is required, for example, to build the infrastructure of Figure 2.2, which is most likely a multimillion-dollar investment.

Corporate cultures can be grouped into three major categories: rational, bureaucratic, or political. My young MBA students often believe that organizations are rational, that is, that the best ideal will prevail. Experienced managers know that this is decidedly not the case. The other two organization cultures are most likely in play: A bureaucratic organization has a very rigid organizational structure, and protocols must be strictly followed in communicating with senior executives. These organizations are militaristic, with the general giving orders from the top, and the commanders ensuring the orders are executed on the front lines. Political organizations, in contrast, have centers of power, with individuals who have kingdoms within the organization, often accompanied by budgetary authority and staff. I work in a university and can testify that universities are the most political places on the planet. As Henry Kissinger once said, "The reason the fights are so fierce in academia is because the stakes are so low."

Navigating a political landscape takes experience, but understanding who has the power in your organization is a useful first step. Seek out senior executive sponsors who have power and appreciate results, and who like to use data-driven decision making. In a large firm to be successful, the broader initiative requires a strong senior executive guiding coalition. This executive council oversees the strategy development and the execution, and it monitors progress. There may be a tendency to make the infrastructure development (Figure 2.2) into a large IT project led by IT. This is the kiss of death for the data-driven marketing initiative—marketers, not technologists, must lead the way.

Although senior executive sponsorship is essential, buy-in from both middle and line managers is also needed for success. Why is change so hard on the front lines? People overestimate the value of what they have and underestimate the value the change will bring. The best motivator to drive change is to have a crisis[6]:

- "Our marketing budget is being cut by 36 percent; we need to justify our future marketing spending."
- "We are losing significant market share."
- "Our discount marketing is killing overall profitability."
- "We are hemorrhaging customers and don't know who are the most profitable."
- "Our competitors are consistently outmarketing us."

These are all motivators for the marketing organization to change. In 2009, the financial meltdown and recession caused massive layoffs and spending cuts across the board. With a recovery of three years or more anticipated to get back to pre-recession levels, now is a great time to change to a data-driven marketing culture with the global financial crisis as a motivator.

How do you get noticed and gain a seat at the table? Everyone loves a winner. So again, start small and get the quick win. People around you will notice. Then get the next win—this builds momentum for change and influencing others, building your credibility and stature within the organization. People want to be on the winning team, so create a buzz around what you are doing and show how good things happen when you follow the principles of data-driven marketing.

Creating Incentives for Change: Measurement and Behavior

Like many Americans, I struggle with my body weight—I travel a lot and eat out often. The result is an expanding waistline. Yet, I have known for a long time that the equation for weight loss is simple: eat fewer calories than you burn through daily activity and exercise. But counting calories is a pain.

Recently I found a free application on the iPhone called Lose It that makes counting calories easy. For each day, you can easily add foods and exercise, and copy, paste, and edit previous meals, so it takes only a few seconds. The result was data-driven transparency in my diet—I realized that my coconut chocolate chip cookie binge each evening was costing 600 calories or more. But my budget was only 1,600 calories a day to lose two pounds a week. This meant I had a decision to make: keep eating the cookies or find an alternative. I found that half a cup of caramel praline crunch ice cream was only 160 calories—what a deal! And more satisfying to me.

My point is that if you can measure something, you can control it. In this case, the measurement was the calories consumed and the exercise calories burned. The result was clarity in decision making for what I eat, which meant I lost the weight and ultimately completely changed my diet. Measurement can also change a culture, especially if you make the measurements public.

Fighter pilots in the United States Navy are highly competitive individuals. There is a scoreboard in the briefing room of the aircraft carrier that rates each pilot's mission on multiple dimensions and is directly compared with scores of peers. The result is transparency in what constitutes an effective mission and peer pressure to improve individual performance.

The Kellogg School of Management is a top management school. Part of the reason for this is that some 30 years ago, Dean Donald Jacobs made the student ratings of the classes "public" information to all students and faculty. There was an outcry from the faculty, but within several months the ratings increased very dramatically across the board: the faculty did not want to look bad compared with their peers, so the teaching quality improved.

For marketing, making metrics and measurement "public" within the organization will incent change. But you have to measure the right things. Many organizations incent activity, not results, so the idea is to focus on the metrics that really value marketing. The next chapter is all about how to do this.

If your goal is to drive new data-driven marketing approaches across a large marketing organization, given executive buy-in and air support, explain to the campaign marketers why they need to do this and demonstrate the results. Training is essential so that they have the skills to use the new approaches and tools. Ideally, there is grassroots support, and the buzz from winning marketing activities creates a snowball effect of positive change. But there will always be laggards. You need to explain the benefits and approach again to those who are not doing it, and put incentives in place for success, such as bonuses for good performance. I believe in second chances, but when it comes to the third time, a big stick can be most effective.

In the mid-1990s, Harrah's Entertainment fundamentally changed its strategy to incent customers play at multiple Harrah's properties. This new strategy required data sharing between casino properties for data-driven marketing (see Chapter 10 for the details). The casino general managers (GMs) had been incented on the profit and loss of their individual property, and some of the casino GMs were very resistant to the new strategy, since they did not want to give data to their "competi-tor" GMs at other Harrah's properties. Harrah's ultimately fired a few of its top-performing GMs who were not in compliance with the new data-sharing policy—the organization instantly got the message across the board.

Overcoming the Data-Driven Marketing Skills Gap

My research points to a significant data-driven marketing skills gap in organizations: 64 percent of survey respondents report that they do not have enough employees who have the skill to track and analyze complex marketing data; 55 percent of respondents said that overall their marketing staff does not have sufficient working knowledge of financial concepts such as ROI, NPV, and CLTV (Chapter 5 and 6 metrics).

The personnel skills gap barrier was echoed in my interviews. For instance, one executive told me, "One of the biggest hurdles is person-nel and their ability to understand this new world of marketing. The number of people that have really deep e-marketing backgrounds plus brand backgrounds could probably measure on one or two hands." Another executive said, "One of the many challenges is that there are lot of processes that still rely on human intervention and human prophecies. Whenever you have that happening, you know there are always going to be human errors."

The theme here is that to bring up the game of the overall marketing organization requires training. You need to give your people the new approaches, tools, techniques, and skills to optimize marketing man-agement and deliver best in class data-driven marketing. Kelly Cook told me, "You have to have a good marketing and business strategy, you also have to have the work processes behind the model and you have to have the technology tools behind that. The fourth critical component is the employees. Data-driven marketing is not a "You build it, they will come" model for employees. They must *want* to deliver exceptional marketing performance. I mean, do you know how fast I can clean my house when I *want* to?"

In my experience, training is an essential component of organiza-tional change. Employee training enculturates the new techniques, approaches, and tools. Don't skimp on the training budget—replace boring rote sessions with energizing group action learning exercises so that the participants are jazzed about data-driven marketing afterward and have follow-up coaching sessions for reinforcement. Dynamic external speakers have another benefit you can use to your advantage—they can be a positive force for the data-driven marketing change initiative by credibly voicing and reinforcing your ideas to the organization.

Top Down and Bottom Up

The strategies given in this book enable you to have a significant impact on your piece of the marketing organization, be it in your own day-to-day activities or on the teams you work with. My experience is that marketers who apply these principles get recognized in their respective organizations, are promoted faster, and are ultimately more successful in their careers. But cultural change for a large organization cannot be accomplished solely from the bottom up.

Over the years, I have come to appreciate how equipping frontline marketers with the right tools and processes is only a piece of the equation of successful firms. For a true cultural change to a data-driven organization, senior executive leadership is essential for success. That is, the top must lead by example.

The need for senior leadership sponsorship and support may seem like scaling Mount Everest in your organization. This is why understanding the political landscape of your organization is so important. You create a powerful guiding coalition by showing like-minded executives what is possible in terms of doing marketing cheaper, better, faster, and smarter by using data. You will know when you are successful when the new data-driven marketing idea is not your idea, but the senior executives.

A Road Map for Implementing Data-Driven Marketing

Let's return to the question "Where do you start?" by defining a road map for upgrading or implementing data-driven marketing (see Figure 2.3). The road map starts at Stage 1 by "designing" the road to the future. That is, this first step is all about defining a clear game plan. At this stage, an initial assessment of the current state is useful. Ask what metrics do you currently use. How do you use data for decision making? Given data, does your organization "'do the right thing"? Think through what you would like to be able to do in terms of data-driven marketing.

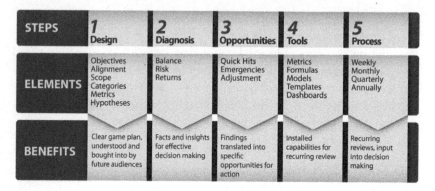

STEPS	**1** Design	**2** Diagnosis	**3** Opportunities	**4** Tools	**5** Process
ELEMENTS	Objectives Alignment Scope Categories Metrics Hypotheses	Balance Risk Returns	Quick Hits Emergencies Adjustment	Metrics Formulas Models Templates Dashboards	Weekly Monthly Quarterly Annually
BENEFITS	Clear game plan, understood and bought into by future audiences	Facts and insights for effective decision making	Findings translated into specific opportunities for action	Installed capabilities for recurring review	Recurring reviews, input into decision making

Figure 2.3 A road map for upgrading or implementing data-driven marketing.

The road map's next step, Stage 2, is Diagnosis, where the idea is to take the current state assessment to the next level. Ask what are the gaps and opportunities? For example, one marketing organization I worked with was focused entirely on unit sales resulting from marketing and was not measuring any forward-looking metrics. Clearly, there was a major gap, and what was needed was a balanced approach.

At the Diagnosis stage, there are most likely multiple options or pathways that you could take for next steps. This is where we need to think about risk and return: of all the options, what are the easy wins that will give the highest impact at the lowest effort and cost? The short list of quick wins is the Opportunities in Stage 3 of the road map.

Once the opportunities are identified, go after the easiest to get the quick win. The Stage 4 focus is on Tools: define metrics and scorecards for success and develop capabilities to support ongoing marketing activities. The quick wins are often one-time proof of concepts. The idea of Stage 4 is to put in place the infrastructure for repeatability.

The last step, Stage 5, is Process—frequent reviews to evaluate performance and change course where necessary. Again you don't need millions of dollars of infrastructure to get started. I advocate using 3″ × 5″ index cards for scorecards and Excel for tracking and initial dashboards. Automate the process once you show repeatability and results.

I have worked with many companies to implement the road map in Figure 2.3. Invariably, a quick 30-day assessment diagnoses problems and identifies quick wins. However, implementing data-driven marketing takes time, so focusing on the quick wins and results is a good first step. Chapter 11 discusses the research on essential marketing processes

(Stage 5 in the road map) and maturity of organizations in the data-driven marketing journey. Chapter 10 is all about the infrastructure component necessary to implement a data-driven marketing strategy, which is the Tools stage of the road map.

Following the data-driven marketing road map will deliver incredible performance improvements to your marketing, which in turn will get you noticed. Results talk, and it is much more fun to be a winner and have respect in the organization than to constantly be questioned about the value of what you do.

Chapter Insights

- Start by collecting the right data to get the quick win—ask what is the 20 percent of data that will give 80 percent of the value?
- Overcome the causality obstacle by using the right metrics and experiment to test marketing ideas. Small experiments can dramatically improve marketing performance.
- B2B companies need a value proposition for channel partners and end customers to share their data.
- Don't have the resources? Marketing measurement is the 1 percent of effort that is the 99 percent of value for justifying spending in the future.
- You need infrastructure to scale a data-driven marketing strategy. The quantity and frequency of customer data to analyze will define how much infrastructure you need.
- Data-driven marketing technology is too important to leave to the technologists.
- Reward results, not marketing activity—align measurement with incentives for change of the marketing organization and train employees to use the new tools and approaches.
- Senior executive leadership is needed for cultural change across a large marketing organization.
- There is a road map for upgrading or implementing data-driven marketing: start with assessment, quick wins, then the development of tools for repeatability, and finally add a flexible review process to act on the results.

The 10 Classical Marketing Metrics

W hen I first started teaching marketing measurement, I was told, rather firmly, by the executive participants that I "did not understand." I had to agree—I was new to the whole marketing thing, since my background was in technology and data analysis.

"Please explain," I said.

"Marketing is creative," I was told, "and you can't measure creativity."

My perspective was, and still is, that you can measure everything. Measurement is powerful, and as we saw in the last chapter, the act of measurement can not only radically improve marketing performance but also dramatically change the behavior of your organization, provided you measure the right metrics in the right way.

So I asked in my survey research, "Do you outsource the creative component of your marketing?" The answer was that 72 percent of firms surveyed outsource the creative. This result has significant implications. *The vast majority of marketing organizations are not in the creative content business, but instead manage the process of marketing.* Optimizing marketing processes, and the four marketing processes to focus on, is the subject of Chapter 11.

I am well aware that most organizations and marketers struggle to measure their marketing activities, given the hundreds of possible metrics. As an example, I once engaged with a major Fortune 100 company, and it shared its scorecard that contained more than 50 metrics. This scorecard took considerable time and effort to put together each month and was providing little benefit; there was too much data, and these data did not provide managers with information they needed to make decisions. Clearly, what is needed is a simple approach to think through which metrics are important for a specific type of marketing activity.

Linking Marketing Activities to Metrics

The fact that an idea is old does not mean that it is not good. The marketing behavioral impact model, sometimes called the purchasing funnel, was first published in the 1960s. The idea is that different marketing activities take the customer through the stages of awareness, evaluation, trial, and loyalty. That is, marketing activities are designed to "funnel" customers from awareness to ultimately become loyal customers. This 40-plus-year-old idea has new significance today as technology enables measurement across this spectrum like never before.

Figure 3.1 is my modern interpretation of the marketing behavioral impact model. In this picture, the purchasing "funnel" is a continuous cycle where loyalty feeds awareness. Let's review this cycle from a modern marketing measurement perspective and also make the connection to the first 10 essential marketing metrics—the "classical" metrics.

Awareness Marketing

Awareness marketing comes in many forms such as TV advertising, billboards, sports sponsorship, naming rights to stadiums, print advertising emphasizing a brand, and creative use of the Internet. Awareness and branding are intimately related. Simply put, a brand is a consumer perception of a particular product or service and may encompass the whole company, such as Disney or Apple. This perception is driven both by marketing and experience with the product and by recommendations of friends and colleagues. Branding is incredibly important, because it often drives the consumer to take a first look at your product or service

Figure 3.1 The marketing behavioral impact model with example
marketing activities.

and can have the advantage of enabling a firm to charge a price premium
over nonbranded competitors.

In the purchasing cycle, awareness is the furthest removed from the
customer purchase, and there can be a significant time delay between
awareness marketing and actual sales. Hence, financial metrics are not
particularly useful for measuring awareness and brand marketing. Firms
often conduct large brand awareness surveys, which track customer
awareness across geographies and over time. These qualitative data are
collected using large sample surveys, 350 people or more in each segment
and geography, and are very costly and time consuming. Hence, large
organizations undertake their brand survey once or at most twice a year.

In addition to brand awareness surveys, typical metrics to measure
efficacy of awareness marketing are number of attendees at events,
eyeballs on a web site, or media impressions. Joyce Julius, for example,
measures sports sponsorship brand exposure. They have sophisticated
systems that track where the corporate branding from the sponsorship
appears on TV, and they then calculate the equivalent cost of purchasing this TV advertising time.

Tiger Woods's win in the 2005 Masters, for example, received $10.4 million of TV exposure for the Nike logo, and Jeff Gordon received $9.9 million of exposure for DuPont brands when he won the 2005 Daytona 500. In total in 2005, DuPont received $85 million in TV exposure due to the Jeff Gordon sponsorship. The challenge with these metrics is that they do not connect to purchase intent and do not capture efficacy of the marketing. The chief marketing officer of DuPont, David Bills, voiced his frustration to me with this measurement approach for DuPont's sponsorship of Jeff Gordon in NASCAR: "DuPont is fundamentally a business-to-business company and we would not ordinarily spend $85 million on consumer advertising."

Clearly, there is a gap between impressions and marketing value. So what is the essential metric? The key metric is ability of the customer to recall your product or service:

Metric #1: The Essential Awareness Metric

Brand awareness = Ability to recall a product or service

Top-of-mind recall means that in the purchasing cycle (Figure 3.1), your product or service will be one of the first the consumer thinks about to consider purchasing. There are a few more sophisticated metrics related to metric #1, but all are essentially a measure of the ability of a customer to name a company or product. I discuss branding impact and how to actually measure awareness in more detail in the next chapter.

But what if you do not have the resources of a large firm or the time to wait for the global brand awareness survey results? The new medium of the Internet and/or cell phone text messaging can be used to connect awareness, trial, and demand generation marketing. In a sports stadium, for example, placing a uniform resource locator (URL) or text message number on a billboard can quantify the impact of the marketing. I advocate that all TV, print, and billboard advertising should have a URL or texting number.

By slightly changing the URL or text message number, one can quantify how many people acted as a result of the awareness advertising. In Chapter 8, we will come back to this concept in detail and show how you can use these techniques to build agility into the design and execution of a marketing campaign. This agility can improve performance by factors of five or more.

Evaluation Marketing

Evaluation marketing is designed to drive customer purchase intent by enabling customers to compare different products or services. Examples include product white papers, print ads with a breakdown of the benefits and features, product brochures, and web sites with product descriptions. As a specific example, Dell predominantly competes based on price because it has a low-cost direct channel to the customer (its web site) and outstanding supply-chain management that drives low-cost manufacturing. The price of the product is prominently featured in Dell's evaluative marketing, and it tends to take a commodity approach to both the product and advertising, providing a list of the facts. This is a good approach if the consumer's primary criterion is price, allowing a quick evaluation of competing product features and the customer to weigh the price performance trade-off.

Apple takes a different approach in its evaluative marketing, emphasizing the cool designs and product innovations. Apple iPhone ads highlight the innovative benefits of the technology, such as the App Store that has many thousands of apps for every conceivable need. Specifically for laptops, Apple charges a price premium over Dell, and tends to deemphasize price in the evaluative marketing: you don't see the price on the Apple web site, for example, until you actually start to custom configure your computer.

Evaluative marketing articulates the value proposition of the product or service, the benefits, and cost trade-offs. There are many ways to present the relevant information to the customer, but there are commonalities in marketing measurement. A challenge for evaluative marketing measurement is that there is a time delay between evaluation and purchase that could be weeks, months, or longer, depending on the product. Another related challenge is linking the evaluative marketing to an actual purchase. For these reasons, financial metrics do not work particularly well for evaluative marketing unless one can track who looked at the evaluative marketing and then subsequently purchased.

Standard metrics for evaluative marketing include product information downloads for a web site or impressions of evaluative marketing print ads. But these metrics do not measure the impact of the evaluative marketing particularly well. So how does one quantify the efficacy of evaluative marketing? The answer is to find metrics that point to future sales.

Anyone who has purchased a car, even a used car, has probably gone to a dealer and picked up brochures for new cars that fit their purchasing criteria, and then done a side-by-side comparison of these glossy picture-filled documents. These brochures, and the related web sites, are examples of evaluative marketing in the auto business. What is the value of the glossy brochure? That is hard to quantify; however, we can define a metric that is a measure of future purchasing intent that embodies the collective impact of the evaluative marketing activities: the test-drive.

It turns out that someone who test-drives a car is very likely to purchase the car. The purchase probability is not 100 percent given a test-drive; instead, there is a probability of purchase. By measuring the number of test-drives and the number of customers who subsequently purchase, one can calculate this average probability of purchase; it's just the number of purchases divided by the number of test-drives. Another related metric worth measuring is foot traffic in a car showroom, since higher foot traffic should result in more test-drives, of which a fraction will convert to sales. The idea is similar to how American football coaches keep score. Their key metric is not the actual score on the scoreboard but the number of first downs (each 10 yards the team advances on the field). Given enough first downs, the team should get a high score and win the game.

Test-drives are a leading metric that point to future sales. In the auto business, evaluative marketing activities should therefore be designed to increase the number of car test-drives and showroom foot traffic. One can therefore design experiments and measure foot traffic and test-drives resulting from specific evaluative marketing activities and optimize based on this metric. One can also utilize focus groups and qualitative methods to estimate "intent to purchase" following exposure to different evaluative marketing materials, such as the new car brochures.

I discuss the test-drive metric in more detail in the next chapter. As we will see, the test-drive is applicable to much more than just cars, and I will give several examples, including Intel chip sales, sunglass purchases, and medical system sales.

Metric #2: The Essential Evaluative Metric

Test-drive = Customer pretest of a product or service prior to purchase

---

Loyalty Marketing

Loyalty marketing activities may include customer assistants such as the Nordstrom Concierge Service to high-value customers. Other examples include proactive event-driven marketing, such as Jiffy Lube sending customers a marketing offer for an oil change soon after the customer has driven 3,000 miles. In addition to repeat sales, a key metric for loyalty is churn rate:

Metric #3: The Essential Loyalty Metric

Churn = Percentage of existing customers who stop purchasing your products or services, often measured in a year

---

Customer churn is a particularly interesting metric and impacts some industries more than others. The U.S. cell phone industry, for example, has a churn rate on average of 22 percent per year. I once shared this statistic with an executive from a major South American telecommunications company, and he exclaimed, "Wow, that's really good!" I inquired what churn he experienced in South America. The answer: 50 percent per year. I have difficulty imagining the challenge of potentially losing all the firm's customers in two years.

For loyalty marketing, there may be a significant time delay between the marketing activity and the repurchase, especially if the product is something like a car, a computer, or a washing machine—a product with a long product life. This is in part why churn is such an important metric; reducing the average annual churn rate over the product life cycle can be directly translated to improving annual sales, although there may be a time delay before the impact is realized.

Firms that do not know who their customers are often do not know what their churn rate is. As a result, once these data are obtained, the measured churn can come as a big surprise. For example, I worked with one major company that did not think it had a churn problem, only to find that some parts of the business had customer churn as high as 45 percent. As we will see in the next chapter and in Chapter 6, marketing activities for retention of high-value customers can have a very significant impact on firm profitability.

The Golden Marketing Metric: Customer Satisfaction

What is missing from our discussion of awareness marketing measurement is a metric tied to awareness, which is a leading indicator of future sales. This essential metric is customer satisfaction (CSAT). CSAT is

Figure 3.2 Metrics for measurement at each phase of the marketing cycle.

not the same as awareness and is more closely related to loyalty. But loyalty and awareness are intimately related; as seen in Figure 3.2, loyalty feeds awareness in the purchasing cycle. Indeed, large firms have established customer bases, and these customers have experiences with the product or service that defines their perception of the brand.

As an example, a major automaker measured CSAT and brand purchase intent and found a one-to-one correspondence between CSAT and repurchase intention. Interestingly, consumers who had problems with their car were more satisfied *and* had higher repurchase intent than those that did not have a problem. Why? The excellent customer service if there was a problem with the new car measurably changed perception positively toward the brand.

CSAT is therefore the "golden" marketing metric that bridges both loyalty and brand awareness, and it can be used as a leading indicator of future sales. Measurement of CSAT is best done by asking customers a simple question: Would you recommend this product or service to a friend or colleague? On a 10-point scale, only those who circle a 9 or 10, for definitely recommend, are highly satisfied and loyal customers.

> ## Metric #4: The Golden Marketing Metric
>
> CSAT = Customer satisfaction measured by asking, "Would you recommend this product or service to a friend or colleague?"

There are a few derivative CSAT metrics, such as Net Promoter Score, but the essential measure is given above. The next chapter describes additional examples of CSAT measurement in practice.

The Essential Marketing Operations Metric

At this point, it is useful to introduce a metric that quantifies the performance of marketing campaigns. There are several metrics that can be defined to measure operational performance of a marketing campaign, such as cost; spend managed per employee; on-time, on-budget delivery; and so on. Many are important and can be tracked, but from an essential metrics perspective, I focus on one:

> ## Metric #5: The Essential Operational Effectiveness Metric
>
> Take rate = Percentage of customers accepting a marketing offer

For example, if you have 100 marketing offers sent by direct mail, telemarketing calls, TV ads, and the like, and 3 people out of the 100 who receive it accept the offer, then the take rate is 3 percent. Take rate defines how well the marketing is working from a tactical perspective, and focusing on increasing the take rate can dramatically improve marketing performance.

Take rate is most often applied to demand generation marketing, discussed in the next section. However, take rate is applicable to any marketing that has a call to action, that is, a clear activity that the marketing is intended to produce from the customer. For example, the call to action for an evaluative campaign might be for customers to download a 10-day free trial of a software product. The take rate to this call to action can be measured from the number of marketing impressions delivered and the number of downloads. By the way, in Internet marketing, click-through rate (CTR) multiplied by transaction conversion rate (TCR) is the take rate measured by clicks on Internet impressions. We will discuss Internet metrics in detail in Chapter 7.

Demand Generation (Trial) Marketing

Trial marketing in Figure 3.2 is synonymous with demand generation marketing, discussed in Chapter 1. These are marketing campaigns that drive sales in a relatively short time period. Examples include grocery store coupons that expire in 30 days, a limited-time sale for 10 percent off, or when GM offered all customers the GM employee discount. These types of marketing activities drive revenues, drive unit volume, and result in sales. Another key metric at the trial stage is lead conversion, which also results in revenue. Since all public companies are required to report their sales and net income quarterly, this type of marketing is the easiest to measure and can be quantified using cold, hard cash. That is, demand generation marketing is quantified using financial return on marketing investment (ROMI).

Chapter 5 is a deep dive into financial ROMI and gives both an introduction to financial concepts and detailed examples for marketing with Excel templates. For now, let's just list the four essential financial metrics. Taken together, these metrics enable you to quantify both demand generation (trial) marketing and new product launch marketing.

The four essential financial metrics:
   #6: Profit = Revenue − Cost
   #7: NPV = Net present value
   #8: IRR = Internal rate of return
   #9: Payback = The time for a marketing investment to pay back
        the cost of the initiative

Note from Chapter 1 that when we examined the portfolio of marketing spending, on average approximately 50 percent of marketing budgets go to demand generation (trial) marketing. In many respects, the end action of loyalty marketing is similar to trial marketing; the customer repurchases a product or service, which results in cash. As a result, loyalty marketing is also often quantifiable using financial metrics. The challenge, however, is that one has to know who purchased the product in the first place. If you don't know who previously purchased your product, then all loyal repurchases look like trials. The trick is to know your customers; this can be particularly challenging for business-to-business (B2B) firms, and I discussed solutions to this challenge in the previous chapter.

The takeaway is that since demand generation, new product launch, and loyalty marketing drive measurable sales revenues, *you can use financial ROMI more than 50 percent of the time for marketing.* This is a significant insight: financial ROMI is applicable to the majority of marketing activities. Of course, financial ROMI is not "the answer" for all marketing measurement, and I advocate taking a balanced approach with multiple metrics in the next section. The point is that financial metrics are applicable to marketing more often than not.

The framework in Figure 3.2 provides a simple and useful guide to figure out what marketing metrics to use depending on the type of marketing activities. For simplicity, so far in this chapter we have discussed the first nine essential metrics; the other essential metrics can be overlaid on the framework in Figure 3.2. Most important is the idea that the type of marketing activity drives what type of metrics to use. Often, marketing campaigns have multiple objectives and may incorporate two or more elements of Figure 3.2, so for each individual campaign a scorecard of multiple metrics defines the value across the spectrum of marketing activities.

A Balanced Scorecard for Marketing

As you drive along a road, there are multiple sensory inputs. You look through the windshield to see hazards ahead. The dashboard with the speed and tachometer are metrics that complement what you see and help you determine whether you are driving too fast or too slowly. The rearview mirror provides sensory feedback on what is behind; the mirror gives backward-looking input. The temperature gauge and oil pressure gauge are additional operational metrics that measure how well the engine is running, and the fuel gauge provides information so you don't run out of gas.

In marketing, measuring only sales revenue is like driving a car by looking only in the rearview mirror, because sales measures what has happened in the past. What is needed is a balanced set of metrics, or scorecard, similar to the complete set of sensory inputs when driving a car. The balanced scorecard was first made famous by Kaplan and Norton,[1] and their original work defined four categories of metrics for the firm: financial, customer, internal processes, and growth and innovation. For marketing, we can use a similar approach where the marketing measurement framework of the previous section forms the foundation.

For marketing, an example of an essential metric that looks into the future is customer lifetime value (CLTV). This metric quantifies the future profitability of a customer and rounds out the 10 classical metrics for marketing:

Metric #10: The Essential Customer Value Metric

CLTV = Future value of a customer

Chapter 6 is devoted entirely to this metric and value-based marketing decision making. Note that CLTV is a forward-looking metric, since it quantifies the future value of a customer. Continental Airlines, Royal Bank of Canada, Harrah's Entertainment, and many other firms given as examples in this book make extensive use of CLTV in real-time marketing decisions.

The scorecard for a marketing program or campaign will be specific to the type of campaign. However, the three broad categories of metrics for a marketing balanced scorecard are strategic (leading/forward), tactical (backward/lagging), and operational (internal). Strategic metrics are forward-looking metrics and include branding, awareness, and customer satisfaction. They also includes test-drive metrics for evaluative marketing initiatives and CLTV for predictive modeling of customer future value. Financial metrics are applicable to demand generation marketing and some customer campaigns. Operational metrics are internal to the marketing function and gauge how well the campaign is running from an operational perspective.

The actual metrics for a specific marketing initiative scorecard will depend on the type of marketing campaign and the context of the business. Figure 3.3 is a summary of the marketing balanced scorecard with some example metrics.

In order to define a scorecard that works, marketers first should think through the marketing campaign objectives and understand where their marketing activities fit in the behavioral impact model in Figure 3.3. The campaign activities follow from the big-picture plan, and metrics are then tied to the activities. For example, if a campaign has dual goals to drive awareness and sales revenues, the metrics focus should be on brand awareness and CSAT, the key financial metrics for demand generation

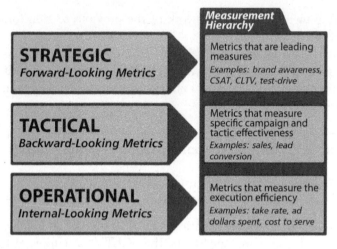

Figure 3.3 A balanced scorecard for marketing.

marketing to drive sales, and take rate for operational performance, along with campaign-specific cost and performance measures.

Figure 3.4 shows the big picture of how marketing scorecards for specific campaigns and marketing activities are connected to an overall chief marketing officer (CMO) balanced scorecard. The idea is to define common performance metrics that roll up to the executive level. At the campaign level, the scorecards contain both common and campaign-specific metrics.

As an example, in the early 1990s MasterCard faced significant competitive pressure from Visa in global credit card business and, as a

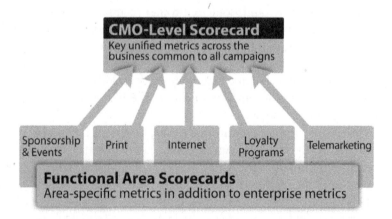

Figure 3.4 Marketing organization scorecards.

result, chose to sponsor FIFA, World Cup soccer.[2] The strategic vision for the sponsorship marketing was clearly defined: "To underscore Master-Card's transformation from a U.S.-oriented credit card company to a truly global brand and payment services organization," said McKeveny, VP Global Promotions, MasterCard International. MasterCard defined the following business objectives tied to its sponsorship strategy:

- Build brand awareness—through the events' television reach and brand exposure of 7.5 minutes per 90-minute broadcast, an advertising cost estimated at $0.40 per 1,000 viewers reached.
- Stimulate card usage and acquisition—by exploiting the global appeal of the World Cup. Members worldwide were given the opportunity to implement customized marketing programs targeted at specific usage, activation, and acquisition objectives.
- Provide business opportunities for members—through in-branch programs to build traffic, cross-sell other member products such as Maestro and MasterCard Travelers Checks, increase automated teller machine (ATM) usage, and execute merchant-driven promotions to increase acceptance and preference for MasterCard products.
- Enhance the perception of MasterCard as a global brand and payment system—by associating for the long-term MasterCard and the world's leading sport.

It is interesting to note that MasterCard is actually a B2B company since its card is licensed to member banks that act as MasterCard's channel partners. The business objectives of the marketing program not only included end consumers, but also specifically included the member banks. Also note that while this was fundamentally an awareness and branding marketing program, an additional objective was to drive sales revenues through card acquisition and usage; this is demand generation marketing measurable by financial metrics. The business objectives drove a tactical execution plan that evolved over several years of the FIFA World Cup sponsorship, and resulted in a scorecard measuring pre-post change across geographies.

The scorecard had two different sets of metrics for consumers and member banks. For consumers, these metrics focused on brand and awareness and pre-post surveys asked questions to measure the brand perception change: Did the sponsorship close the awareness gap compared with Visa?

Did sponsorship awareness increase? And was sponsorship awareness higher than or equal to that of Visa during the Visa Olympics? For all of these measures, MasterCard had significant and measurable pre-post changes across the vast majority of geographies.

The scorecard for member banks was different and focused on how well the sponsorship built business-building opportunities and drove card acquisition and revenues. That is, the member bank scorecard focused primarily on demand generation metrics. Pre-post member surveys across geographies were complemented by card acquisition and revenue data.

The results of the program were impressive. Brand awareness measurably increased globally, and card acquisition and usage very significantly increased, driving measurable revenue and profitability for MasterCard. Member banks also contributed to the campaign. More than 450 MasterCard members, including 75 percent of the top 100 card issuers, participated in one or more aspects of the global promotion. Together they invested $38 million in sponsorship-related marketing. Member satisfaction was measured as part of the scorecard, and 87 percent of the members stated that the sponsorship added value to their own marketing programs.

This example illustrates conceptually where the scorecard fits in the marketing program design and execution. Best-practice marketing program design begins with defining the overarching strategic vision for the campaign. This vision is then translated into key business objectives (KBOs), and these objectives lead naturally to tactical execution. The balanced scorecard provides metrics tied to the key business objectives and tactical execution. All campaigns should have a clearly defined vision statement and KBOs supporting this strategic vision. Given the tactical execution plan for the campaign, the scorecard measures pre-post change on key metrics that define the KBOs.

A useful exercise is to take the scorecard challenge. Early in a campaign design, have the marketing team spend a few hours brainstorming the correct metrics for the scorecard and think through how they will measure these metrics. Note that you want to focus on creating a scorecard with the few metrics that point to value—think 4 or 5 metrics, and not more than 10, for a specific campaign. I have conducted this exercise many times with executives, and invariably teams come back with a well-thought-out scorecard and measurement methodology focusing on the 3 to 5 metrics in each category that define real value.

If marketing campaigns are designed for measurement up front, the impact is easily captured downstream. However, if the vision, KBOs, metrics, and criteria for success are ill defined at the outset, the resulting value of the campaign will be nebulous. So creating the scorecard is the proverbial 1 percent of effort that gives the 99 percent of value later. If the campaign is successful, the scorecard provides factual data to support follow-on funding. If things do not go well, however, the scorecard can provide advanced warning that you are driving a marketing campaign off a cliff.

In summary, creating a marketing campaign scorecard is pretty easy. Given a couple of hours of thought, I have no doubt you can come up with one for your specific campaigns—you can use Figure 3.3 as a starting point. Yet the ability to measure and keep score is an essential first step in the data-driven marketing journey. Marketers who systematically measure are promoted faster and are sought after when times are tough, since they can show the value of what they do and have a track record documented with scorecards.

Facing the B2B Measurement Challenge

B2B companies are one more step removed from a customer. They often "sell" to original equipment manufacturers (OEMs), who then sell the integrated products through a value-added reseller (VAR) or other channel (possibly retail or Internet) to the end customer. Most often, B2B firms that sell through OEMs do not know the end customer, and this is often cited as a major reason why experimental design and marketing measurement are difficult for B2B firms.

Marketing measurement for B2B is challenging, but through an example I will show that it can be done. Microsoft, for example, sells the vast majority of its products indirectly. Its software is loaded onto personal computers manufactured by OEMs such as Dell, HP, Sony, and others, and then sold by these OEMs through channels such as the Internet, Best Buy, Wal-Mart, and other retail stores. A major challenge for Microsoft (as mentioned previously) is that it does not know who actually buys its products. Furthermore, Microsoft spends a significant amount on OEM partner comarketing.

OEM "evaluative" marketing is designed to help consumers evaluate which is the best product from a number of possible choices.

Figure 3.5 Experiential test print advertisement for the Windows 7 new product launch.

Source: Microsoft Marketing.

Typical OEM evaluative ads often have a dense list of the features and functionality of the PC. The OEM comarketing is embedded in the ad through "[the OEM] Recommends Microsoft [Product]," but is this marketing delivering the best bang for the buck for Microsoft?

To find out, Microsoft regularly conducts experiments comparing evaluative advertising with more experience-based advertising. See, for example, the "experiential" test advertisement in Figure 3.5 for the Windows 7 new product launch in 2009. (ConToSo is a fictitious OEM name for experiments.) The new product launch marketing focuses on

Cell	Pre-Post Change			Post-Messaging Impact			
	Likelihood to Purchase Win PC	Intent to Use MCE on Next PC	Intent to Use Win XP on Next PC	Win XP Favorability	MS Brand Recognition	MS Logo Recognition	Detailed MS Product Info Recognition
OEM & MS Feature	++	++	+++	++	+++	++	++
MS Experiential	+++	++++	-	+	++++	++	++
OEM Experiential	+++	++++	++	-	+++	++	++
OEM & MS Experiential (Mercury)	+++	+++++	+++	+	++++	+++	+++

Figure 3.6 Data from the experiential versus traditional Microsoft OEM Media Center Edition print advertising experiment.

Source: Microsoft Marketing.

three major messages: Windows 7 (1) simplifies everyday tasks, (2) works the way you want, and (3) makes new things possible. The experiential ad in Figure 3.5 highlights a few essential elements of these three messages. That is, Windows 7 is faster and more reliable, and has expanded wireless capability, enhanced multimedia, and good energy efficiency, which, taken together, will change your experience and make you "view your PC in a whole new light."

Figure 3.6 shows actual data for the Microsoft Media Center Edition (MCE) evaluative versus experiential advertising experiment. The MCE software is designed to help users manage all of their multimedia on a PC, making you "the center of your media universe." For this example, Microsoft conducted an experiment consisting of four different cells. In each cell, 350 people were individually exposed to different print marketing and asked pre-post questions. Participants in the control group were exposed to traditional feature-based ads. Participants in the three other cells were exposed to "experiential ads" such as that shown in Figure 3.5. In these three cells the branding was varied on the ads so that participants in the three experimental cells were exposed to (1) OEM-only branding, (2) Microsoft-only branding, or (3) OEM and Microsoft joint cobranding advertising, respectively.

The results are shown in Figure 3.6. For confidentiality, the actual numerical changes are not shown. Instead, interpret "−" as a small average negative pre-post percentage change, "++" a small to moderate positive response, "+++" a very good pre-post percentage change, and "++++" a very significant positive change—where pre-post is measured by comparing questions asked before and after viewing the print ad. These questions include "What is your intent to purchase a Windows PC?" and "What is your intent to use Microsoft MCE on your next PC?"

The results are very interesting. First, you see that the control group, the top line of data, faired okay but not great. The challenge, of course, is that feature-based ads are hard for the customer to decipher; they focus on feeds, speed, bits and bytes, and do not clearly define the benefits of the MCE. The experiential ads, in contrast, articulate what the software actually does; it helps you control all of the media in your life.

In the pre-post change data, the experiential ads clearly fare a lot better than the feature-based control group. But what makes this experiment particularly noteworthy is the investigation of which branding is optimal. That is, is it better to just have an OEM-branded ad, to have a Microsoft-only ad, or to cobrand with the OEM partner?

The cobranded OEM and Microsoft experiential ads clearly have the best results, with likelihood to purchase and intent to use rating at the highest end of the scale, and post-message questions for brand and logo recognition rating very high also. This is an example of how 1 plus 1 sometimes equals 10. The OEM- and Microsoft-only branded ads rated poorly on the dimensions of "View Win XP Favorably" and "Intent to use XP." However, consumer perception was significantly more positive when the only difference in the ad was the cobranding of the logos.

This example illustrates multiple important points about marketing measurement and experimental design. First, for a B2B firm, customer surveys can be used as a proxy for actual customer data. Second, nonfinancial metrics can also be used to point to future value. We will discuss this idea further in the next chapter, but for now note that "intent to purchase" serves as a pointer to actual purchasing intent and to the efficacy of this evaluative marketing.

As a result of these experiments, Microsoft committed significantly more funding to OEM comarketing activities, but ensured that the funding was used to optimize the marketing impact as defined by these experiments. The reaction of the OEM partner was extremely positive, as Microsoft added value in the relationship by showing how to optimize the comarketing impact and increase profitability for not just Microsoft but the OEM partner as well.

I have to admit that when I first started on the marketing measurement journey, I had great skepticism about using qualitative data, such as "intent to purchase," from surveys and focus groups. This was due to my heavy quantitative background, coming from science and engineering, where I was used to calculating exactly the "right" answer. But as I conducted more survey-based research, I realized that in marketing it is better to be approximately right than exactly wrong, and I started to appreciate the value of qualitative data.

For sure, if you ask one or two people their "intent to purchase," their opinions are not reliable. However, if you ask 350 people the same question, after exposing them individually to the same advertising, their responses have statistical significance. So the takeaway is that qualitative data can be extremely useful, but you have to be careful that the sample size is large enough.

A rule of thumb for survey-based research is that having more than 100 people in a sample is pretty good, and 300 or more is very good. However, individual in-depth interviews, small intimate focus groups of 6 to 10 people, and quick online surveys with responses from 30 to 50 customers can be invaluable in gaining customer insights. So small samples can be used effectively to rapidly test and experiment with marketing, with the understanding that the insights may be limited, and/or not generalizable to much larger samples or different geographies. I believe that it is infinitely better to fail fast via experiments, rapidly adjusting to find what works, than to crash and burn millions of campaign dollars without any measurement.

Chapter Insights

- A spectrum of metrics exists for marketing, depending on the type of marketing activity.
- Financial metrics quantify more than 50 percent of marketing activities.
- When financial metrics do not work, define marketing metrics that are leading indicators of sales.
- Take the scorecard challenge and design all marketing programs and campaigns to be measured using a balanced scorecard approach.
- B2B companies can use surveys and focus groups effectively to capture metrics in place of direct customer data.

15 Metrics to Radically Improve Marketing Performance

CHAPTER

4

The Five Essential Nonfinancial Metrics

#1 – Brand Awareness, #2 – Test-Drive, #3 – Churn, #4 – Customer Satisfaction (CSAT), and #5 – Take Rate

Shaping Perception: Metric #1—Brand Awareness

Branding is one of the most fascinating and unique aspects of marketing, because branding is all about customer perception. As an example, let's consider bottled water. Pure water is an odorless, tasteless liquid made from molecules of two hydrogen atoms and one oxygen atom (H_2O), and approximately 70 percent of the Earth's surface is covered in water. My point is that, as products go, water is pretty much on the low end of complexity, and it's fairly abundant. Yet, the proliferation of brands of bottled water is amazing: Ice Mountain, Aquafina, Geyser Peak, Poland Spring, and Dasani are a few that are top of mind for me.

So why spend $2 a bottle for the brand and not 25 cents for the generic grocery store brand when the products are identical? I say this and my students have a violent reaction: "It really is different—my water comes from a mountain spring high in the Alps," they say. Yep, and I'm sure the million bottles a month were filled by a guy hand-dipping them in a stream. I agree that Perrier is different—it has bubbles and it has a cool green glass bottle. Dasani claims to have "minerals" as a differentiator, and they went with a blue plastic bottle.

Bottled water emphasizes the power of brand—the product conveys a feeling, an experience, and perception of repeatable quality that the customer is willing to pay a premium for. The value of a brand, or brand equity, is particularly difficult to quantify in hard dollars.

Brand equity is sometimes estimated by subtracting all tangible assets of a firm, derived from various approximations, from the market valuation of the firm based on stock price—the remaining intangible value is attributed to the "brand." The challenge with this approach is that there are so many unknowns that end up multiplying together, that the derived "brand equity" is almost a random number.

A better approach is to use surveys to ask how much more a person will be willing to pay for a branded versus the equivalent nonbranded product. This percentage difference multiplied by the product sales is approximately the value of the brand. The reader should be cautioned, however, that this approach is just an estimate, and in my opinion, the value of marketing to enhance the brand is practically impossible to accurately measure using financial metrics. I, therefore, take a different approach, focusing on the essential nonfinancial metric to measure brand marketing effectiveness, and I show how to use this metric to optimize brand-marketing campaign performance.

Consumer Product Brand Marketing

From a purchasing perspective, a strong brand awareness gives your product or service first consideration, or first look, as the customer moves into the evaluative stage of the purchasing cycle (see Figure 3.2). Over time, customer perception about brands changes, and hence branding is an ongoing activity. For example, Philips Electronics manufactures electric shavers that produce an extremely close shave. Over time, electric shavers have waned in popularity, and there is a perception that

(a)   (b)

Figure 4.1 Philips Nivea for Men Shaver brand advertising: (a) TV and (b) poster and direct mail.

Source: Philips Consumer Lifestyle and Ipsos ASI.

blades give a better shave, in large part due to the good branding of Gillette. Gillette blade versus Philips electric shavers underscores how perception is reality, independent of the technical specifications of the product.

For the 2007 Christmas season, Philips launched a new product-branding campaign in the Netherlands for the Philips Nivea for Men Shaver. The theme was a sensuous female robot helping a guy shave with an electric shaver in the shower, obviously designed to appeal to the male demographic. The campaign included integrated media with TV, MTV promotions, train station billboards, direct-mail postcards, and a dedicated web portal. See Figure 4.1 for representative campaign media.

Ipsos ASI, a United Kingdom-based advertising research agency, conducted weekly surveys of 120 men in the target demographic to track both brand- and product-specific awareness. Questions included:

- "Thinking about all the different places you have seen, heard, or read about electric shavers recently, including all the different kinds of advertising, sponsorship, and other activities that promote them, have you seen, heard, or read anything about the following brands of electric shavers recently?"
- "Have you seen/heard/read/experienced [specific TV, print, etc., advertising]?"

For aided recognition, they also showed the various impression media and asked: "What brand was the ad for?" and to understand

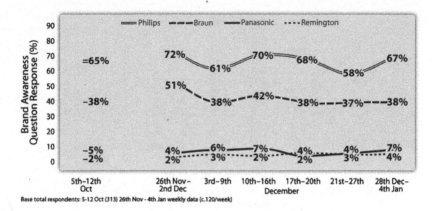

Figure 4.2 Sample Philips Nivea for Men Shaver campaign weekly claimed advertising tracking data.

Source: Philips Consumer Lifestyle and Ipsos ASI UK.

how awareness of the specific advertised product had changed from week to week, they asked: "You said you were aware of Philips electric shavers. Which of the following Philips electric shavers have you heard of?"

Intent to purchase was captured through the request: "Please tell me which of the following best describes how likely you are to consider purchasing a Philips Nivea for Men Shaver in the future."

Figure 4.2 is the response to the first question. The baseline survey, October 5–12, showed 65 percent brand awareness for Philips and 38 percent for its nearest competitor. The campaign data show a peak at the initial launch and then in mid-December at the peak of the advertising. In this same time period, 86 percent of the target audience claimed to recognize some element of the campaign when shown prompts from the advertising. However, overall claimed advertising awareness is often simply mirroring market share, so it is more interesting to look at the pre-post change of the product-specific brand awareness.

Figure 4.3 shows the pre-post change in product-specific brand awareness and intent to purchase over the life of the campaign. For the Philips Nivea for Men Shaver, there is a change in product-specific brand awareness of 22 percent before the campaign versus 25 percent after the campaign, and intent to purchase changed from 9 percent to 12 percent after the campaign. These data suggest an impact of the product launch marketing over a relatively short three-month time

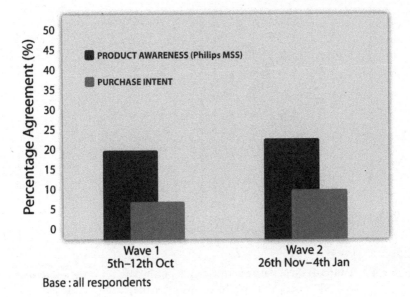

Figure 4.3 Philips Nivea for Men Shaver pre-post product awareness and intent to purchase impact.

Source: Philips Consumer Lifestyle and Ipsos ASI UK.

frame. In addition, as discussed in Chapter 3, intent to purchase is a leading indicator of future sales, so the survey is measuring product brand awareness at the beginning of the purchasing cycle and pointing to trial near the end (see Figure 3.2).

However, it is not enough to get the "answer" in term of the pre-post change of awareness. You need to understand why—what caused the awareness impact, what's working, and what's not? A common approach to quantify advertising awareness is based on cost per 1,000 impressions (CPM). The idea is to estimate the number of impressions and then calculate the cost per impression for each media channel: TV, print, direct mail, online, and so on. The lowest cost per impression is then perceived as the winner. The challenge with this approach is that it does not measure the efficacy of the marketing. That is, did the marketing influence perception?

Most ads fail because people don't realize which brand the creative is communicating for. Figure 4.4 is the results of the Philips Nivea for Men Shaver campaign on the dimension of those who recognize the touch point against those who attribute the communication to the correct brand. Survey participants are asked whether they have seen

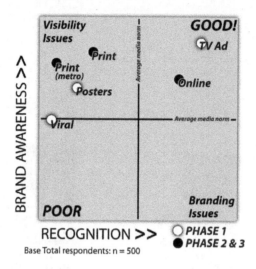

Figure 4.4 Awareness campaign performance optimization on the dimensions of brand awareness and recognition of the touch point.

Source: Ipsos ASI UK.

the ad (unaided awareness that is recognition), and for the brand linkage, they are exposed to the advertising and asked, "What brand was this advertising for?" (aided brand awareness).

High brand awareness and recognition is the top right quadrant of Figure 4.4; this is ideal and, for Philips Nivea for Men Shaver, TV and online adverting are performing particularly well. Poor brand awareness and high recognition are bottom right. Campaign components in this quadrant could be placed well but have branding issues. For Philips Nivea for Men Shaver, there are no campaign activities in this quadrant. There are, however, multiple components in the high brand awareness, low recognition, top left quadrant of Figure 4.4. These components are working well, except that they have visibility issues—for these components, question whether the creative is impactful enough to reach the consumer and the efficacy of the placement: is there a better location to advertise?

Poor visibility and brand awareness marketing clearly have problems, shown in bottom left quadrant, and "viral" is in this category. Jamie Robertson, director of Ipsos ASI UK, told me: "Just because a campaign component is not working well does not mean we should not do it at all. We need to reevaluate how we are doing the marketing and look for opportunities to improve the effectiveness."

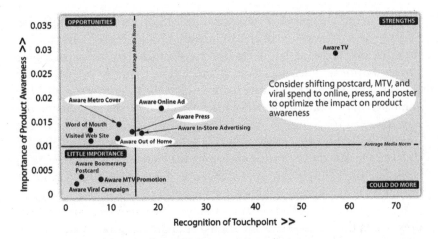

Figure 4.5 Awareness campaign optimization on the dimensions
of perceived importance of the specific campaign media on product
awareness and recognition of the touch point.

Source: Ipsos ASI UK.

Figure 4.5 dissects the awareness campaign on the dimension of
perceived importance of the specific campaign media (TV ad, postcard,
poster, MTV ad, etc.) to product brand awareness and the dimension of
recognition of the TV ad, postcard, poster, MTV ad, and so on. This
more fine-grained analysis identified the postcard, MTV, and viral
spending as not contributing significantly to the product brand awareness (bottom left quadrant of Figure 4.5). Ipsos therefore made the
recommendation to shift future campaign spending from these touch
points to online, press, and poster, which have high perceived product
brand awareness but just above-average recognition.

Sabrina Tucci, Global Communication Intelligence, Philips Consumer Lifestyle, told me:

> The awareness marketing measurement not only provided insights
> into product brand awareness and future purchasing intent, but also
> allowed us to optimize the campaign for future launches. The data-
> driven approach to awareness marketing gave us a very valuable
> insight into the specific market and target audience. These learnings
> are extremely valuable for our business units and marketing team to
> develop the communication strategy for the product and category.

What I admire is that the campaign was designed for measurement
and optimization of future campaigns: weekly surveys were conducted to

capture brand and product awareness and to uncover the component effectiveness. As a result of the campaign, Philips shaver sales did not dramatically increase but were on target with expectations. Some Philips business executives voiced frustration that the campaign did not generate a financial return on investment (ROI) during the time the campaign ran. But this was not the objective of the campaign; the objective was to change awareness and influence future purchase intent toward the Philips shaver for a demographic that is not buying electric shavers. Measured against this objective, the campaign was a success. In addition, the data-driven approach gave deep insights into how to optimize the marketing spending for future iterations of the campaign.

The good and the bad of data is that you see when you win and lose. Given data the business can and should ask hard questions, for example, "Was the change in perception worth the marketing investment?" Asking and answering these questions is a valuable discussion that is needed for healthy alignment of marketing investments and business objectives. But education is needed to help business executives understand that not all marketing investments need to show a financial ROI, and branding in particular is almost impossible to quantify with financial metrics. However, you can define nonfinancial brand awareness metrics that point to future sales, and you can measure marketing impact through changes in customer perception.

The brand campaign optimization (Figures 4.4 and 4.5) may seem intimidating. But realize that you can get started by conducting a simple brand survey in a limited geography, and see if the needle moves on customer awareness as a result of the campaign. As a next step, it is not so hard to add a few questions in the survey to probe brand/product awareness and recognition for specific advertising media—with these data you can generate Figures 4.4 and 4.5 for your campaign. You can then see which specific media is creating a brand impact, and what's working and what's not.

Brand Marketing for Business-to-Business

Consumer products and business-to-business (B2B) are surprisingly similar from a brand measurement perspective. The branding goal in B2B is to change customer awareness toward a product or service that may not be obvious to the consumer. Intel, for example, revolutionized the PC industry by branding "Intel inside," and DuPont uses NASCAR to brand its auto paint.

The big difference between B2B and consumer products is that often B2B has more than one customer. That is, there may be specific brand marketing to channel partners and manufacturers and different marketing to end consumers. DuPont, for example, hosts more than 20,000 B2B "partners" at NASCAR events each year in large part to build brand and relationships. Yet, the principles of brand marketing measurement are universal.

Navistar, Inc., is a $14.1 billion revenue manufacturer of large 18-wheeler International® brand trucks, school buses, and military vehicles. IC Bus™ is a subsidiary of Navistar and is the market leader in school buses. The economic downturn of 2009 hit the company hard as industry truck and bus sales slowed significantly. But, in spite of these challenges, IC Bus continued to innovate and build brand, given a lean marketing budget. In 2009, global warming and the environment came to the forefront of national attention, and IC Bus was uniquely positioned with the only plug-in electric hybrid school bus on the market.

As a first step, IC Bus started small with a pilot campaign purchasing radio spots in Sacramento, California. The overarching goal was to increase awareness of a very powerful demographic—moms aged 25 to 49. The radio spots emphasized the benefits of riding a school bus as explained by a young child[1]:

- According to the American School Bus Council, just one school bus is equal to taking 36 cars off the road. This equates to 17.3 million cars taken off the road annually by children riding school buses.
- Every year, 3.1 billion gallons of fuel are saved by students riding school buses.
- If another 10 percent more children rode school buses, another 300 million gallons of fuel could be saved annually.
- An estimated $663 in fuel costs and 3,600 miles per family could be saved annually by putting their child on a school bus. From kindergarten to 12th grade, that is 46,800 miles or $8,619.
- The average daily fuel cost to transport a child to school is $3.68 for a private vehicle but only $0.73 if that child rides a school bus.

The brand was slipped in at the end of the radio spot as a public service announcement, "Brought to you by IC Bus."

The results from a brand metrics perspective were impressive. Pre-post phone surveys of 300 moms aged 25 to 49 with at least one child in kindergarten through high school were conducted in January, then in April 2009. The survey first asked the unaided reception question: "Have you recently seen/heard any advertisements for school buses being environmentally conscious or green?" There was a 29 percent increase in unaided recall of an ad promoting riding the school bus as environmentally conscious. This means nearly a third of the target demographic had unaided recall of hearing the ad. Follow-on questions revealed that respondents could also recall the main messages of the ad.

For the next set of survey questions, the ad was played and the aided recall question was asked: "Have you heard this advertisement on the radio before today?" There was a 32 percent pre-post measured positive response, suggesting that those who claimed to have heard the ad were likely recalling the IC Bus ad. The phone survey then probed potential impact of the ad by asking: "What impact does the advertisement you heard have on how likely you are to have your children ride the school bus in the future?"—this question is the branding equivalent of "intent to purchase." For the income demographic above $75,000 per year, there was a 13 percent increase in positive response.

What I like about this example is that the marketers started small, in a limited geography, and measured pre-post perception change of the major components of the branding business objectives. They demonstrated that one third of the demographic could recall the ad and measured a very significant perception change toward "intent to use" school buses.

As a next step, the marketing team came up with the idea of a school essay-writing contest, America's Greenest School (AGS) contest, where the student with the winning essay received a scholarship and their school received a hybrid school bus from IC Bus. Dena Leuchter, marketing communications manager of IC Bus, told me:

> As rounds of budget cuts came through [in 2009], we were faced with decisions on what to cut. We needed a significant budget to launch a new customer brand campaign. As a completely new effort and target audience, AGS could have been the first area to slice. However, I held onto the budget for AGS with a tight grip—when you have an idea that is so simple and you have a gut feeling that it will be groundbreaking for your company and industry, you cannot sacrifice it. If AGS was the last thing standing, I knew we had to make it happen and aim for the fences with its full budget intact.

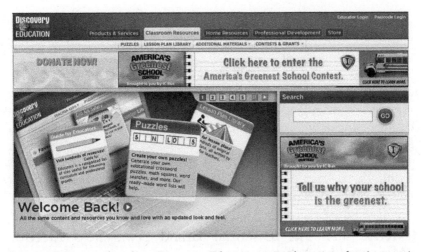

Figure 4.6 Screen shot from DiscoveryEducation.com featuring the America's Greenest School contest impression advertising.

Source: Discovery Education and IC Bus™ Marketing Communications.

The branding initiative was undertaken on a relatively small $350,000 budget. The prize was a $5,000 scholarship for the student with the winning essay and a $200,000 IC Bus hybrid school bus donated to the school. Marketing consisted primarily of public relations press releases and e-mail and web impressions on Discovery Education.com (see Figure 4.6). Due to the educational component, Discovery Education enabled an e-mail blast to 94,000 teachers as part of the campaign. Of 94,000 total e-mails sent, 13 percent were opened and 16 percent clicked through. The contest received enthusiastic support from kids, parents, teachers, schools, and school boards—all of whom influence the purchasing decisions of their school district— generating awareness of the environmental impact of riding a school bus, and especially the IC Bus hybrid bus.

From January 1, 2009, to June 12, 2009, when the winner was announced, the campaign generated nearly 300 million media impressions, including TV news broadcasts in 10 major metro markets, *USA Today*, and online sites and mom blogs. But most important is customer engagement for the campaign. Writing an essay is a lot of work, and whole households got involved. Over 20,000 people voted, and over 30,000 votes were placed for the 10 finalists (people could vote more than once). Furthermore, of the nearly 80,000 visits to the AGS web site, more than 40 percent opted in to receive future e-mails from IC

Bus. Leuchter told me, "We were hoping we would get at least 100 entries, and when we saw that we received nearly 2,000 we knew we had a success on our hands."

The AGS campaign highlights how creativity in campaign design and execution can drive incredible performance gains. The branding initiative was designed for measurement and had a high level of customer engagement. Taken together, this is a winning combination for data-driven branding.

In summary, the following two simple questions asked of customers enable the measurement of brand awareness from both a consumer product and a B2B perspective.

Metric #1: The Essential Brand Awareness Metric Measured by Asking

For [product or service], what is the first [company or product] name you think of?
For [product or service], what other [companies or products] have you heard of?

These questions uncover unaided reception of your product or service and the relative ranking of brands relative to competitors. These questions are a starting point and should be refined for the specific campaign. Follow-on questions can show example marketing for aided awareness and ask questions to uncover brand and messaging impact and intent to act.

How do you actually do this? Brand awareness measurement is easily accomplished with relatively low-cost phone interviews and surveys to gather the data. If the marketing is combined with the Internet, as in the AGS campaign, the call to action can be captured. Action is related to customer engagement and is another measure of the brand marketing impact.

At the next level, you can relatively easily apply the principles of the Philips Nivea for Men Shaver example to optimize your brand marketing and ensure you get the biggest bang for the brand-marketing buck. You don't have the resources to do this? I suggest you cut the advertising spending by 10 percent and invest the money in measurement—if you apply the optimization approach you will get much more than 10 percent improvement in performance. Ipsos, for example, documented a more than 20 percent performance gain for future Philips Nivea for Men Shaver brand marketing.

Comparative Marketing: Metric #2—Test-Drive

On March 9, 2009, the Dow Jones Industrial Average hit a 12-year low of 6,547 points. On March 6 of that same week, Porsche Cars North America launched an aggressive marketing campaign. "The Porsche brand is about being confident and taking control, and Porsche owners share this confident spirit. We wanted the Porsche First Mile campaign to give prospective customers the confidence to test-drive our product," said David Pryor, Porsche Cars North America's vice president of marketing: "We know that when a prospective buyer drives a Porsche, he or she is much more likely to buy one. We also understand that many people think our cars are out of their reach and simply inaccessible."

In April 2009, the U.S. campaign delivered more than 241 million online display impressions and 17 million in print. See Figure 4.7 for print and Internet advertising. These impressions resulted in more than 2,000 test-drive sign-ups. "Dealers were doubtful at first, but within three to four weeks had sales that would not have happened without the campaign. These results changed the dealers mind-set toward the importance of marketing the test-drive," Pryor told me.

The Porsche First Mile campaign illustrates best-practice data-driven marketing principles. All elements of the campaign were tracked. Note, for example, the SMS text number and Internet URL in the print advertising of Figure 4.7(a). Weekly leads generated were tracked by geography and the campaign was dynamically tuned to improve performance while it was running, this is the essence of Chapter 8, Agile Marketing.

For example, the marketing team realized that the southern U.S. states were getting less leads than they should have based on their overall sales contribution. As a result, they used targeted online and print advertising in May 2009 to bring up the number of leads in this geography. Said Scott Baker, Porsche Cars North America manager of marketing communications: "Other auto companies have marketing budgets 5 to 50 times bigger than Porsche's. We therefore have to be very focused on optimizing efficiency and delivering high-value marketing activities."

While fairly obvious for a car, the test-drive metric is relevant in practically all purchase decisions. Intel, for example, has a greater than 80 percent market share in central processing units (CPUs) for

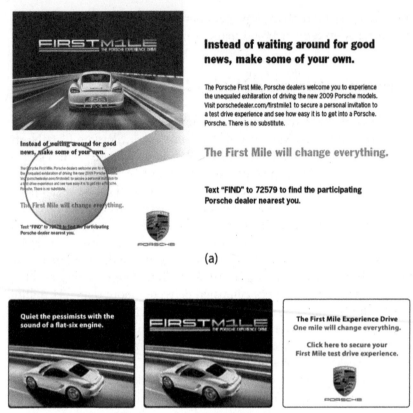

Figure 4.7 Example of Porsche First Mile (a) print and (b) online impression advertising. Note the Internet URL and SMS text messaging number in the print advertising (a).

Source: Porsche Cars North America.

Windows-based PCs and servers. This almost monopoly power drives Intel's sales model: it has a very large direct sales force that engages original equipment manufacturer (OEM) partners with the goal of selling additional Intel chips on the motherboard around the CPU. Intel's sales cycle typically takes 18 months, from initial discussion to manufacture with the OEM shipping boards with new Intel chips. This relatively long sales cycle poses a challenge for incenting the sales force and measuring evaluative marketing efficacy.

However, within a few months of the initial Intel and OEM dialogue, in order to move forward the OEM must create a team to study the feasibility of incorporating the Intel product into the mother-board. This constitutes a "design win" for Intel; it is the proverbial test-drive that points to future revenues. Why? The OEM has had a series of conversations but has not yet committed skin to the game. For the OEM, pulling together a team to investigate manufacturing feasibility requires people and money, which is not possible without an implied commitment to purchase. By collecting data in its operational customer relationship management (CRM) system, Intel can measure the conversion rate from design wins to sales and can predict the probability of future sales revenues more than 12 months in the future. For marketing, the focus is then on improving evaluative marketing materials for the Intel sales force to drive more design wins.

As another example, Philips Medical Systems manufactures and sells large, expensive magnetic resonance imaging (MRI) and computed tomography (CT) scanners to hospitals. The purchasing decision in a hospital is a group decision, often requiring buy-in of multiple stakeholders of doctors, nurses, management, and support staff. Philips has noted the equivalent of a test-drive for MRI and CT scanners. In order to facilitate the purchase decision buy-in, the hospital will often request a test-drive for the doctors and staff to test the product. This is a signal of future purchasing intent that may be several months in the future.

The Internet provides new and unique opportunities for marketing measurement at the evaluative stage. Navistar, for example, tracks the number of users who design virtual trucks online. This is a virtual test-drive, and improvements in web evaluative marketing can be quantified by an increase in this metric. A particularly innovative use of the Internet in this same theme is from Luxottica, a global fashion company, with $9 billion annual revenues, based in Milan, Italy.

Luxottica has consolidated the global high-end sunglass business, with products ranging from a few hundred dollars to $1,500. The Luxottica brands include Ray-Ban, Oakley, Maui-Jim, Prada, Dolce and Gabbana, and many more. In addition, Luxottica is vertically integrated and owns Sunglass Hut and LensCrafters in the United States.

The traditional sunglass purchasing experience involves going to the store and trying on different sunglasses in front of a mirror. Luxottica has simulated this experience through an evaluative marketing initiative. The Ray-Ban web site, for example, has as an innovative web application that enables users to try on sunglasses in a "virtual mirror" (see Figure 4.8). Combined with a PC webcam, customers can try the glasses and see how they look in the virtual mirror, moving their head

Figure 4.8 The Ray-Ban Virtual Mirror with an online sunglass simulated test-drive. See www.rayban.com.

Source: Luxottica Group.

similar to an in-store experience. Users can print their final selection of how they look with the sunglasses; the number of printouts is the key test-drive metric for Luxottica.

Not only does the sunglass test-drive metric point to the efficacy of evaluative marketing, it has important supply-chain management implications. A challenge in the sunglass business is that the sales window is only seven months, tied to the summer season. Plus, a new product life cycle is only one season long, because next year's fashion has to be different. Since there is a four-month lead time in sunglass manufacturing, Luxottica has only two chances at guessing demand during a product life cycle: once at the start of the season and once a few months in.

By releasing new designs on the web site several months before they hit stores and measuring the number of printouts for a particular design, Luxottica can estimate demand and adjust manufacturing accordingly. This leading metric is therefore a powerful tool for Luxottica to maximize product profitability by ensuring that the right product mix and volumes are shipped to stores in the season.

There are limitations, however, as Internet-based evaluative marketing appeals to select demographics. Generations X and Y are much more likely to preview products online, and the Ray-Ban application is a hit with these demographics: This online application has more than 3 million unique users. Dolce and Gabbana sunglasses, however, appeal to women over 40, who rarely visit the Web for a product evaluation prior to purchase. So the virtual mirror evaluative marketing does not work for them.

If you can measure who did a test-drive and purchased, you can also calculate the conversion rate. The test-drive conversion rate is just the number of purchases divided by the number of test-drives. Let's assume the test-drive conversion rate is 20 percent; then each 100 test-drives add 20 product purchases. So test-drives can be linked to cash, but you need to track both test-drives and purchases for specific customers.

In summary, the test-drive is the essential metric at the evaluative stage of the purchasing cycle. You should therefore define the test-drive for your product or service and then design evaluative marketing campaigns to incent the test-drive; the resulting change of this metric evaluates efficacy of evaluative marketing campaigns and is a leading indicator of future sales.

Metric #2: The Essential Evaluative Metric

Test-drive = Customer pretest of a product or service prior to purchase

---

Loyalty Marketing: Metric #3—Churn

I live in a 75-year-old house, and the garage door opening is rather small. One Saturday I succeeded in scraping the left quarter panel of the family Lexus down the side of the door. The lecture on my driving skills lasted for about three days, and shortly thereafter I went to the dealer to get the car fixed. I have limited experience with auto body repair, except to know that usually a small dent knocks a hole in $1,000. So I was expecting the worst.

The cheerful Lexus dealer took the keys and gave me the free loaner, and I returned at the end of the day.

"What was the damage?" I asked, fumbling for my credit card.

"There is no charge sir. Touch-ups are free."

Talk about surprise and delight. I couldn't believe it. How was I to know—the side of the car is mostly plastic and the three-foot-long scrapes apparently "buffed right out." I ecstatically returned home to share my good fortune with my wife.

The essential metric to quantify customer loyalty is churn rate. Churn is the percentage of existing customers who chose not to do business with you, often calculated on an annual basis. So, for example, let's assume your customer churn is 20 percent in a year. If you have 100 existing customers at the beginning of the year, then at the end of the year you will have only 80 customers, assuming you do nothing to retain the 20 customers who leave.

In the auto industry, Lexus has incredibly loyal customers; approximately 70 percent of Lexus owners repurchase a Lexus as their next car. If we assume on average that a car is purchased every five years, this means that Lexus has a 30 percent churn over five years. Churn is usually calculated on an annual basis, so in one year Lexus has a customer churn of approximately 6 percent (that is, 6 percent churn/year × 5 years = 30 percent churn over 5 years).

Reducing churn rate can have a very significant impact to the bottom line. Some other luxury carmakers have repeat purchase rates of approximately 50 percent. Assuming a five-year purchase cycle, a 50 percent repurchase rate corresponds to 10 percent per year churn. For Lexus, the difference between 10 percent and 6 percent churn a year is huge—it corresponds to approximately 20 percent more repeat sales revenues relative to some competitors![2]

Loyalty marketing initiatives for Lexus include a free loaner car, free car washes, and breakfasts on Saturday mornings at certain dealers, a free subscription to the *Lexus* lifestyle magazine, and marketing offers to attend "drive tee to green" golf events tied to new car product launches such as the LS 450. Of course, the loyalty initiatives also include free touch-ups.

Free touch-ups also have a significant benefit to Lexus. Since customer loyalty is so high, the vast majority of existing Lexus owners trade in their old Lexus for a new one. It is therefore advantageous for Lexus to offer free touch-ups, since this is a low-cost service that prevents rust and increases the resale value of the "pre-owned" Lexus after trade-in. This example illustrates the best type of loyalty marketing—offer a "free" repeat product or service that is relatively low cost to you, but has high-perceived value to the customer. The repeat customer interaction enables the sale of additional high-margin products or services, builds loyalty, and increases retention. That is, the loyalty, marketing reduces churn.

These principles are not limited to large firms. Dental Care Partners (DCP) was founded in 1981 by Dr. Edward H. Meckler. Meckler owned and operated a successful dental practice in Cleveland, Ohio, for many years. Although he took great satisfaction in treating his patients, Meckler became troubled by how many people were not receiving the dental care they needed. He also realized how challenging it was to run a dental care practice as a business and treat patients.

Meckler came up with a solution that addressed both problems. He developed a business model that would supply doctors with the facilities, equipment, and administrative and marketing support they needed, leaving them free to spend more time with their patients. The resulting cost efficiencies would be passed on to the patients, many of whom would be otherwise unable to afford professional dental care. In 2009, DCP managed 162 practices, including 80 DentalWorks and Sears Dental offices in 10 states, generating annual revenues in excess of $100 million.

DCP uses innovative loyalty marketing with their "Free Whitening for Life" program. The idea is to offer patients free teeth whitening for a lifetime, after the initial whitening procedure. Dr. Charles Zasso, chief dental officer, told me: "We combine the guidance of a dentist, custom-made trays, and professional products to deliver a superior service. The follow-up whitening is perceived as very high value by the patient, but does not require a very significant time commitment of the doctor or high cost in additional dental supplies." The patient is incented to come back periodically into the office and as a result gets continuous dental care with DCP.

As a result of this loyalty marketing, DCP measured a significant churn reduction, and this improvement in churn has important implications for the bottom line. But beyond the revenue impact from the churn reduction, marketing for dental services most often focuses on price, with low-cost price promotions. Said Brian Kovach, director of DCP Marketing, "The program works for both acquisition and retention marketing, and enables us to focus more on the value, rather than the cost, of dental services."

Although churn is often defined on an annual basis, for customer retention in a high-churn business, what is really important is to proactively market to customers who are about to churn. As an example,

Input Variables	
Customer Base	100,000 *
Annual Revenue per Customer	$1,000 *
Annual Churn Rate	30.0% *
Churn Rate Reduced by 5%	28.5%
Churn Rate Reduced by 10%	27.0%
Churn Rate Reduced by 25%	22.5%
Annual Churn Analysis	
Total Revenues (No Churn)	$100,000,000
Customers Lost to Churn	30,000
Revenues Lost to Churn	$30,000,000
Revenues with Churn	$70,000,000
Revenues Lost with 5% Churn Reduction	$28,500,000
5% Churn Reduction Revenue Impact	$1,500,000
Revenues Lost with 10% Churn Reduction	$27,000,000
10% Churn Reduction Revenue Impact	$3,000,000
Revenues Lost with 25% Churn Reduction	$22,500,000
25% Churn Reduction Revenue Impact	$7,500,000
*Change these cells for your business	

Figure 4.9 Churn reduction impact template. Downloadable at www.agileinsights.com/ROMI.

EarthLink is a midsized, $955 million revenue company that provides dial-up and broadband Internet access. Sam McPhaul, senior manager, Business Intelligence for EarthLink, pointed out to me, "We focus on the shortest amount of time to get out in front of the customer to stop them from churning." EarthLink specifically does loyalty marketing to reduce 30- and 90-day churn. See Chapter 9 for a detailed example from EarthLink on churn reduction.

Figure 4.9 is a template to calculate the revenue impact of reducing churn. The template assumes a 30 percent annual churn rate, $1,000 annual revenue from a customer, and 100,000 customers—these variables can easily be changed for your business in the template. The annual revenue impact of reducing churn by 5 percent, 10 percent, and 25 percent are calculated. To calculate the 30- or 90-day impact of retention marketing, just divide the annual churn rate by 12 to get the monthly rate, or by 4 to get the 90-day churn rate. You can plug your business-specific numbers into the template, which is downloadable at www.agileinsights. com/ROMI. The online template gives 30- and 90-day churn analysis.

Most business-to-consumer (B2C) companies have direct access to customer data. For these companies a loyalty card and/or branded credit card is often the key to measuring and tracking churn, and frequent flyer point rewards or card-only discounts incent continuous purchases. Churn measurement may seem challenging, though, especially for B2B companies, if you do not know who your customers are. You can start by using surveys to estimate the churn rate. That is, for a sample of 300 customers, measure the percentage of them who stop doing business with you in six months or a year. This is an estimate of the churn for your larger customer base.

Specifically for B2B you can also focus on channel partner churn. The channel partner is the customer before the customer, and churn in B2B is the percentage of channel partners that stop selling your products or services in a year. For B2B, partner loyalty marketing such as golf events, executive summits, and reward programs can be used to ensure that your products or services are well placed by the channel partner and to reduce partner churn.

In summary, churn is the essential metric to measure customer loyalty through repeat purchases, by monitoring the fraction of customers who stop doing business with you in a time period—often a year, 90 days, or 30 days. Reducing the churn rate can significantly impact the bottom line and loyalty marketing should therefore focus on this essential metric.

Metric #3: The Essential Loyalty Metric

Churn = Percentage of existing customers who stop purchasing your products or services, measured in a year, 90 days, or 30 days

---

How do you get started? As a first step, you should measure your customer churn rate either directly by tracking customer repeat purchases or indirectly through customer surveys. More likely than not, the churn is higher than you think. Then start with loyalty marketing campaigns to the highest-value customers and conduct experiments on small samples to measure the efficacy of the loyalty marketing initiatives. See Chapter 6 for more in-depth examples of value-based marketing.

Customer Satisfaction: Metric #4—CSAT

When I was growing up, I wore eyeglasses as thick as the bottom of Coke bottles. Yes, I was a nerd. In 2002, I went to a party and the host, Jackie, was raving about her Lasik surgery. We talked about it, and I explained that my problem was that I was really blind (minus 11), so Lasik would not work for me. She then explained that her friend who was as nearsighted as me had Lasik—she was also at the party and raved about the results and their doctor. It turns out Jackie had recommended the doctor to her friend (and Jackie had the doctor recommended to her). I'm pretty nervous about doctor-type things, but I was sick of waking up in a complete blur every morning, so I checked out Jackie's doctor and ultimately went through with the procedure. Today, I have better than 20/20 vision—for me it was a life-changing experience.[3] This is a personal story about the power of someone you trust making a recommendation for a product or service.

I asked my executive and MBA classes to describe a product or service that they recommend to a friend. A sample of the brands they recommend: Jet Blue, Blue Nile, Lexus, Netflix, and Shutterfly. Students fairly frequently rave about Jet Blue: they like the leather seats and the personal TV. Blue Nile, www.bluenile.com, sells high-quality diamonds over the Internet with a 100 percent satisfaction guarantee or money back. One student explained how he purchased an engagement ring on Blue Nile and was impressed by the good customer service and reasonable price. He had the diamond independently appraised and verified the quality and value. He has subsequently told hundreds of people about his positive experience.

"Would you recommend to a friend?" is the essential question to define satisfied customers: meaning only customers responding 9 or 10 on a 10-point scale, with 10 being "would definitely recommend and I am truly satisfied." Fred Reichheld has used this question to define the "net promoter score," which is the subtraction of the average number of detractors (those who answer 0 to 6 on the 1 to 10 scale of "would you recommend?") from promoters (those who answer 9 or 10).[4]

Academic research has debated Reichheld's claim that asking "Would you recommend?" is better than asking "Are you satisfied?" and the validity of subtracting the detractors from the promoters. From my perspective, it costs nothing to ask both "Would you recommend?" and "Are you satisfied?" in a survey—the answers should be correlated.

But I agree with Reichheld's overall idea—for actionable metrics, it is better to ask a few simple questions that focus management attention.

Certainly, how you ask a question can influence the answer. For example, a major garbage and recycling company in the United States used to ask a series of survey questions to measure customer satisfaction. These questions started with a drawn-out discussion on the customer's garbage, pickups, cleanliness of garbage trucks, and friendliness of workers, and then finally asked how satisfied the customer was. Not surprisingly, the detailed discussion of garbage made most customers neutral in satisfaction. Simply asking "Would you recommend?" at the beginning of the survey added clarity to customer satisfaction for this company.

DSW is an example of the importance of CSAT in practice. DSW is a $1.4 billion discounted brand-name footwear retailer that focuses primarily on women, but also sells men's shoes. DSW offers more than 2,000 styles of dress, casual, and athletic shoes, and in addition sell handbags, hosiery, and accessories. DSW operates 300 stores in more than 35 states and also sells online. The company is opening new stores at a pace of about 10 per year through 2010, and also operates more than 375 leased departments inside stores operated by other retailers.

To measure CSAT, DSW asks survey questions such as:

- "How likely would you be to recommend DSW to a friend, relative, or colleague?"
- "All things considered, how satisfied are you with DSW?"

And to link to future spending, DSW asks:

- "Thinking about the past four months, approximately how much have you spent on shoes for yourself at DSW and other stores?"
- "Now thinking about the next four months, approximately how much do you plan to spend on shoes for yourself at DSW and other stores?"

For the first question, "Would you recommend?" 37 percent of DSW customers responded that they would highly recommend. The reason for the high CSAT is in part due to DSW's award-winning rewards program, which is free to all store and online shoppers. Customers accrue points with each purchase, which provide reward certificates. Of

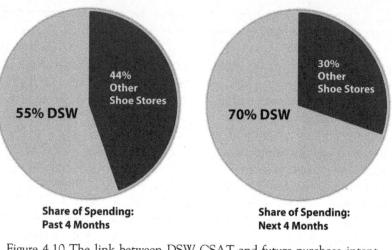

Share of Spending:
Past 4 Months

Share of Spending:
Next 4 Months

Figure 4.10 The link between DSW CSAT and future purchase intent
for highly satisfied customers.

Source: DSW research.

a sample of DSW "advisor" customers, a full 68 percent are highly
satisfied with DSW rewards. Most important, these shoppers anticipate
increasing their spending with DSW in the next four months (see
Figure 4.10). This is a significant result, since it shows the link between
customer satisfaction and future sales. Of course, you have to be careful,
since some customers overexaggerate their future spending intent.
However, the survey results suggest DSW is heading in the right
direction and the idea is to be directionally correct.

Derek Ungless, DSW executive vice president and chief marketing
officer, told me, "Our customers are shoe lovers. There is strong product
attraction and brand affinity by our customers. We have always observed
and acted upon the correlation between their satisfaction and spend
performance. The more satisfied our customers are, the more shoes
they buy."

From my perspective, the ultimate for marketing is when your
customers are so excited about your products or services that they
recommend to friends or colleagues. Said Ungless: "Customer evangel-
ists and fans demonstrate their emotional connection to your brand, so
they become your marketing department. Everywhere. And what's even
better? The passion adds authenticity to that connection—a customer's
recommendation is the best compliment your customer can ever give
your brand."

Customer satisfaction is a double-edged sword. A related question is "What product or service would you not recommend to a friend?" This question can elicit a strong response. My students have reported luxury car dealers unable to resolve simple maintenance issues, a phone company incapable of getting the bill correct, and an airline with terrible customer service. These students also told many more people how bad their experience was with these companies. Hence, if customer satisfaction starts to decline, this is a leading indicator of future sales decreasing, and is clearly damaging to the brand. I view CSAT as the golden marketing metric, since it links brand and loyalty in the behavioral impact model (see Figure 3.2).

In summary, CSAT is a leading indicator of future sales and can be measured by asking a simple question: "Would you recommend?" Related questions can link to future purchasing intent. Obviously, CSAT trending upward over time is good, and CSAT trending down is bad. The final takeaway: you need to actively manage CSAT just as you would sales revenue.

Metric #4: Customer Satisfaction (CSAT) Measured by Asking the Essential Question

How likely would you be to recommend [product, service, or company] to a friend or colleague?

If you are not currently measuring CSAT, it's easy to get started by doing some surveys in specific segments or for specific products and services you offer. I believe CSAT is one of the most important marketing metrics for your firm—you can be a hero by explaining to the CFO and CEO that you have a golden metric to predict future financial performance.

Campaign Effectiveness: Metric #5—Take Rate

The last metric of this chapter is the essential operations metric: take rate. This metric measures internal effectiveness of a campaign and can be linked to campaign cost. Take rate is just the percentage of customers who accept an offer. For example, if you send out a demand generation marketing offer with 1,000 direct-mail pieces (or make 1,000 telemarketing calls) and 50 people accept the offer, then the take rate is $50 \div 1,000 = 5$ percent.

For this example, let's assume the contact cost is $5 for each direct-mail piece or telemarketing phone call. Since we made 1,000 contacts, the cost of the marketing is 1,000 contacts × $5/contact = $5,000. But 50 people accepted the offer, so the acquisition cost (AC) per customer is:

$$AC \, per \, customer = \$5,000 \div 50 = \$100$$

That is, the customer AC is the total cost of the marketing divided by the number of customers who accept the offer. In summary:

Metric #5: The Essential Marketing Performance Metric

$$\text{Take rate} = \frac{\text{Number of accepted offers}}{\text{Number of contacts}}$$

And AC is calculated from:

$$AC = \frac{\text{Cost per contact} \times \text{Number of contacts}}{\text{Number of accepted offers}} = \frac{\text{Cost per contact}}{\text{Take rate}}$$

We will discuss profitability in the next chapter. For now, realize that if the net money you can make from the product or service being sold is less than the $100 AC, then this is a losing demand generation marketing campaign.

The AC equation is very simple but has incredibly profound implications for your marketing cost performance. Notice how AC is equal to cost per contact divided by the take rate. So if you reduce the cost per contact, the AC goes down, and if you increase the take rate, the AC also goes down. So what? Realize there is a multiplier effect. Let's assume the cost per contact is reduced by a factor of two, and the take rate increases by a factor of two. The AC is then reduced by a factor of four!

$$\frac{1}{2} \div 2 = \frac{1}{4}$$

Reducing the contact cost and/or improving the take rate can therefore dramatically reduce the AC per customer, which can save you lots of marketing dollars. As another example, if the take rate is

Input Variables	
Take Rate	3.00% *
Cost per Contact	$5.00 *
New Take Rate	3.50% *
(a) Analysis with a Fixed Number of Marketing Contacts	
Total Marketing Contacts	100,000,000 *
Customers Acquired	3,000,000
Total Marketing Cost	$500,000,000
Acquisition Cost (AC) per Customer	$166.67
With a 3.5% Take Rate	
Customers Acquired	3,500,000
Acquisition Cost (AC) per Customer	$142.86
(b) Analysis with a Fixed Number of Acquired Customers	
With a 3.5% Take Rate	
Customers Acquired (Fixed Target)	3,000,000 *
Total Marketing Contacts	85,714,286
Total Marketing Cost	$428,571,429
Acquisition Cost (AC) per Customer	$142.86
Total Contact Cost Saving	$71,428,571
*Change these cells for your business	

Figure 4.11 Take-rate analysis template (a) for a fixed number of contacts and variable acquired customers and (b) for a fixed number of acquired customers. Downloadable at www.agileinsights.com/ROMI.

6 percent and the contact cost is $4, for 1,000 contacts the customer AC is: $1,000 \times \$4 \div 60 = \$66$. This is 33 percent less cost than with a $5 contact cost and a 5 percent take rate, for which the AC was $100. For your reference, Figure 4.11 is an Excel template linking take rate, contact costs, and customer acquisition cost. The template is downloadable for free at www.agileinsights.com/ROMI.

The relationships of the template in Figure 4.11 have important implications for both small and large marketing budgets. Clearly, the idea is to make the contact cost as low as possible and make the take rate as big as possible. For demand generation marketing, you should carefully track AC and stop marketing campaigns where the AC is greater than the money made from the products or services sold.[5] I sometimes hear the argument that even though the campaign is losing money, you should do the marketing anyway, from a branding perspective. I agree that if the objective is branding then financial metrics are not applicable. But if the marketing objective is demand generation and the campaign is losing money, a rational manager should stop and try something different.

For large marketing budgets, small changes in take rates can have huge implications. For example, telecommunications companies in the United States can contact 100 million customers or more per year with direct mail or telemarketing. At $5 per contact this is $500 million per year in direct marketing! A take rate of 3 percent versus 3.5 percent means you can contact the same number of customers and get more customers accepting the offer. How many more accept the offer? 100 million × 0.5 percent = 500,000 additional customers.

Or you can send out fewer offers to get the same number of customers. With a 3 percent take rate, the 100 million offers are accepted by 3 million customers. But I only need to send out 85.71 million offers to get 3 million customers if the take rate is 3.5 percent. This is calculated from 100 million × 3 percent/3.5 percent (see Figure 4.11). (You can check to see if this is right: 85.71 million offers × 3.5 percent take rate = 3·million accepting the offer.)

What does this all mean? If I want to get the same number of customers to accept the offer, 3 million customers, the difference between a 3 percent take rate and a 3.5 percent take rate is 100 million contacts less 85.71 million contacts, or 14.29 million less contacts—at $5 per contact, this is a $71 million savings in marketing costs to get the same results (see Figure 4.11).

Of course, most likely you don't have several hundred million dollars of marketing budget to play with (I like to think big), but the point of this exercise was to show the huge impact that improving take rate can have on marketing cost performance. For large-customer-base direct marketing, the impact is amplified. You can plug your business-specific numbers into the template in Figure 4.11, downloadable at www.agileinsights.com/ROMI.

Note that take rate can also be applied to branding, evaluative, and loyalty marketing activities. In this case, accepting the offer is equivalent to acting as a result of a specific call to action, such as downloading free trial software or a white paper, or texting a branding ad in a sports stadium.

The summary takeaway is that improving the take rate and decreasing the contact cost per customer dramatically impacts the cost side of marketing performance. This is why analytics, which targets marketing to increase take rates, can have such a high return on investment. Chapters 6 and 9 discuss how to use analytics and event-driven marketing to improve take rates and reduce churn, amplifying marketing performance by a factor of five or more.

Cutting marketing costs can be a great place to start, since you can free up cash for other data-driven marketing initiatives. This is why understanding the simple relationships of take rate and contact cost is so important—simultaneously improving take rate and reducing contact cost has a multiplier effect for saving money in your marketing.

Chapter Insights

- Brand awareness (metric #1): A strong brand drives initial preference in a purchasing decision and enables a price premium over nonbranded products or services. Use nonfinancial metrics from surveys to track brand awareness and the impact of brand marketing.
- Test-drive (metric #2): The essential metric for evaluative marketing. Develop evaluative marketing to incent test-drives of your products or services and measure conversion rates to sales.
- Churn (metric #3): The essential loyalty metric. Reducing customer churn can have a profound impact on firm profitability.
- CSAT (metric #4): This golden marketing metric links branding and customer loyalty. CSAT should be actively managed just like sales revenues.
- Take rate (metric #5): The essential marketing operational metric. Increasing take rate and reducing customer acquisition costs dramatically improves the cost side of marketing.

Show Me the ROI!

The Four Essential Financial Metrics: #6–Profit, #7–Net Present Value (NPV), #8–Internal Rate of Return (IRR), and #9–Payback

Finance is the language of business, and marketers who learn to speak this language gain respect in the boardroom. One chief marketing officer (CMO) I know once went into the office of the chief executive officer (CEO) and explained that if they did a certain marketing initiative, it would increase share price by 40 cents a share: this got the CEO's attention, and the program was funded in short order.

As we discussed in Chapter 1, financial return on marking investment (ROMI) is applicable to more than 50 percent of marketing activities. These include trial and demand generation marketing and new product launch marketing. In this chapter, we will delve into both of these and provide insights into how to quantify marketing using financial metrics. In my research, 55 percent of CMOs surveyed reported that their staff does not understand financial metrics. I realize that math and finance may not be your strong suit, so my intention is to make this chapter as painless as possible. Readers who are familiar with finance can skip the section on Finance for Marketing Managers and can dive into the detailed examples.

Metric #6: Profit

Put simply, profit is defined as:

Metric #6: The First Essential Financial Marketing Metric

Profit = Revenues − Cost

There is nothing mystical in the definition of profit, but there are a few important points to consider based on the discussion of Chapter 1. First, realize that the marketing divide exists because some firms choose to invest more in demand generation marketing, running sales and promotions, which drive sales revenues but kill profits. The leading firms invest more in branding and customer equity, and as a result are able to charge a price premium, which means higher profit. This is why I do not include sales revenues as one of the "essential" 15 metrics, although, of course, revenues resulting from marketing are incredibly important.

Competing on price is most often a losing game, since it kills profitability. A few firms, such as Wal-Mart and Dell, have been effective with this strategy. These companies compete because they have exceptional supply-chain management capabilities that drive cost down to a minimum. If operational efficiency is your core strategy, then by all means consider competing on price. But for the remaining firms, using marketing to drive profits is a better strategy.

This brings us to profit versus market share. When dealing with large firms, I often hear that "grabbing" share is most important. Certainly, market share (the percentage of the market you own) is important, but if you consistently lose profits to gain share, then over time this is a losing strategy.

There is a conflict here between marketing and sales, since sales is most often incented on volume, not profits. An analysis of sales force effectiveness often reveals that the highest-performing salespeople, those who get the Hawaii vacation reward each year, are often the least profitable, and may even be negative in profitability.

In order to combat this, when Mark Hurd became the CEO of Hewlett Packard in 2005, one of his first acts was to change the incentive system for HP enterprise sales force—he incented the sales-people based on the profits of the products they sell, not the volume. In part as a result of this change, and significant cost management throughout the enterprise, HP overall revenues grew by 20 percent between 2005 and 2007, but the net income grew from $2.4 billion to $7.3 billion per year, increasing the stock price by 243 percent.

Solving for the "right" price point to maximize profits and sales revenues is a pricing exercise, and one can easily travel down the road of complex math in an attempt to figure it out. At the end of the day, price is set by what the market is willing to pay for the value of the products or services you provide. A brute force approach that can work in some situations is to jack the price up 5 to 10 percent a month and see when sales start to drop off: this is the optimal price maximizing sales and profits. This book is not a pricing book, however, but a book on marketing metrics, and the interested reader should consult a few good references on pricing strategy.[1]

The insight, though, is that facing difficult times and competitive pressures, the inclination is to compete by cutting price, to the detri-ment of profitability. This leads to the death spiral of losing money in the majority of marketing activities. A better strategy is to build brand and customer equity so that you compete on value, not price. Value-based marketing is the subject of Chapter 6.

Finance for Marketing Managers: Metrics #7—NPV, #8—IRR, and #9—Payback Defined

Ask someone with a golf handicap if he or she keeps score and that person usually laughs: the answer is, of course, yes. Why does he or she keep score? Most often, the response is, "To know if I am improving or not." The purpose of this book is to articulate how to keep score for marketing and improve its performance. There are several parallels to playing sports.

A golf handicap is calculated by taking the average golf score over the last 10 rounds of golf played. The handicap is the average number of shots over par. For those who don't play golf, you know there are 18 holes. Some of these holes are par 3, par 4, and par 5. Par is the number of strokes (long shots and puts) expected for an "expert" golfer. Adding up the 18 holes, par for playing a golf course is typically 72 strokes. Realize that golf is an incredibly difficult sport. When Tiger Woods, for example, shot 16 under par to win the 2001 Masters, this meant that he was an average of 4 under par in each of the four rounds.

Why this digression into the intricacies of golf scores? I would like to draw some parallels between golf and marketing and articulate the essentials of finance using a golf analogy. If you don't like golf, not a problem, just substitute your favorite sport. Albert Einstein was famous for his "thought experiments," which were daydreams connected to the real world, to help articulate the principles of physics. Let's do a thought experiment about golf. But don't panic—finance, it turns out, is much simpler than Einstein's theory of relativity.

Let's assume that you have a golf handicap of 10 (yes, for me it's a fantasy thought experiment). This means that you routinely keep score and on average you shoot 82, or 10 strokes over par. Now you get an opportunity for the first time to play Pebble Beach, one of the top golf courses in the world, located in Monterey County, California. Will you shoot exactly 82 at Pebble Beach? Very doubtful. Most likely, you will shoot more; let's say 90. Exactly 90? Well, no, there is a range perhaps from 82 to 100.

What does this all mean? We have ascertained (1) that good golfers keep score so that they know how well they played and (2) that they keep score multiple times to have a handicap. That is, they have trend data. With this trend data, they can predict the future. However, when experiencing a new golf course, there is risk. (3) Because of risk, it is not possible to predict the future exactly: there is a range of possible outcomes. For financial return on marketing investment (ROMI), these are the three major takeaways that we will return to in the examples of the subsequent sections.

Every year in February, there is a pro-amateur golf tournament at Pebble Beach. The usual suspects show up: Michael Jordan, Bill Murray, Kevin Costner, and many more celebrities, along with the pros like Tiger Woods and Phil Mickelson. Let's assume you enter this tournament and have an amazing four rounds of golf: you win the tournament!

Very excited, you get the large trophy and a check for $1 million, only to find to your dismay that there is fine print on the bottom of the check that you have the choice of winnings: $100,000 per year for

10 years or $520,000 cash today. You have to make a decision. What would you choose?

This is clearly a financial decision, and to answer the question it would be helpful to know how much the $100,000 ($100K) per year for 10 years is actually worth today. Intuition tells us that a dollar (or yen, pound sterling, euro, or baht) today is not worth a dollar a year from now. How much is it worth? The answer is that if we had a dollar today we could invest it, so that in one year:

$$\$1 \text{ today invested for one year} \rightarrow \$1 \times (1 + r)$$

where r is the rate of return we expect to get. So the $1 today should grow to $(1 + r)$ dollars with interest in a year. This is an equation, and we can divide both sides by $(1 + r)$. This means that a dollar obtained a year from now is worth $\$1/(1 + r)$ in today's dollars (see Figure 5.1(a)).

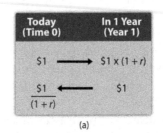

(a)

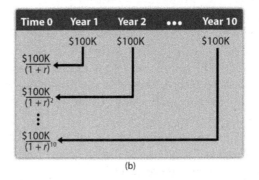

(b)

Figure 5.1 Conceptual diagram of the time value of money: (a) $1 today can be invested and will earn interest $(1 + r)$, meaning $1 received in one year is worth only $\$1/(1 + r)$ today. (b) $100K received at the end of each year are discounted by factors of $(1 + r)$, $(1 + r)^2$, etc., to put each amount in today's dollars at Time 0.

Specifically, if *r* was 10 percent, then a dollar received a year from now would be worth 91 cents today.

For our thought experiment, if we had $100K per year for 10 years, with payments at the end of each year, the value today is:

$$PV = \frac{\$100K}{(1+r)} + \frac{\$100K}{(1+r)^2} + \frac{\$100K}{(1+r)^3} + \cdots + \frac{\$100K}{(1+r)^{10}}$$

where PV is called present value and is the value for the cash discounted to include the time value of money, the $(1 + r)$ factors, so that money in the future is worth less. How much less? Divide by $(1 + r)$, $(1 + r)^2$, and so on, in each time period. So we are taking the payments in the future, bringing them back to today, and then adding them up. See Figure 5.1(b) for a schematic of how this works.

In this calculation, *r* is the rate of return you expect to get on your investments and is called the discount rate, cost of capital, or hurdle rate. Prior to 2008, during informal discussions, executives would often tell me that their expected *r* is 12 percent or more per year; today, I hear 5 percent or less as the economy is not doing so well. For now, let's assume we are in business school; in business school, *r* most often equals 10 percent for convenience. If we fill the squares in Excel, click on the correct function (NPV with *r* of 10 percent and click and drag the squares of 100K), and hit Return, we get: PV = $614,457. See Figure 5.2, and for free Excel spreadsheets of all the financial examples given in this book, please visit www.agileinsights.com/ROMI.

This is the value of the $100K per year for 10 years in today's dollars, assuming a discount rate *r* = 10%. So which would you choose? A total of $520K cash today or cash over 10 years worth $614K today?[2] Clearly, the $614K is worth more today in dollar terms, but the decision is very personal. Perhaps you will retire in 10 years and the winnings of $100K per year could help fund your retirement. In this case, the $100K per

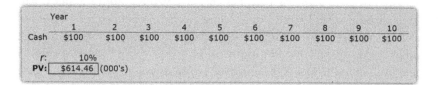

Figure 5.2 Template for present value calculation using the Excel NPV function. Downloadable at www.agileinsights.com/ROMI.

year is the best choice. However, perhaps you would like to purchase a house and need the money today, making the $520K is a better choice.

This example highlights that calculating the metric "number" is only the first step in management decision making. The context is incredibly important, and there are many factors that will influence the decision. In management, unlike physics, one can argue that there are no wrong answers. However, I believe there are "better" answers.

In summary, we have discussed how decision making depends on much more than the "metric" number, and we have also defined the time value of money, the rate of return r, and the present value of cash

---

Metric #7: The Second Essential Financial Marketing Metric—Net Present Value (NPV)

$$NPV = PV - Cost$$

---

flows. These are the ingredients in the second essential financial metric for marketing:

For the golf thought experiment, fees for entering the tournament, travel on your private jet, and the cost of the suite overlooking the 18th hole at Pebble Beach were a sunk cost: they were the same for $520K or $100K per year choices. NPV enables you to compare marketing campaigns or initiatives that have different costs; hence, the cost of the campaign is subtracted from the present value. More specifically, the cost of the marketing is spread over time, so metric #7 can be written:

$$NPV = -C_0 + \frac{(B_1 - C_1)}{(1+r)} + \frac{(B_2 - C_2)}{(1+r)^2} + \frac{(B_3 - C_3)}{(1+r)^3} + \cdots + \frac{(B_n - C_n)}{(1+r)^n}$$

This looks complicated, but the idea is straightforward and is the same as in Figure 3.1. In time zero, there is startup marketing cost C_0 and in each subsequent time B_n is the cash benefit, or revenues, from the marketing in each time period and C_n is the cost of the marketing. So we are just calculating the benefit minus cost in each time period, which is just the profit metric #6, and discounting by the $(1+r)$ factors for the time value of money. This is the idea that the profit is worth less in the future. See Figure 3.3 for examples of marketing campaign NPV calculations.

So what is r, the discount rate, for a firm? The answer is that r is the rate of return investors expect to get by investing in similar firms. So, for example, manufacturing companies typically have rates of returns of 12 percent and software firms approximately 18 percent, since they are both more risky and have higher growth potential than manufacturing firms. The idea is that investors have freedom to choose where they invest their money, and as a result, the return of your company should be comparable to that of similar firms in the same industry.

For management decision making, the idea is to invest if NPV is greater than zero and to not invest if NPV is less than zero.[3] Why? If NPV is greater than zero, the average benefit is larger than the cost in each time period, taking into account that money in the future is worth less.

Essential marketing metric #7, NPV, has broader implications than just making funding decisions. For example, the value of a firm is calculated by estimating the net cash the firm will generate in the future and discounting it back to today.[4] If the company has no debt, this number divided by the number of shares outstanding is how the share price can be calculated.[5] This is why the CMO at the beginning of this chapter was able to say if she did the marketing campaign, the share price would go up by 40 cents.

For example, let's assume that you have a new product launch, a digital book. It will take a year to deliver the new technology, and with marketing and the cost of developing the e-book, the NPV is $50 million.[6] Following the press announcement of your company's intention to launch the new product, financial analysts worldwide will evaluate this investment and, if they agree with your estimates, will start to buy shares of the company. Assuming no debt and 100 million shares outstanding, the announcement of the new e-book product will make the share price go up by 50 cents a share ($50 million/100 million shares): the shares are now worth a 50-cent premium because of the new product announcement.

Now let's say that you get six months into the new product launch and the product development is way behind schedule. As a result, the product launch will be delayed by one year, and you will have additional costs for a year of development and lose new revenues for a year. As a result, let's assume instead of making an NPV of $50 million, you now expect to make $25 million NPV. What happens to the share price? It goes down. How much? $25 million/100 million shares is a decrease of 25 cents a share.

So the reason to invest in positive NPV marketing programs and campaigns is that the share price will go up, and for negative NPV projects the share price will go down. Senior business executives are intimately aware of the relationship between NPV and share price, primarily because their bonuses are tied to share price in public companies. As a result, marketers who speak this language are now able to speak the language of the boardroom.

This discussion assumes rational and efficient trading markets. Clearly, those of us who experienced the market crash of 2008 and 2009 will question this assumption—there are times the market indeed goes stark raving mad. In the case of the modern financial crisis, there was great uncertainty about the economy and what the future value of firms would be, and a panic in the market led to massive selling of equity shares. I want to be clear that calculating NPV is an inexact science because there is risk in the assumptions, the benefits, costs, and discount rate r. However, this does not mean NPV should be discarded in difficult times. On the contrary, in difficult economic times, mangers need better tools to make more informed management decisions, and NPV is one of those tools.

So what is ROI? From my experience, if you ask five marketing managers to define ROI, you will hear about seven different definitions. This is not the fault of the marketers, but the definition of ROI typically found in most marketing textbooks and articles. Most often this definition is:

$$ROI = \frac{Benefit - Cost}{Cost} \times 100\%$$

where benefit is the net sales revenues that result from marketing and cost is the cost of the marketing—realize that this is just the profit metric #6 divided by the cost of the marketing.

There are two problems with this definition; both have to do with time. First, the ROI defined above does not include the time value of money. We have discussed that money in the future is worth less than money today, but this ROI definition assumes all time periods are equal. The other major challenge is the length of time. For example, one can have an ROI of 100 percent for a campaign that is nine months or three years. The ROI number is the same but the campaigns are clearly completely different. This is why ROI defined above is *not* one of the essential marketing metrics in this book. A better metric is:

Metric #8: The Third Essential Financial Marketing Metric—Internal Rate of Return (IRR)

IRR = Rate that money is compounding internally to the campaign or program

For example, if in the first time period there is a $100K profit (Benefit − Cost) of the campaign and the IRR is 25 percent, in the second time period the $100K will grow to $125K. Now add another profit of $100K in the second time period, in the third time period you will have $225K (1 + 0.25) = $281K.

IRR is technically calculated by setting the NPV equation to zero and solving for $r = \text{IRR}$.

$$0 = -C_0 + \frac{(B_1 - C_1)}{(1 + \text{IRR})} + \frac{(B_2 - C_2)}{(1 + \text{IRR})^2} + \frac{(B_3 - C_3)}{(1 + \text{IRR})^3} + \cdots + \frac{(B_n - C_n)}{(1 + \text{IRR})^n}$$

Now I know this looks really complicated, but it can be accomplished with a few mouse clicks in Microsoft Excel, where both IRR and NPV are standard financial functions.[7] See Figure 5.3 for a template with example campaign IRR calculations.

Financial decisions with IRR are made by comparing the IRR to the discount rate r, also called the hurdle rate. If IRR is greater than r, in principle, one should invest, and if IRR is less than r, then one should not.

Figure 5.3 is an Excel template for calculating the essential financial metrics. Two examples are given: (a) a three-year marketing program and (b) a nine-month campaign. In both cases, the total costs and revenues are input first to calculate the profit metric #6 in each time period. These profit numbers are then discounted assuming the annual discount rate r is 15 percent. In both examples, the NPV is greater than zero and the annual IRR is greater than 15 percent, which suggests these programs/campaigns are good potential investments.

The last essential financial metric for ROMI is payback.

Metric #9: The Fourth Essential Financial Marketing Metric

Payback = The time for the cash benefit out to equal the cost

---

The payback period is usually not discounted, but it is used as a rule of thumb for decision making. In Figure 5.3, the payback is calculated in part for the three-year and nine-month campaign examples. Calculating the payback is easy—just cumulatively sum (add the previous cells) of the profit line. The payback is the time period when the profit goes from negative to positive, so the campaign or program has paid back the cost so far. In Figure 5.3(a) the payback is in about 18 months, and in (b), it is at the end of 8 months; both are good. I give a more detailed example

	Year 0	Year 1	Year 2	Year 3
Marketing and All Other Costs	(100)	(250)	(250)	(250)
Revenues	-	300	300	300
Profit (Revenues – Cost)	(100)	50	50	50
r	15%			
NPV	$12.31			
IRR	23%			
Incremental Cash Flows	(100)	(50)	-	50
		Payback ==>		
		Middle of Year 2		

(a)

	Month								
	1	2	3	4	5	6	7	8	9
Marketing and All Other Costs	(60)	(20)	(20)	(10)	(20)	(20)	(10)	(20)	(20)
Revenues	-	25	25	15	30	30	20	30	30
Profit (Revenues – Cost)	(60)	5	5	5	10	10	10	10	10

Annual r 15.0%
Monthly r 1.25%
NPV $1.04 (000s)
Monthly IRR 1.6%
Annual IRR 19.21%

Incremental Cash Flows	(60)	(55)	(50)	(45)	(35)	(25)	(15)	(5)	5
							Payback ===>		
							End of Month 8		

(b)

Figure 5.3 Templates calculating the four essential financial metrics (a) for a three-year marketing program and (b) for a nine-month campaign. All dollars are in units of thousands. Downloadable at www.agileinsights.com/ROMI.

tying all of these metrics together for marketing in the following sections. For now, the takeaway is that they are easy to calculate with the template downloadable at www.agileinsights.com/ROMI.

In summary, financial return on marketing investment is not one metric but three: essential metric #7, NPV; metric #8, IRR; and metric #9, payback. Using these three metrics to quantify the value of marketing is what I call ROMI. Intuitively, NPV is just the benefit minus cost, or profit, in each time period discounted for the time value of money. IRR is the rate that money is compounding internally to the campaign, and payback period is how long it takes so that money put into the campaign equals the money out. For management decisions, think NPV > 0 IRR > r, good; and NPV < 0 IRR < r, bad. Similarly, also think short payback, good; long payback, bad. As we will see, taken together, these financial ROMI metrics enable much better decisions than the traditional ROI metric.

Return on Marketing Investment (ROMI) Framework for Management Decisions

So how do you actually figure out the ROMI of your campaigns and/or new product launches? A systematic framework for ROMI is shown in Figure 5.4. The approach to ROMI analysis is straightforward and is the same for a new product launch, a line extension, or a demand generation marketing campaign or program. The first steps are business discovery to understand the impact of the existing marketing and product and to

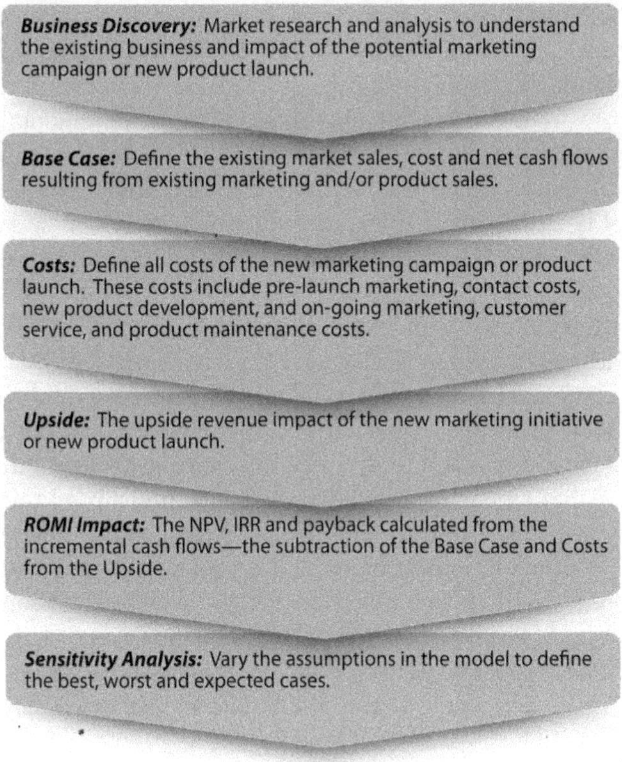

Business Discovery: Market research and analysis to understand the existing business and impact of the potential marketing campaign or new product launch.

Base Case: Define the existing market sales, cost and net cash flows resulting from existing marketing and/or product sales.

Costs: Define all costs of the new marketing campaign or product launch. These costs include pre-launch marketing, contact costs, new product development, and on-going marketing, customer service, and product maintenance costs.

Upside: The upside revenue impact of the new marketing initiative or new product launch.

ROMI Impact: The NPV, IRR and payback calculated from the incremental cash flows—the subtraction of the Base Case and Costs from the Upside.

Sensitivity Analysis: Vary the assumptions in the model to define the best, worst and expected cases.

Figure 5.4 ROMI framework for a demand generation marketing initiative or a new product launch.

research the potential impact of the new marketing or product launch. The next step is to calculate the base case revenue and costs expected in the future if the business continues as it is now. The base case analysis is straightforward if the organization has "kept score" previously; however, it may require some work if the past marketing impact is ill defined.

The third step of Figure 5.4 is to define the complete costs of the new initiative. For a new marketing initiative with existing products or services, these costs include collateral development, contact costs, staff salaries and overheard, and agency costs. A new product launch should also include the product development cost, prelaunch marketing, and all ongoing costs, including marketing and customer support, in addition to the base case.

The upside is then calculated and is the revenue impact of the new marketing and/or product launch. The upside will include assumptions about the impact of the new marketing or product launch. Finally, we get to the ROMI: the base case cash flows (net profit) are subtracted from the projected cash flows with the new project (net upside profit). The results of these subtractions are called the incremental cash flows for the new product or campaign—this is just the incremental profit as a result of the new initiative. The ROMI (IRR, NPV, and payback) is then calculated from these incremental cash flows. The last step in Figure 5.4 is sensitivity analysis, to define the best, worst, and expected case. Sensitivity analysis is discussed in detail in the last section of this chapter.

Figure 5.5 is a general spreadsheet template that can be used for your marketing campaign ROMI, and Figure 5.6 is for ROMI of a new product launch. The base case is calculated at the top and the upside with the new marketing campaigns is on the bottom. In this example, COGS is cost of goods sold and EBIT is earnings before interest and taxes. The incremental cash flows are calculated by subtracting the base case cash flows from the upside cash flows. This is the proverbial "bottom line" and is the difference in profit with and without the marketing initiative. The NPV and IRR are then obtained from standard Excel functions by clicking and dragging across the incremental cash flow bottom line. (For free Excel template spreadsheets of all the financial examples given in this book, please visit www.agileinsights .com/ROMI.)

The spreadsheet in Figure 5.5 is for a multiyear marketing program, but it can also be used for monthly campaigns—just change the years to months and divide r by 12. Note that the IRR you calculate

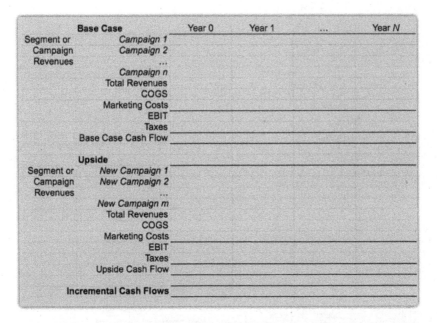

Figure 5.5 Campaign ROMI template. In this example, there are n campaigns in the base case and m new campaigns in the upside. The analysis is for N time periods—in this case, years—but it can be for months also. Downloadable at www.agileinsights.com/ROMI.

will then be a monthly IRR. You have to multiply the monthly IRR by 12 to answer the question,[8] "Is the annual IRR greater than r, and should we invest?" See the template of Figure 5.3(b) for an example of how to do this.

An equivalent approach to the framework in Figure 5.4 is to calculate the additional benefits of the marketing campaign directly to obtain the incremental cash flows. When similar products or marketing activities already exist, however, separating out the additional benefits when there are multiple variables can be more difficult than calculating the total cash flows with the new product, line extension, and/or marketing and then subtracting the base case.

As discussed in the previous section, if the IRR calculated from the incremental cash flows is greater than the project discount rate, the new product and/or campaign should be considered for funding—this is equivalent to a positive NPV. The challenge is to accurately incorporate the business drivers in the base case and all of the costs, and potential revenue benefits, since there are often many assumptions.

Base Case		Year 0	Year 1	...	Year N
Segment or	Segment 1				
Campaign	Segment 2				
Revenues	...				
	Segment n				
	Total Revenues				
	COGS				
	Marketing Costs				
	EBIT				
	Taxes				
	Base Case Cash Flow				
Upside					
Segment or	Segment 1				
Campaign	Segment 2				
Revenues	...				
	Segment n				
	Total Revenues				
	COGS				
	Marketing Costs				
New Product Development Cost					
	Depreciation				
	EBIT				
	Taxes				
	Net Income				
	Plus Depreciation				
	Upside Cash Flow				
Incremental Cash Flows					

*Assumes base case product is fully depreciated.

Figure 5.6 New product launch ROMI template. Rather than campaigns, as in Figure 3.3, the impacts are for n segments over a time period of N years. You can substitute campaigns for segments and months for years, although a new product will usually have a useful life of a few years. Downloadable at www.agileinsights.com/ROMI.

I have engaged several times with organizations that, after the marketing campaign ran, wanted to figure out the ROMI of their marketing. Most often, they were interested in justifying future spending and had a gut feeling something good happened from their marketing. These engagements are similar to an archeological dig, or *CSI* episode, where one has to reconstruct the base case from limited measurement after the fact. The result is burning lots of resource hours in interviews and analysis to figure out the baseline.

These challenges can largely be avoided by simple measurement before the campaign starts. The idea is to track the sales of a product or service with the existing marketing, and then measure the percentage increase, or lift, in sales resulting from the new campaign. Keeping score is an essential element of ROMI and is engrained in the cultures of high-performing marketing organizations.

An alternative to prebaseline measurement is to have a control group that is not exposed to the campaign and to measure the lift relative to this control group. For example, Nissan conducted a "Drive to a Million" sweepstakes marketing initiative continuously from February 14 through March 31, 2005, supported by national and regional media. To help create a sense of urgency, the interactive marketing contained a countdown communication as the March 31 end date neared, such as paid search, online advertising, direct marketing programs, and so on. Lift relative to a control group was measured for each of the marketing channels: direct mail had a 10 percent lift, and e-mail had a 50 percent lift in some cases, compared with that of the control group. The control group was the base case in Figure 5.4, and the upside was the result with the new "Drive to a Million" marketing. Given the cost of the marketing, you can use the framework in Figure 5.4 for this example and calculate a financial ROMI.

Since the Nissan marketing was for only a few months, one can argue that the simple ROI formula is fine, since the time value of money is not so important. However, the challenge, as we discussed, is that the formula is ambiguous and it is not an apples-to-apples comparison between campaigns if, say, one ran for 18 months and the other for 6. As I mentioned earlier, for relatively short campaigns, monthly increments in the spreadsheet template in Figure 5.3(b) can be used to calculate IRR and NPV, where the annual discount rate is divided by 12 and is a monthly discount rate. So you can calculate ROMI on a monthly or annual basis.

ROMI for Sports Sponsorship

Demand generation marketing, also known as trial marketing, discussed in Chapter 1, is a marketing initiative that results in sales revenues during or shortly after the marketing campaign and is therefore directly attributed to the campaign. Examples given previously were coupons, sales, or "act now for a limited time" events. These marketing activities directly result in sales revenues and are therefore quantifiable using financial ROMI.

Let's see the ROMI approach in action for a real marketing program consisting of multiple campaigns. This ROMI is for an actual client engagement and is for a three-year sponsorship of a major sports team in Europe. The client has been disguised for confidentiality reasons. The sponsorship was a third-tier sponsorship; this meant the client's logo appeared on the sports team web site, promotional materials, and posters at events but did not appear on the team players' jerseys or other sports equipment easily seen by spectators. What is the ROMI of this investment? To find out, it is important to understand a little more about sports sponsorship marketing.

Typically, sponsorship is viewed as branding and awareness marketing and is quantified by nonfinancial metrics, as discussed in Chapter 4. However, this sponsorship is an example of both awareness and demand generation marketing combined. I have seen the dual approach multiple times,[9] and it is certainly possible to drive both objectives of increasing brand awareness and revenues simultaneously with sponsorship. The key insight, however, is that it is not the cost of the sponsorship that counts, but the activation, that is, the marketing you combine with the sponsorship.

This client's sports sponsorship was by definition low budget, but as we will see, due to excellent activation, was very high impact. It turns out that one of the athletes on the sponsored team was extremely popular in eastern Europe. In order to capitalize on this popularity, the company partnered with a Romanian manufacturer and distributor of its products to make commercials and run a sweepstakes-type offer at stores. The sponsorship cost was $850,000 per year, and under the contract the athlete agreed to participate in filming a commercial. The partner distributor agreed to pay for the commercial airtime and in-store displays.

The sponsor firm acted as the facilitator, orchestrating the promotion, and benefiting as the manufacturer of the product. The resulting lift in sales and profit was impressive, increased by 108 percent and 164 percent, respectively. The marketing also measured 7,870 valid text messages related to the promotion. As a result of these positive results, the sponsor firm expanded the marketing to Poland and the United Kingdom. The results of these campaigns were measured by controlled marketing experiments. In the United Kingdom, similar positive sales were observed, with a lift of 20 percent in sales and profitability in test stores.

Figure 5.7 is a summary of the three-year ROMI analysis for the sports sponsorship. This illustrates a best practice for a marketing program ROMI: individual campaigns and initiatives that are less

	Year 0 ($)	Year 1 ($)	Year 2 ($)	Year 3 ($)
Sponsorship Related Sales		500,000	750,000	1,000,000
Romania Campaign		2,500,000	2,500,000	2,500,000
UK Campaign			2,500,000	2,500,000
Bulgaria Campaign			2,500,000	2,500,000
Poland Campaign			2,500,000	2,500,000
Total Revenues		2,500,000	10,000,000	10,000,000
COGS		(1,750,000)	(7,000,000)	(7,000,000)
Net Profit		750,000	3,000,000	3,000,000
Sponsorship Cost	(250,000)	(850,000)	(850,000)	(850,000)
Marketing Activation Cost		(250,000)	(600,000)	(750,000)
Total Costs	(250,000)	(1,100,000)	(1,450,000)	(1,600,000)
EBIT	(250,000)	(350,000)	1,550,000	1,400,000
Tax	96,250	134,750	(596,750)	(539,000)
Net Profit (or Loss) after Tax	(153,750)	(215,250)	953,250	861,000
IRR	132%			
NPV	$916,813			
Payback (Years)	1.4			

Figure 5.7 Example sports sponsorship ROMI analyses. The numbers are disguised for confidentiality. Downloadable at www.agileinsights.com/ROMI.

than one year in duration are components of the bigger three-year marketing program. In this case, the baseline in Figure 5.7 has been removed to show only the incremental improvement in sales resulting from each of the marketing activities. The numbers have also been disguised for confidentiality reasons, but they are approximately correct.

In Figure 5.7, COGS, sponsorship costs, and activation marketing costs are subtracted from the incremental revenue improvements. The resulting NPV is a positive $917K and 132 percent IRR, and the payback is 1.4 years. The positive NPV, high IRR, and less-than-two-year payback make this a very good ROMI program and warranted a closer look to potentially increase funding.

In my experience, however, when you present an ROMI analysis such as the one shown in Figure 5.7, there is always someone in the back of the room who says, "How do you know the 150 percent improvement in Romania is real?" That is, "How do you know the marketing campaign caused the increased sales?" This question is always asked, and should be, when hard numbers are presented. So you need to think through the answers before the meeting. A good answer is to discuss how in Romania, the company had no other marketing initiates under way, so the 150 percent lift in sales must be due to the sponsorship marketing. The U.K. marketing was done in a controlled way to isolate out confounding effects, using experimental design, discussed in Chapter 2.

In my experience, there will always be skeptics—so be ready with good answers when they ask the question about your analysis. The next section goes deeper into assumptions and the interpretation of the ROMI metrics for management decisions. The last section of this chapter discusses sensitivity analysis—tools and techniques to make you look brilliant and dazzle skeptics in meetings.

ROMI for a New Product Launch

Given the discussion of the previous sections of this chapter, you are now armed and dangerous to show the financial ROMI for 50 percent of all marketing—demand generation marketing. The templates and examples of the previous sections will enable you to directly apply financial ROMI to your marketing, either several month-long campaigns or programs consisting of multiple campaigns over multiple years. You can speak the language of finance and, I have no doubt, will impress the socks off folks in the boardroom. The rest of this chapter is about making you a true financial genius in marketing. In this section, I want to give an in-depth example of a new product launch financial ROMI. I realize this section might be a bit heavy going, but realize when it comes to ROMI, the devil is in the details. (If new product launch marketing and/or the intricacies of financial ROMI are not your cup of tea, you might skip this section in the first read.)

My next case example is ROMI analysis applied to a new web portal product and the related marketing campaign. Please note that although this example is for a web portal, the approach is completely generalizable to any new product launch or a line extension of an existing product. The best practices are also applicable to marketing campaigns that drive revenues discussed in the previous section.

The web portal in this example is a web sales channel, where customers can purchase products online instead of by fax and phone, and the marketing is designed to drive users to the new web channel. The new web portal product was for a midsized B2B electronics distributor. However, the numbers have been changed to protect confidentiality, and the example has been simplified for the discussion.[10] The cost and revenue numbers in this example are therefore for illustrative purposes only. The objective of this case example is to illustrate the general framework in Figure 5.4 and the important mechanics for calculating ROMI from the template in Figure 5.6 rather than calculating the exact costs and benefits of a web product launch.

Base Case

The first step in setting up any ROMI analysis is to understand the base business case. That is, what are the primary costs and revenues expected if the firm continues operations and does not implement a new web sales channel? Answering this question should focus on the major costs and revenue drivers that the new product is expected to impact. The process of understanding the existing business is called business discovery and is the first step in the ROMI framework Figure 5.4.

A best practice of business discovery is to understand the business drivers in a particular market and then benchmark against competitors in the industry. Where benchmarks are not available, market research will be necessary. For the web portal product case example, we can assume that the business discovery yielded a set of assumptions that are summarized in Figures 5.8 and 5.9.

(a) *Base Case (U.S. $1,000s)*		
Revenues	Year 0	
Diamond	554	
Platinum	252	
Gold	103	
Silver	55	
Total Revenues	964	
Units of U.S. $1,000s		
Annual Marketing Costs (U.S. $1,000)	80	
Base Case Annual Inflation Factor	3%	
Tax Rate	38%	
Discount Rate:	12%	
(b) *Upside Costs (U.S. $1,000s)*		
New Product Development	275	
Product Launch Marketing	100	
(c) *Upside Revenue Lift*		
Order Size Increase	Expected	Best
Year 1	5%	10%
Year 2	10%	20%
Year 3	13%	25%
Worst case is zero revenue lift		

Figure 5.8 Assumptions for the web portal new product launch ROMI. (a) Base case revenue and costs in Year 0, (b) new product development and marketing costs, and (c) order size upside revenue lift (% improvement) from market research.

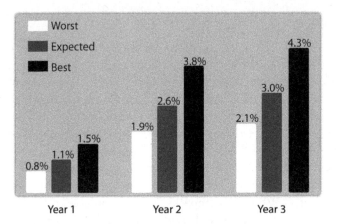

Figure 5.9 Market share increase assumptions: worst, expected, and best cases from market research.

The base case assumptions in Figure 5.8(a) are the Year 0 revenues from existing sales to the four market segments: diamond, platinum, gold, and silver. Other findings from the business discovery were the year-over-year sales increase, the tax, and discount rate (or hurdle rate), r. These numbers are based on the existing sales force and marketing with no web-enabled order entry and limited market penetration.

Incorporating the New Product and Marketing Costs

The new product will have product development and ongoing maintenance costs. In addition, there will be product launch marketing and ongoing marketing to drive users to the web site. These costs are summarized in Figure 5.8(b) and include the web portal development and annual maintenance. Costs are often the easiest to quantify—the upside revenue projections resulting from the new product sales and marketing are usually more challenging.

Upside Assumptions

Business discovery yielded two major drivers of ROMI. The first is increased market penetration. The first driver of revenues from the new product web portal was increased revenues per customer, as product bundling and targeted marketing could be implemented on the web site. The expected case revenue lift is summarized in Figure 5.8(c).

Since this firm had a small number of direct sales personnel, its market share was limited. The second driver of revenue from the web portal is increased market share; however, there is a risk in how much new market share the portal could capture. Market research suggested a best, worst, and expected case increase in market penetration for the next three years, which is summarized in Figure 5.9. Business discovery suggested that a 1 percent increase in market share into the B2B customers corresponded to $105,000 in new sales for a particular product line.

Pro-Forma Cash Flows

Given the base case revenues and costs, the costs of the new product development and launch marketing, and estimates of the upside revenues, the template in Figure 5.6 can be filled out and is shown in Figure 5.10. The result is the pro-forma, or future estimated, cash flows for the new product launch. The base case on the top is just the Year 0 assumptions of Figure 5.8 growing at 3 percent per year; this is business as usual for this company. The upside includes the expected case market share and revenue increase assumptions, and the cost of the new product development and product launch marketing.

Depreciation for New Product Development

To complete this discussion, we need a word on accounting for new product development costs. I know, talking about accounting can make most marketers glaze over, but the devil is in the details when it comes to ROMI. Furthermore, with Sarbanes-Oxley legislation, officers of public firms can go to jail if the firm does not follow accounting rules. So this aside on accounting is worth reading—if you are an officer, it might keep you out of jail!

Marketing costs can be expensed in the year they occur, but in the United States, for tax reasons, new product development cannot be expensed in the year when the money is actually spent (capitalized), with the possible exception of 2008 to 2010 due to the federal government's economic stimulus package.

For the calculation of net income in Figure 5.10, we subtract out the depreciation of the product development, assuming a three-year straight-line schedule with equal expenses in each year. The hardware, software, and professional service costs must be depreciated using a

Units of U.S. $1,000s					
Base Case		Year 0	Year 1	Year 2	Year 3
Segment	Diamond		571	588	605
Revenues	Platinum		260	267	275
	Gold		106	109	113
	Silver		57	58	60
	Total Revenues		993	1,023	1,053
	COGS		(675)	(695)	(716)
	Marketing Costs		(82)	(84)	(87)
	EBIT		236	243	250
	Taxes		(90)	(92)	(95)
	Base Case Cash Flow		146	151	155
Upside					
Segment	Diamond		765	1,080	1,183
Revenues	Platinum		438	727	812
	Gold		277	553	629
	Silver		225	497	570
	Total Revenues		1,704	2,857	3,193
	COGS		(1,159)	(1,943)	(2,171)
	Marketing Costs	(100)	(82)	(84)	(87)
	Product Maintenance		(50)	(52)	(53)
	New Product Development Cost	(275)	-	-	-
	Depreciation		(92)	(92)	(92)
	EBIT		322	687	790
	Taxes		(122)	(261)	(300)
	Net Income		199	426	490
	Add Back Depreciation		92	92	92
	Upside Cash Flow	(375)	291	517	582
	Incremental Cash Flows	(375)	55	275	331
	Cumulative Cash Flows		(320)	(45)	286
	NPV	129.3			
	IRR	27%			
	Payback	2.2 Years			
	Discount Rate	12%			

Figure 5.10 ROMI analysis for a web portal new product launch. Downloadable at www.agileinsights.com/ROMI.

five-year modified accelerated cost recovery schedule (MACRS). This is an accelerated depreciation schedule described in any good accounting textbook.[11] Although the accounting books may use MACRS, depreciation for ROMI analysis is most often incorporated using three- or five-year straight-line depreciation. That is, we expense the new product development equally over a period of several years, usually three.

Straight-line is a conservative compromise, because it weights the expense equally in each year, whereas accelerated depreciation weights the capital expense more in the first few years than in the last. Once the system is operational, ongoing costs such as maintenance, professional service support, and marketing can be expensed when they occur.

So to calculate the free cash flow with the new web portal product, Figure 5.10, the last step is to add back the depreciation expense to the net income after tax. The depreciation expense was included in the calculation of net income in order to correctly include the tax advantage of this expense. However, for the final free cash flows, the total depreciation is added back to the net income because depreciation is not a "real" expense that actually impacts the cash flows, other than for tax reasons.

I realize this discussion of depreciation sounds rather esoteric—the takeaway is that you need to account for depreciation for new product development. So you can't expense the product development costs all in the year(s) you do the development, but have to spread them out over the life of the product to get the tax deduction. Marketing is an expense, though, and these costs can be deducted as they occur. I suggest you find an accountant if you have questions about this.

ROMI Metrics: #7—NPV, #8—IRR, and #9—Payback in Action

Okay, we are almost done. Once the pro-forma base case and new project free cash flows have been calculated, the calculation of NPV and IRR is straightforward. The base case cash flows are subtracted from the cash flows with the new web project; these are the incremental cash flows (see the bottom of Figure 5.10). The incremental cash flows are the net positive or negative cash in each time period that occurs in addition to the base case. The IRR is calculated from these incremental cash flows.

Using Microsoft Excel, the NPV and IRR of the project are calculated to be $129K and 27 percent, respectively, for the expected case. Assuming the assumptions are correct, the positive NPV and IRR greater than the firm's discount rate of 12 percent suggests that this is a product the firm should consider funding. The other metric to consider is the payback. A rule of thumb for new products is that they should payback within one or two years of launch. There are exceptions, however, that depend on the product and strategy. For example, the Microsoft Xbox took several years to pay back and was a strategic investment for Microsoft to gain a foothold in the home.

The payback for this product is calculated in Figure 5.10 from the cumulative cash flows at the bottom of the cash flow statement. Payback occurs when the cumulative cash flows (the sum of previous cash) transitions from negative to positive. For this example, this transition occurs in the third month of the third year. The payback is therefore anticipated to be over two years, which is potentially a little long, so one possibility is to consider adjusting the total project expenses to enable an earlier payback. The complete analysis for the new product launch case example is summarized in Figures 5.10. This spreadsheet can be used as a template and starting point for any product launch ROMI calculation and is downloadable for free at www.agileinsights.com/ROMI.

The new product will produce revenues over a long time period into the future, so an important question is, "What time period should be taken for a particular ROMI calculation?" The time period for the analysis should match the time period used to calculate ROMIs for similar investments in the firm. Often, the one-, two-, and three-year ROMI numbers are calculated for an investment decision and, depending on the firm, management decides which one to use for comparisons with other marketing and product initiatives.

Most often for new products, the ROMI is calculated over the useful life of the product, up to the next major upgrade of the product. For the web portal product, for example, 36 months was chosen as the length of time for the analysis. For technology products, ROMIs for time periods longer than three years are usually not considered when projects are compared, even though the project may have benefits in additional years. However, if the new product was a car, which is more durable than electronics, then the ROMI would be calculated for the product life of the car, approximately seven years, and would also include the two-year development time, so a nine-year analysis.

Note that the 27 percent IRR calculated in this example does not include additional benefits such as improved information on customers, and improved customer satisfaction, because customers can place orders 24/7 and have access to up-to-date product data. You can attempt to quantify these benefits and include them in the model; however, soft benefits such as improved customer satisfaction and better information are extremely difficult to quantify using financial metrics.

The approach most often used is to realize that the calculated ROMI does not include these benefits, and hence the actual ROMI of the new product should be somewhat higher. In addition, the case example does not include the strategic value of the initiative. Specifically, the web portal may be a "table stake"—an investment that is required to stay in business in a particular industry. Hence, even if the IRR is less than the hurdle rate for the company, management must invest in the product, or risk losing market share to competitors. There is a note of caution, however—just because you have to do it does not mean you have to do it with the original plan. So I suggest you look for alternatives, and if the NPV is negative, choose the alternative that loses the least money for the firm.

Stress-Test the Numbers: Sensitivity Analysis

Have you ever presented a campaign-funding request with the chief financial officer (CFO) or someone from his or her office in the meeting? Often, you don't get far into the presentation before you hear a question from the back of the room:

"Excuse me, how much will this marketing cost?"

But the questions don't stop there. They often come in a cascade: "How long will it take?" "When will we see a return [payback]?" And then the question that is pointed like an arrow: "Please tell me about your assumptions." In my experience, these questions are always essentially the same and are pretty annoying, since most likely the CFO or his or her report has no concept of your marketing campaign. But you can prepare for these questions, like a student studying for an exam where you have an old version. From the discussion earlier in this chapter, you should know the cost and, for a demand generation campaign or new product launch, the payback from your ROMI calculation.[12] Before going into the "exam," it is most important is to answer the last question—what happens if you change the assumptions?

To answer this question you need to do something called sensitivity analysis to your ROMI Excel spreadsheet model. The idea is conceptually simple: vary the input assumptions and figure out what happens to the output. But the answers provide you with deep insights into whether you have a chance of realizing the campaign returns. That is, they enable to you to answer the question, What is the best, worst, and expected case of your campaign or program ROMI?

This section is truly advanced, but the techniques are amazingly easy to do in Microsoft Excel. As you will see, with just a few clicks of the mouse, you can take the Excel templates of this chapter to the next level. These sensitivity analysis tools are used by best-in-class CFO offices, and if you use them for marketing, I guarantee a "wow" in the next meeting.

One of my favorite features of Excel is the table function—I know, I'm a nerd—this function enables you to change the numbers in a model

		Order Size (%)					
		100	83	67	50	33	17	0
Market Share (%)	100	68	64	60	56	52	48	44
	83	59	55	51	47	43	39	35
	67	49	45	41	37	33	29	25
	50	38	35	31	27	23	19	15
	33	27	23	20	16	12	8	4
	17	15	11	8	4	0	-4	-9
	0	2	-2	-6	-10	-14	-19	-23

Figure 5.11 Table function sensitivity analysis. The ranges of market share and order size (0 to 100 percent) are scaling the assumptions in Figures 5.8 and 5.9 from the worst to best case. Downloadable at www.agileinsights.com/ROMI.

and see what the output looks like.[13] For example, Figure 5.11 is a table for the new product launch example of the previous section, where the market share and revenue lift assumptions were changed and the IRR calculated. For each parameter range, zero corresponds to the worst case and 100 percent, the best case. What I especially like about the tool is the ability to color-code the squares: green is good (IRR above the hurdle rate) and red is bad (IRR below the hurdle rate, dark grey in Figure 5.11).

I believe a picture is worth a thousand analysts: Figure 5.11 is a picture that can give invaluable insights into the ROMI. In the section on Finance for Marketing Managers, we discussed how good golfers (1) keep score, (2) have trend data to predict the future, and (3) know they can't predict the future exactly, so there is a range of possible outcomes. Figure 5.11 is the range of possible outcomes for the new product launch example, and I'm not kidding—it only took me a few minutes to do this!

The power of Figure 5.11 is that managers can have an objective discussion about the campaign or new product launch initiative and discuss what the best, worst, and expected case will be. Sensitivity analysis enables you to vary the assumptions and understand the impact. It can also help identify critical assumptions in the model.

The table function is used to vary one or two input parameters. However, if there are many parameters in an ROMI model, an even better approach is to use Monte Carlo analysis. This may sound complicated but, again, is surprisingly easy to do and provides powerful insights.

The idea is as follows: First, realize that each of the inputs assumptions in an Excel spreadsheet model has a range of possible outcomes. Most often, this range can be approximated by a bell curve with a best (top 5 percent), worst (bottom 5 percent), and expected case (mean). So that the best and worst case are both two standard deviations from the average, where the standard deviation is a measure of the "spread" of the curve. Next, roll dice to choose random inputs, using the ranges for each input assumption. Finally, calculate the output of the model using the random inputs.

Intuitively, one Monte Carlo cycle (one roll of the dice for each variable) is a possible outcome of the ROMI model with one particular set of variations in the inputs. This is a simulation of what might happen if the campaign were run and were impacted by random risks given by the distributions of input assumptions. Now, by rolling the dice thousands of times (running thousands of cycles), you are effectively finding out what might happen for thousands of identical campaigns given many different variations of risk inputs—the output is plotted as a bar graph and is a distribution of the possible outcomes.

So the idea of a Monte Carlo simulation is to generate a set of random numbers for key variables in the model. Past experience, market research, and the judgment of the management team are all factors to consider when defining the statistics of the input variables. The random numbers are then put into the analysis spreadsheet, and the output (the IRR and NPV) is calculated. New sets of random numbers are then generated, based on the statistical functions defined for each input variable, and the output is recalculated. This process is repeated a large number of times to calculate the distribution of the output.

Packaged software is available that can perform Monte Carlo simulations in spreadsheet software, Palisades @RISK and Crystal Ball, for example. This software is easy to use—the user selects specific cells and specifies distribution functions for the variables. The software then varies the values of the cells with random numbers. The output, in this case the IRR or NPV, is automatically calculated for a large number of cycles and statistics of the possible outcomes are generated.

Figure 5.12 is an example of the Monte Carlo output for the case example of Figure 5.10 for 5,000 rolls of the dice for the input variables. The project cost, increase in market share, and order size improvement were varied simultaneously. The distribution functions chosen for the inputs were all normal distributions, with standard deviations defined by the approximate best and worst case for each variable. The average NPV, or expected value, is $171K with a standard deviation of $153K.

But wait—what is so incredibly cool about this is that the numbers change on the screen. So you see the cells for the model dancing for a

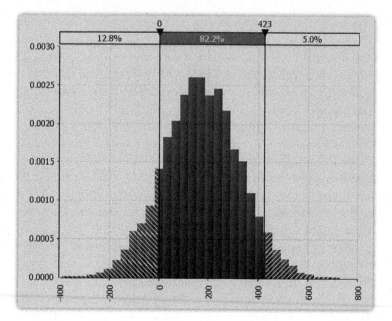

Figure 5.12 Monte Carlo simulation for the new product launch ROMI example. Downloadable template at www.agileinsights.com/ROMI and a 10-day free trial of the @RISK Monte Carlo software is available at www.palisade.com.

minute or so, and then the "answer" such as Figure 5.12 pops up. I've run these simulations in executive programs and in client engagements and invariably hear the audience go, "Wow." Again, with the @RISK software, it took me about 10 minutes to do this for the example in Figure 5.10, and the result is to look like a genius.

The power of this approach is that now you can visually "see" the best, worst, and expected case for the ROMI model and estimate the probability of each. For this example, there is a 12.8 percent chance that the NPV will be negative, with IRR less than the hurdle rate (see Figure 5.12). Management can then ask hard questions about whether this risk is acceptable and may decide to implement a risk management strategy to reduce this downside risk, changing the input assumptions.

In summary, in this chapter I have discussed absolute best practices for financial ROMI analysis applicable to more than 50 percent of marketing activities. This analysis uses the four essential financial metrics for marketing: metrics #6, profit; #7, NPV; #8, IRR; and #9, payback. You have templates to calculate ROMI for your specific demand generation campaigns and programs and for new product launch marketing. The framework in Figure 5.4 is a systematic approach to gather the essential inputs for the templates and calculate the ROMI. I have also discussed how to interpret the "answer" and make a campaign funding decision based on the essential financial metrics. Once the campaign is complete, you should go back and proactively keep score—plug the actual numbers in the spreadsheet and see how you did.

Realize that there is one thing you know with certainty about the number calculated in the spreadsheet before the campaign runs: the single number point estimate is wrong. That is, I have never seen an actual campaign deliver on the exact financial ROMI number at the end of the day. Why? The world is fraught with risk and variability. Hence, it is imperative to always ask and answer the questions for any ROMI: What is the range of possible outcomes—the best, worst, and expected case? What are the assumptions in the model, and if we change them, how does the answer change? Sensitivity analysis discussed in this last section is the essential tool to use to answer these questions for any financial ROMI and will make you look like a genius in the boardroom.

Chapter Insights

- Profit (metric #6) is an essential metric that should be managed for long-term sustainability.
- ROI as traditionally defined is ambiguous and is not the best metric for marketing.
- The essential financial metrics for ROMI are NPV (metric #7), IRR (metric #8), and payback (metric #9).
- Financial ROMI is a template-able process that can be applied to more than 50 percent of marketing activities. These include demand generation marketing and new product launch initiatives.
- Sensitivity analysis is essential to define the range of possible outcomes given the market risks and is surprisingly easy in Microsoft Excel.
- Always ask what is the best, worst, and expected case of any ROMI analysis, and question the assumptions.

CHAPTER

6

All Customers Are Not Equal

Metric 10 – Customer Lifetime Value (CLTV)

Several years ago, my cell phone stopped working and I went to the store to get a replacement. I arrived at 8:55 AM to find there was already a long line. When the door of the store opened at 9:00 AM, I signed my name and explained that I had a flight to Washington, D.C., and needed a phone. I was politely but firmly told that I had to wait my turn, and it would be about 45 minutes before I could see a representative. I attempted to explain that I really needed a phone and had to leave for a flight. I was told:

"But sir, all of these people are ahead of you; they are just as important."

I had been a loyal customer for seven years, and as a result of this interaction when I returned from my trip, I canceled my cell service, data plan, family plan, and home fixed-line service that were all with this same company. The customer service representative at the store had given the "right" answer, following the policy of that store, but the result was the loss of a high-value customer who defected to a competitor.

134

Egalitarian marketing and sales are not limited to business-to-consumer (B2C) companies. As another example, I once worked with a Fortune 500 business-to-business (B2B) company with a very large direct sales force. The sales force had just undertaken an analysis that showed that 8 percent of the company's B2B customers were 93 percent of its revenues. Yet the direct sales force treated every B2B customer equally. Clearly, 8 percent of the customers were more important than the other 92 percent, and if one of the 8 percent were to defect, the impact could be devastating. A better approach is to realize that all customers are not equal and develop a marketing and sales strategy grounded in this reality.

Metric #10—Customer Value Defined

The essential metric that is the focus of this chapter is customer lifetime value (CLTV).[1] This metric is the most advanced in this book, and value-based marketing strategies often require industrial-strength infrastructure (see Chapter 10). As a first step, most organizations often start by looking at plain vanilla sales revenues so that marketing effort and the sales force are directed at the customers with the most revenues. The problem with this approach is that it does not include the cost of serving the customer, which may be considerable, and a customer's revenues today do not accurately tell us about the value of the customer in the future. CLTV addresses both of these issues and, in my opinion, is the most important metric in marketing. Even if you don't use CLTV, I believe everyone in marketing should understand the concepts of value-based marketing.

For readers without a technical background, don't panic when you see the following equation! Metric #10, CLTV, looks very complicated but is actually straightforward and easy to understand given the introduction to finance from Chapter 5.

Metric #10: The Essential Customer Value Metric, Customer Lifetime Value (CLTV)

$$\text{CLTV} = -AC + \sum_{n=1}^{N} \frac{(M_n - C_n)p^n}{(1+r)^n}$$

---

where AC is the acquisition cost, M_n is the margin produced by the customer in each time period n, C_n is the cost of marketing and serving the customer, p is the probability the customer will not defect in a year, and N is the total number of years or time periods (the Greek sigma means sum).

To understand metric #10, realize that CLTV is just the net present value (NPV) of a customer. We defined NPV in Chapter 5. To see this, let's write out metric #10 as follows:

$$\text{CLTV} = -\text{AC} + \frac{(M_1 - C_1)p}{(1+r)} + \frac{(M_2 - C_2)p^2}{(1+r)^2} + \cdots + \frac{(M_n - C_n)p^n}{(1+r)^n}$$

Comparing this with NPV defined in the last chapter, see that the cost at time zero is the acquisition cost of the customer (AC). Then in each time period 1, 2, 3, . . . , n, we have margin minus the cost; this is the profit of the customer in that time period. And we are discounting by $(1 + r)$ because profit in the future is worth less.

The difference between the CLTV equation and traditional NPV is the p, the probability the customer will stay, also known as the retention rate. The probability is just 1 minus the probability the customer will leave:

$$p = 1 - c$$

where c is the churn, essential metric 4. That is, the probability the customer will stay in a year, p, is just 1 minus the probability that the customer will leave, or churn. So we can rewrite CLTV as:

$$\text{CLTV} = -\text{AC} + \frac{(M_1 - C_1) \times (1 - c)}{(1+r)} + \frac{(M_2 - C_2) \times (1 - c)^2}{(1+r)^2} +$$
$$\frac{(M_3 - C_3) \times (1 - c)^3}{(1+r)^3} + \cdots + \frac{(M_n - C_n) \times (1 - c)^n}{(1+r)^n}$$

Again, this looks really complicated, but in summary we are just taking the profit in each time period (margin minus cost) and discounting for the time value of money. The $1 - c$ factors are just the probability the customer will stay in a year; this is 1 minus the probability they will leave, or churn. At time zero there is an acquisition cost, AC, to acquire the customer. CLTV is not a standard function in Excel, but Figure 6.1 is a template to calculate this essential metric for a single customer. (For free Excel spreadsheets of all the financial examples given in this book, please visit www.agileinsights.com/ROMI.)

	Year 0 ($)	Year 1 ($)	Year 2 ($)	Year 3 ($)	Year 4 ($)	Year 5 ($)
Discount Rate r	12% *					
Acquisition Cost (AC)	$100 *					
Churn Rate	15% *					
Retention Rate p = (1 − Churn)	85%					
Margin *		60	55	75	95	100
Marketing Cost *	(100)	(10)	(10)	(15)	(15)	(15)
Other Costs to Serve *		(5)	(7)	(6)	(7)	(8)
Customer Profit	(100)	45	38	54	73	77
Profit x $p^n/(1 + r)^n$	(100)	34	22	24	24	19
CLTV	$23					

* Type your numbers here

Figure 6.1 Customer lifetime value (CLTV) Excel template for a single customer. The numbers can be changed for your customers. Downloadable at www.agileinsights.com/ROMI.

A natural question to ask is, "What is the correct length of time to use for calculating CLTV?" At the extreme, I saw in one case CLTV calculated over 85 years for the natural "lifetime" of a customer. This length of time is not realistic, however. A best practice is three to five years. The reason, similar to return on marketing investment (ROMI) for Chapter 5, is that the future is very difficult to predict, and although the value of a customer may be for longer than three or five years, it is better to focus on a shorter time period for decision making, grounding the analysis with some semblance of reliability.

A note of caution, though—the template in Figure 6.1 assumes you know the acquisition cost, the cost to serve, and the profit for the customer over time. Obtaining these data can be very challenging, especially for a large enterprise. On the cost side, we need to understand all touches of the customer with the call centers, web site, customer service, marketing communications, and so on. On the profit side, we need to know what we sell to the customer, the profit margin of each product, and so on.

So although the calculation of CLTV is easily done in Excel, getting the data is not so easy and may require an enterprise data warehouse and industrial-strength analytics infrastructure for a large firm. Chapter 10 is all about this infrastructure challenge and answers in detail the question "What's it going to take?" for small, medium, and large customer bases. In the rest of this chapter, I focus on how to use CLTV for marketing management and strategy.

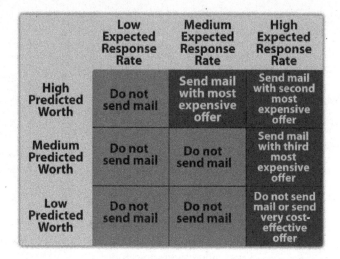

	Low Expected Response Rate	Medium Expected Response Rate	High Expected Response Rate
High Predicted Worth	Do not send mail	Send mail with most expensive offer	Send mail with second most expensive offer
Medium Predicted Worth	Do not send mail	Do not send mail	Send mail with third most expensive offer
Low Predicted Worth	Do not send mail	Do not send mail	Do not send mail or send very cost-effective offer

Figure 6.2 Value-based direct-mail marketing strategy.

The New Marketing Strategy: Value-Based Marketing

Value-based marketing drives significant performance gains, and firms that bridge the marketing divide focus on customer value in all marketing activities. As an example, Figure 6.2 is a value-based direct-mail marketing strategy. In Figure 6.2, each individual customer's value is calculated using metric 10, CLTV, prior to the marketing mailing.

The dimensions of Figure 6.2 are CLTV and response rate. Low to medium CLTV and low to medium response rate customers are not sent a mailing. The ROMI for these customers will be low, or even negative, for the low take rate, so why waste marketing dollars here? High CLTV and low response rate customers are also not sent a mailing. Again, the cost of the mailing is not justified. Instead, the focus is on medium to high CLTV and medium to high response rate customers.

Note that highest CLTV customers with high expected response rates get the second most expensive offer. The high CLTV customers with the medium response rate get the highest value offer. Medium CLTV high response rate get the third most expensive offer. Those with low CLTV but high response rate either do not get an offer, since they are most likely coming anyway, or they get the lowest, most cost-effective offer. By focusing the direct-mail strategy, the marketing costs are halved, since we now focus on less than 50 percent of the potential

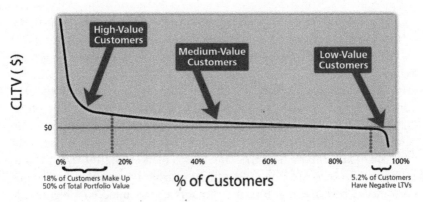

Figure 6.3 Spectrum of CLTV for existing wireless customers.

Source: Adapted from Mercer Management Consulting.

customer base, but the impact is significantly higher because we are focusing on profitability.

The spectrum of CLTV for wireless customer is shown in Figure 6.3. We see the 80/20 rule in play—in this case, 18 percent of the customers are 55 percent of value. These high-value customers are incredibly important. The acquisition cost for a high-value customer is very high, and the revenue and profitability impact to the business is very significant if they leave.

What are the characteristics of high-value customer? This is an important question to ask of your business, and focus groups and analysis may be necessary to answer this question. In banking, a high-value customer has a portfolio of services: significant cash deposits, credit cards, auto loans, and perhaps a mortgage. The strategy for managing this type of customer is to ensure, first and foremost, that they do not leave; and, second, the strategy is to up-sell and cross-sell additional products and services. That is, sell deeply to high-value customers. In banking, for example, selling retirement and investing services can broaden the pie of high-value products.

In the wireless industry, a high-value customer may have multiple cell phones, a family plan, a data plan, and perhaps fixed-line service at home with the same company. One could sell deeper by targeting marketing for high-speed Internet and TV services. If they bite on the TV services, then there is an up-sell opportunity for high definition, premium channel packages, and a digital video recorder (DVR) rental.

The sale of bundles of products to high-value customers has the advantage of creating lock-in; there becomes a significant switching cost to the customer if they want to change to a competitor. However, beware of customer lock-in backlash; poor service can result in negative customer satisfaction (CSAT) that results in mass defections as a competitor enters with a low-switching cost alternative. Therefore, customer service and service recovery become much more important to retain high-value customers.

The next component of the value-based marketing strategy is to focus on customers who are one cross-sell away from becoming a high-value customer. There are a group of customers in the middle of Figure 6.3, and the customers who are close to the 18 percent of high-value customers are particularly important. The goal is to up-sell and cross-sell to these customers to move them up the customer value chain.

At the other end of the spectrum, in Figure 6.3, note that 5.2 percent of customers actually have negative profitability. Negative-profitability customers are just as important as high-CLTV customers: these customers are sucking the lifeblood out of the firm. A few examples illustrate the importance of managing negative profitability.

Best Buy analyzed the profitability of stores and found that a certain segment of customers were purchasing products, often on sale, then returning the products for a full refund. These customers then came back to the store shortly thereafter and purchased the exact same product, which was now "open box," at a 20 percent discount. These customers had a negative CLTV. Note that without value-based analysis, negative-profitability behavior often goes unnoticed. So what is the best way to deal with negative-CLTV customers? Do you fire these customers?

In Best Buy's case, the company realized that the problem was not the customer but the process. That is, it had a policy of 100 percent money back guaranteed, no questions asked, and then resold the product at a discount. The essential realization is that the process needed to be changed to stop this behavior. As a result, Best Buy implemented a 15 percent restocking fee for all items that were opened. Furthermore, the company analyzed stores, and in geographies where it had specific high incidence of this problem, resold the open box items at different stores or through its inline channel.

Negative-CLTV customers are in every business. As another example, most airlines offer discounts for last-minute flights when there is a death in the family, called a bereavement fare. Continental Airlines started to analyze customer value and found that one customer had made

44 trips in a year for a single bereavement. As another example, Intuit, found that one small business customer with a single-site license for Quickbooks, had made 800 calls to the service desk in one year.

The theme is to identify negative-CLTV processes and then change the process. In banking, the cost of seeing an in-person teller is approximately $6 per transaction, yet an automated teller machine (ATM) costs less than 25 cents. Fees can be implemented so that low-CLTV customers pay to see a teller but get the ATM and Internet access for free.

In the wireless business, there are three drivers of negative profitability. The obvious is not paying the bill. For these customers, there is a late payment fee, and service is disconnected after a certain time period. The wireless provider often subsidizes the handset, so another source of negative CLTV is canceling early in the contract—hence the need for a $150 fee for early contract termination. The most insidious driver of negative CLTV, however, is phone calls to the service desk. There is an overhead cost of a person in a call center; his or her salary, overhead, and the cost of the phone call. This cost can range from $2.50 to $7.50 per service call, depending on whether he or she are outsourced offshore in India or Asia, or anywhere else in the United States. The reason is that there are only so many service calls someone can answer in a day—each call therefore costs a significant amount. Some low-CLTV customers can make a disproportionate amount of calls to the call center, perhaps to understand how features on the phone work or to protest a phone call charge on the bill. These calls can add up and actually make certain customers negative profitability. Again, how do you manage this?

Once the customers have been identified, the idea is to move them to a lower-cost-of-service channel. As an example, they may experience relatively long hold times for phone calls to the service desk but hear a message directing them to the web site. High-CLTV customers, however, should get fast-tracked through to the call center. This may sound like a very expensive proposition, requiring a significant infrastructure investment. And, indeed, leading firms do make real-time routing decisions based on CLTV. However, there is a low-cost alternative used by airlines. High-value customers get a special phone number to call, which automatically segments them for the call center.

In summary, the new marketing strategy is to first understand the spectrum of lifetime value for your customer base. There are most likely three broad value segments: high, medium, and negative. For negative-value customers, the strategy is to move the customers to a lower cost of service and aggressively manage costs. For high-value customers, the strategy is customer retention and cross-sell and up-sell of products and services. And for medium-value customers, figure out the one cross-sell that will make them a high-value customer, and focus marketing on moving them into the high-value bucket. Value-based management has implications beyond traditional marketing. In high-performing firms, value-based management infuses all aspects of an organization's processes. To illustrate the implications, let me share a few more case examples.

Sainsbury's

Sainsbury's is the United Kingdom's second-largest food retail chain, with more than 400 stores. These stores process 10 million transactions per week, with 200 million items of data, and have a total of 75,000 scannable units (stock-keeping units [SKUs]). Sainsbury's used a data warehouse to analyze the large amount of customer transaction data, and it created 10 segments based on spending and foods selected.

The result was that Sainsbury's was able to identify two major segments of customers: "quality-oriented" and "less affluent family." The latter "basic food" segment was primarily interested in essential food at a reasonable price. The former group was the key segment, however, and Sainsbury's called this group the "foodies." It was passionate about food, and while 21 percent of customers accounted for 24 percent of spend. Note, however, that from a value perspective, these customers were highly profitable, purchasing higher-margin food products within stores.

The idea that there are two major groups of customers that shop at grocery stores is not earth shattering. However, what is interesting is that based on these analyses Sainsbury's was able to know where the customers actually live. It found, for example, that 70 percent of some London branches are foodies, and only 6 percent in parts of West Midlands. It turns out I am originally from the West Midlands and can attest that the inhabitants eat traditional bland English food. I remember well how my grandmother used to say with pride about her cooking: "When it's black, it's done!"

For Sainsbury's, the stores were then remodeled and customized based on these data. The foodie stores were remodeled to create a more upscale food-shopping experience, with greater selection of gourmet and natural foods. The "basic food" customer stores were similarly rationalized to stock the foods these customers primarily purchased. A result of the analysis was a realization that, of the 75,000 total SKUs, 30,000 contributed less than 1 percent of revenues.

One might consider delisting all of these 30,000 SKUs. However, one must analyze which SKUs are really important—this analysis is called market basket analysis, or cluster analysis. The idea is to see what related products customers put in their basket as they shop. For example, in Chicago, if a person likes olives in his martini, and the store does not stock olives, he will most likely not shop at the store when he is in the market for martini ingredients, where the vodka is very high margin.

The results for Sainsbury's were impressive. Overall revenues increased by 12 percent; however, profit increased a lot more, since there was now a focus on providing the right products to the high-value customers, the foodies. Furthermore, 14,000 SKUs were candidates for delisting, resulting in £12 million of purchasing spend that could be shifted to bestsellers.

3M

The value-based approach to sales and marketing is not limited to B2C companies. In the mid-1990s, 3M had a major challenge that it could not accurately price deals with major channel partners, such as Wal-Mart. 3M has $25 billion in revenues and more than 79,000 employees, and is best known for Post-It notes and Scotch Tape brand products, but it makes thousands of other products, including surgical gloves, masks, masking tape, and automotive components.

Before 1995, 3M was product-center focused; it could tell which channel partner sold the most Scotch Tape or Post-Its, but it could not tell which customer purchased the most total products. As a result, 3M could not calculate the value of its channel, the profitability, and hence price large-volume contracts.

The solution to the challenge was to move to a market-centered organization and centralize data across the enterprise. 3M built a single centralized global data warehouse in place of 30 decentralized systems. The initial benefits were cost savings from the decommissioning of dozens of small data marts (databases). However, the real benefit came from understanding the value, from a profit perspective, of customers across the enterprise.

Specifically, 3M was able to create a profitability spectrum, similar to that in Figure 6.3, for its channel partners. This analysis then enabled focused marketing and sales to high-value customers (channels) and cost management for negative-profitability partners. The documented ROMI for this initiative was 56 percent.

Continental Airlines

Continental Airlines illustrates value-based marketing and management at the highest level. As I mentioned in Chapter 2, in the mid-1990s, Continental ranked dead last on every conceivable airline metric. In 2005, Continental ranked number one and was awarded the Gartner Business Intelligence award across all industries. The worst-to-first transformation provides useful insights on the value-based, data-driven marketing journey.

In the mid-1990s, Continental's processes and systems were a disaster. It didn't know who its best customers were, had incomplete and inaccurate data, could not quickly react to industry or market changes, and could not differentiate customer service and products. There was no opportunity to calculate value, and 45 separate customer databases, including an outsourced marketing data mart, compounded the challenge. Marketers were struggling to define customer value.

Continental started small, with focus groups of customers. Approximately 80 percent of Continental's customers travel less than three times per year, and for this segment price is the primary consideration. In focus groups of these customers, Continental's marketing team heard consistently what the customer wanted: clean, safe, and reliable air travel at a low cost. Clean, safe, and reliable are hygiene factors, that is, what customers explicitly expect of the product and service, and which are often taken for granted. Beyond hygiene factors, in focus groups Continental consistently heard that high-value, "elite" customers wanted employees to smile, call them by name, and treat them like they are "more than just another customer." They like to feel different, special, and important, boarding the plane first on the Elite Access blue carpet, for example. These are the elements of good customer service and are the important human component of any customer interaction with your firm.

I have young kids, and they are still pretty excited about riding on an airplane. But, for most adults, the destination is the goal, and the focus groups highlighted how customers just want a hassle-free experience. Customers realize, however, that not all will go well. That is, occasionally the flight will be delayed or canceled, connections missed, or the bags lost. When problems arise, what is important is *service recovery*. This became the insight that led the team to start with the "we are sorry" letter, sent within 12 hours of an event to change customer perception around service recovery (see Chapter 2).

As a next step, Continental started to calculate customer profitability; this is the first element of CLTV metric and is the margin for a customer on a flight. It found, for example, that the traditional ranking of customers from high to low value by "miles flown" was a completely inaccurate metric. When it started to factor in the type of ticket purchased (first class, discount economy, or last-minute full fare) and the cost to serve the customer, the ranking was dramatically different— so much so that "silver" customers became "platinum" and vice versa. What also came to light after the first-cut analysis was the large number of negative-value customers.

As an example, customers can be compensated if their flight is delayed or canceled or their bags are lost. Figure 6.4(a) is a sample of compensation for 100 customers, low-value customers are the light dots, and high-value customers are dark dots. One customer in particular received an $800 compensation for a $300 ticket! Note that the low-value customers receive on average much higher compensation than the high value. Why? There are squeaky wheel customers who have figured out how to game the system and continually call up to complain, expecting compensation. High-value customers are less likely to call and complain, and to expect compensation, but they are much more likely to churn to a competitor.

Figure 6.4(b) is compensation for 100 customers after instituting value-based management. Compensation is now based on value and severity of the incident. Continental's average used to be a $300 compensation per event, and now the average is $195 per event— this is a multimillion-dollar cost saving. Note, though, that high-value customers, dark dots with a + in Figure 6.4(b), are now receiving consistently higher compensation than the low value customers, light dots with a −. The result is higher CSAT for high-CLTV customers, which translates to measurably lower churn.

Mike Gorman from Continental pointed out to me, "Our very best customers tend not to complain. There is a danger point if they have three bad experiences in a row—for this specific customer we are not doing 'clean, safe, and reliable,' and they are at risk of defecting to a competitor. So we need to be proactive with these customers; we intervene with marketing and improve our service game."

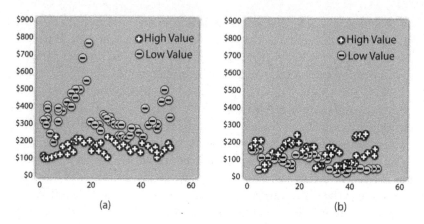

Figure 6.4 Representative compensation for 100 high-value (dark dots) and low-value (light dots) Continental Airlines customers. (a) Before value-based management and (b) after.

Source: Continental Airlines.

Balancing Short- and Long-Term Customer Profitability

The next level of CLTV strategic thinking is to understand how to balance short- and long-term customer profitability. Why is this important? Focusing solely on long-term profitability is not a viable strategy for public companies that have to make quarterly earnings. As an example, a major energy company systematically "fired" its low- and negative-value customers, and as a result significantly damaged its customer base for future growth and killed their revenues.

Figure 6.5 shows short- and long-term customer profitability data for Royal Bank of Canada (RBC). These data have been disguised for confidentiality reasons but are directionally correct. There are three customer segments: key, growth, and prime. For each of these segments, the percentile of value is plotted for the short term (annual profitability) in Figure 6.5(a) and for the long term (five-year CLTV) in Figure 6.5(b). The annual profitability is just the profit metric 6 of Chapter 5 calculated for one year, and long-term profitability, CLTV, is calculated using the template in Figure 6.1 over five years.

The idea of the percentile in Figure 6.5 is to rank-order the customers of each segment from high to low value. So, for example, for 100 customers in each segment, sort the short- and long-term customer profitability in Excel from high to low value, then plot. For

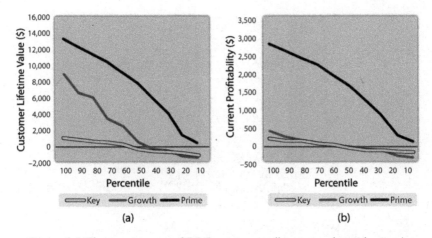

Figure 6.5 Three segments of RBC customers (key, growth, and prime). (a) Customer lifetime value (CLTV) and (b) current profitability. This data is disguised for confidentiality but is directionally correct.

Source: Cathy Burrows, RBC, and Mark Jeffery, Agile Insights LLC.

more than 100 customers, it is impractical to plot every customer, so you can make buckets of, say, 10 or 100 customers. Again, rank-order from high to low, and plot the average customer value in the bucket of 10 or 100 customers. So if you have 10,000 customers, rank-order the spreadsheet and plot the average of each 100 points, making a 100-point plot total. For a very large customer base, you won't be able to use Excel on a PC but can easily do this with SAS or an equivalent.

The Royal Bank segmentation into key, growth, and prime is predominantly age based. That is, key are the younger demographic, 18- to 29-year-olds just starting out and most often with little money. Growth customers tend to be middle-aged, 30 to 49 years old; and prime customers are established, often retired, age 50 years plus. Note that almost 50 percent of the customers are negative profitability in Figure 6.5, in both the short term and long term! Interestingly, the negative-profitability customers are the most loyal. Why? Because they are receiving more services than they are paying for.

What should you do—fire these customers? One approach is to sock the negative-profitability customers with high fees. But firing customers by using fees or other incentives to leave can have a significant backlash in the media, resulting in very negative customer perception (overall declining brand awareness and CSAT). In the United Kingdom, for

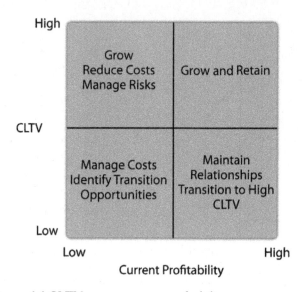

Figure 6.6 CLTV versus current profitability strategy matrix.

example, laws have been enacted to prevent high fees in banking, since they are said to discriminate against the less affluent. Furthermore, if you fire the key segment negative-profitability customers, then there will be few growth segment customers in the future.

Figure 6.6 is a 2-by-2 matrix to help you think through the optimal strategy for balancing the short- and long-term customer profitability challenge. The low-current-value, low-future-value customers, in the bottom left corner of Figure 6.6, are the negative-value key and growth segment customers. For these customers, we want to aggressively manage costs and risk—they should be encouraged to move to a lower cost of service, such as the Internet. We should also look for transition opportunities to higher value.

Obviously, the strategy for high current profitability and high future profitability customers (predominantly the prime segment) is customer retention and cross-sell marketing to grow their value. The high-current-profitability, low-future-value bottom right of Figure 6.6 is interesting. How is this possible? The answer is a customer who has only one product with the bank, such as a car loan, which is highly profitable. But the customer doesn't have anything else, so his or her future profitability is low. The strategy for this group is to maintain relationships and seek opportunities to transition these customers to high CLTV. The top left of Figure 6.6 has high future value, low current profitability. For this group, we need to manage costs and grow the customers, while actively managing risk.

RBC identified the nexus segment as a key transition segment. Nexus customers are a younger demographic, a subsegment of key segment customers, who are about to undergo a significant life-changing event such as getting married, graduating college, buying a car, or buying a first house. These nexus events are accompanied by a "first experience" that involves a financial product. For example, buying a home requires a mortgage; buying a car, a car loan; and a first investment, an investment account.

RBC created partnerships with real estate web sites and wedding sites, such as wedingbells.com. They then provided nexus customers tools for financial planning for their wedding and/or home sales. The results were impressive. Understanding the nexus customer and taking a holistic approach resulted in 200 percent balance increase in some cases, with significant cross-sell opportunities once client needs were identified. Specifically, 30 percent of new mortgages and 21 percent of new loans went to the nexus segment. In addition, 36 percent of nexus customers migrated over the next two years to higher-profitability and lifetime-value segments.

Figure 6.7 shows how RBC translates its short- and long-term strategy into tactical execution. This decision tree is a set of business rules that works as follows: At every interaction of the customer with RBC, and for all outbound marketing, the decision tree is analyzed in the background. That is, if the customer talks to a teller in the bank, contacts the call center, or reviews his or her account online, then the following questions are asked and answered by the RBC information technology (IT) systems: What is the short-term profitability? What is the client's risk? Vulnerability to churn? And what is the client's long-term value, five-year CLTV? The RBC response is then defined by where the customer ends up at the bottom of the tree.

That is, the bottom of Figure 6.7 shows the spectrum of marketing and customer relationship tactics depending on the key variables for RBC: profit, risk, churn, and CLTV. Within each of the buckets at the bottom of the tree are specific marketing campaigns and predefined customer interactions. For example, if the person is low profitability and CLTV and is high risk with high chance of churn, he or she ends up on the far right in the decision tree. This is the foundation risk control—these customers do not receive any marketing materials and are encouraged to use the lowest cost of service channels.

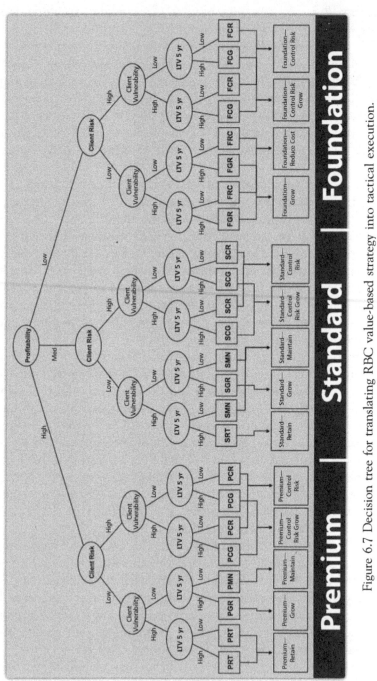

Figure 6.7 Decision tree for translating RBC value-based strategy into tactical execution.

Source: RBC.

However, consumers with high current profitability and CLTV and low risk and churn end up on the far left of the tree. These customers end up in the second box from the left: the premium growth. They are cross- and up-sold in the marketing interaction. If the high-value customer has high probability of churn, then he or she is in the far left bucket: in this case, the customer receives premium retention marketing activities. The call center agent may be prompted to apologize for the problem with the account and provide immediate compensation, for example.

Will the tree look the same for your business? No, but the important insight is how to translate value-based strategy into execution—the decision tree helps define specific marketing tactics given the key value-based metrics for a customer. An additional insight is that the original customer segments—key, growth, and prime—are not the best segments. Figure 6.7 shows three new value-based segments: premium, standard, and foundation. These segments are defined by the customer service and marketing interaction appropriate given their specific profit, risk, churn, and CLTV. From my perspective, Figure 6.7 is perhaps the most important diagram in this book, since it shows how to operationalize a value-based marketing strategy.

Customer Life Cycle Management

Customer life cycle management is just the idea of using marketing across the customer life cycle to (1) acquire, (2) grow, and (3) retain customers. CLTV adds the important dimension of value-based customer life cycle management. Ideally, the goal is to (1) acquire high- or medium-value customers, not negative-profitability customers. Then (2) grow these customers over time, with marketing to cross-sell and up-sell. But most important, you don't want your high-value customers to leave, so (3) retention is extremely important. In Chapter 8, I give a detailed example of customer retention marketing for EarthLink. Here, let's focus on growth of high-value customers, since this is often the easiest place to start. At the end of the section, I will also touch on customer acquisition.

Carnival Corporation is the world's number one cruise operator, with $14.6 billion annual revenues. It operates more than 85 ships with a total passenger capacity of nearly 170,000. Carnival operates in North America primarily through its Princess Cruise Line, Holland America, and Seabourn luxury cruise brand, as well as its flagship Carnival Cruise Lines unit. To develop its data-driven marketing strategy, Carnival followed the framework discussed in Chapter 1 (see Figure 1.7).

Carnival's marketing team started by understanding how to define its valuable customers and by thinking through what behavior it wanted to change. The marketing team realized that it was not individuals, but households, that were important and that without good household data, Carnival could not understand the true value of a customer. That is, one person in a family may inquire about a cruise and book the trip, but Carnival's customers cruise as couples or families, so the value of the customer is closely related to the value of the household, not the individual. Therefore creating good household data for segmentation was the essential early step for Carnival.

Householding is also important in other B2C industries, and in retail these data are often obtained from credit card transactions and purchased data. But households move around, and their value grows and changes, so continual updates are necessary. Carnival therefore runs more than 20 business rules each day to update their household data, and each quarter it sends the database to an external vendor who cross-checks all the records against United States postal addresses to see if anyone moved.

With the household data foundation, as a next step, Carnival segmented customers based on household value and potential future profitability (CLTV). In the cruise business, a guest's current profitability comes from two components: the actual value of the booking and the onboard spending during the cruise. Carnival did a value-based segmentation of more than 10 million guests with multiple years of prior historical data. Note that for 10 million customers you can't do this analysis in Excel 2007 (but you potentially can in Excel 2010), and Carnival used the SAS Enterprise Miner tool. In SAS, there is a function that enables the analysis of natural breakpoints in a multi-variable data set called the Proc Univariate. The idea is similar to looking for the cutoff of A's and B's in students' graded exam data, and the function looks for natural gaps in the household value data to define the cutoffs.

Based on this analysis, Carnival was able to undertake a detailed value-based segmentation that separated customers into high, medium, and low value. It found, for example, that more than 50 percent of customers were less than 50 percent of revenues—these were the low-value customers. This analysis shows that although it is important to identify your best customers, it is even more important to identify your worst customers—this is where not to spend your marketing dollars.

As it built the value segments, Carnival thought through the important decision metrics that predicted behavior. The established thinking was that marketing had to focus on "how to get people to sail." But analysis revealed that the important behavior was booking the cruise, and this occurred several months before the ship sailed. This meant a shift in marketing focus to "how to get people to book." Carnival looked at each piece of the sales cycle and asked, "What can marketing influence?" The marketing team also worked to simplify and translate the results into actionable recommendations the executive team could understand.

For each value segment, it looked at many different parameters and asked questions like, "Do you travel with children?" "Do you book in April?" "How many days do you typically cruise?" and "What is the average spending on a ticket and onboard during the cruise?" The answers to these questions for the various value segments helped define the targeted marketing offers. For example, only a small percentage of the high-value segment travels with children. Since most of the high-value segment don't travel with children, there is a good chance these customers will be receptive to marketing featuring "adults-only decks" on the cruise ships.

Booking the cruise was the key event identified by Carnival marketing. By analyzing past booking data, Carnival predicts when the high-value customers will be in the market to book their next cruise. Two months before the predicted booking date, it sends a targeted marketing offer to save by booking now. If the customer does not accept the offer, and does not book on the predicted booking date, two months after the predicted booking date the customer is sent a more expensive marketing offer. The results were impressive—repeat bookings increased more than 10 percent over a two-year period. But just as important, Carnival significantly reduced its marketing spending by not sending offers to customers who were low value.

In summary, Carnival started by creating a solid database to predict the household value of existing customers and it then segmented these customers based upon value. The cruise line thought through the behavior it was trying to influence—booking the cruise—and defined clear objectives for the marketing initiative. The Carnival example illustrates how the bigger the database is, the more important it is to keep things simple. Carnival started with big buckets of high-, medium-, and low-value households. The value-based segmentation defined who should receive the marketing, and Carnival experimented to figure out the best offers within the segments.

Growth of existing customers is a natural first place to start value-based marketing, since you can collect data on these customers. (See Chapter 2 for strategies for collecting customer data for B2B companies.) Customer acquisition marketing takes various forms, but at essence, it is the first three stages of the purchasing cycle described in Chapter 3 (awareness, evaluation, and trial) and is measured through the metrics of brand awareness, test-drive, and sales revenue. Customer acquisition may require purchasing of lists for targeted marketing. Alternately at the test-drive stage, customer data can be collected via a "car configurator" or "free 10-day trial software download," for example, and acquisition marketing triggered through these leads. For value-based customer acquisition marketing, one may need additional data to qualify the leads and to purchase lists.

The customer lists can be augmented and segmented by purchasing additional value-based data. For example, a few companies have compiled detailed transactional data on all United States individuals and households. A potential customer's complete file can be purchased by a business, but is rather expensive for mass marketing. Specific elements of the file can be purchased at a relatively low cost, however, of a few cents a record, so that customer lists can be purchased and targeted with value and event data. I suggest continual experiments in specific geographies, demographics, or segments to test the performance of acquisition campaigns, since purchasing data for direct mail, e-mail, and telemarketing can quickly get expensive.

Chapter Insights

- Metric #10—customer lifetime value (CLTV)—is the essential metric for the future value of a customer.
- The new marketing strategy is to actively manage CLTV across all your customers: retain and up-sell/cross-sell high-CLTV customers, cross-sell and up-sell medium-value customers to make them high-CLTV customers, and reduce cost to serve of negative-CLTV customers.

- B2B companies can start by calculating the spectrum of CLTV for their channel partners.
- There are no negative-profitability customers, only negative-profitability business processes or service channels. You have to identify processes that subtract value from the firm, and then change the process or service channel.
- Long-term thinking with CLTV is only one dimension: you have to manage short-term profit and CLTV.
- The customer life cycle consists of acquiring, growing, and retaining customers. For each component, take a value-based approach and use data-mining to target marketing.

From Clicks to Value with Internet Marketing Metrics

#11–Cost per Click (CPC), #12–Transaction Conversion Rate (TCR), #13–Return on Ad Dollars Spent (ROA), #14–Bounce Rate, and #15–Word of Mouth (WOM)

A challenge writing this book is that in many respects Internet marketing is the Wild West: the Internet is the new frontier for marketing and is not yet completely figured out. In the American West of the 1800s, there was lawlessness, bandits, and ad hoc laws and approaches for survival. Internet marketing is similar—innovation is occurring rapidly, and the rules are continuously being rewritten. Just like a gunfight, the major players in the game are also changing quickly—in 2007 with Google purchasing DoubleClick for $3.1 billion, followed by Microsoft's acquisition of aQuantive for $6 billion, for example.

In Chapter 1, I discussed what I called the marketing divide—that a few organizations "get" data-driven marketing and the majority do not. This divide is alive and well for Internet marketing, with a relatively small group of established marketers in the game for several years, and many more marketers struggling to get started. For marketers beginning the journey, Internet marketing is indeed the Wild West, and this chapter will answer the questions of where to start and how to deliver measurable value. For experienced Internet marketers, this chapter will provide insights to take your existing Internet marketing to the next level.

My approach is to start by focusing first on the biggest piece of online marketing budgets: search engine marketing (SEM), which in a November 2008 eMarketer study was found to be 45 percent of online marketing spending and was predicted to be 49 percent of spending in 2010. To get started with SEM there are a few essential metrics that can be analyzed with Microsoft Excel to deliver real results.[1] These metrics have acronyms such as CPC, TCR, and ROA (essential metrics numbered 11 to 13) that take a little getting used to, but, like juicing a fresh lime for a margarita, the effort is worth the squeeze. If you are presently not optimizing your SEM, then the first part of this chapter will provide you with actionable frameworks to drive significant performance gains out of your existing search marketing.

But beyond traditional SEM and optimizing your marketing web sites (with essential metric #14, bounce rate), I want to go to the frontier and provide insights into how Internet marketing is rapidly evolving. As examples later in the chapter, I discuss attribution modeling, the impact of targeted impressions in social media, and how to track and measure word of mouth (WOM, essential metric #15) on the Internet. Mastering the five new-age metrics of this chapter will make you a genius, Internet-savvy marketer in your organization.

CPC versus CPM: Optimizing Metric #11—CPC Is the Google Innovation

In 2002, on a flight from Washington, D.C., to Chicago, I happened to sit next to a senior partner from a big five consulting firm. Google was in the news, again, and he exclaimed, "I don't get it; search is easy, what's the big deal about Google?" He had a point—search is not rocket science—so what's the Google innovation?

It turns out that it is fairly straightforward to make computer program "robots" that scour the Web and tabulate all the web pages in existence and the keywords on these pages. You can then search this very large table for specific web pages with corresponding keywords. The challenge is ordering the very big list of web pages with keywords you want in some way that makes sense. That is, you can search all the web pages on the planet, but how do you list them in an order of most important to least important?

In the early days of the Internet, circa 1995, search engines counted the number of keywords on a page to define the search order—more occurrences of the keywords ranked the page higher in the search order. So web developers just listed their keywords lots of times on each page to influence the search order. To circumvent this, Yahoo! had buildings full of people who manually reviewed web pages and rated them.

In 1996, Larry Page and Sergey Brin had an insight that would change the world. They had the idea to rank-order search web pages by the number of links to a given web page.[2] That is, people who link to a page are effectively voting for the importance of a web page, so Google search is, in principle, democracy in action. Page and Brin incorporated Google on September 4, 1998, and at that time the Google patent gave them the best search algorithm on the planet. From my perspective, it is amazing that Google is just over 10 years old. Yet, my six-year-old comes home from kindergarten each day and Googles web sites with kids' games, such as Bubble Trouble and Nick Jr., that his friends have told him about at recess.

The marketing business model for the Internet up until 1997 had been based upon a CPM (cost per thousand impression) model. That is, the revenue model for advertising was based on the cost per impression. In 1997, Overture[3] was the first to put sponsored search advertising around the natural search and charge based on cost per click (CPC), which is now the de facto measure for SEM.

Metric #11: The Essential Search Engine Marketing Metric

CPC = Cost per click on a sponsored search link or banner advertisement

---

CPC versus CPM is a subtle shift in Internet marketing strategy. In the CPM model, the person doing the search is most important and advertisers pay to just be seen by the searcher. In the CPC model, the company being searched is most important, and advertisers pay for a click-through that has good odds of resulting in a purchase. A Media Contacts study has shown that 46 percent of searches are to find a product or service to buy, and advertisers are willing to pay a premium for a click-through for a qualified lead to a potential purchase. SEM therefore focuses on the cost per click-through—this is in the category of demand generation marketing, defined in Chapter 1.

However, for Overture in 1997, the highest bid for the keyword won, so marketers could always secure top placement by bidding the most. The Google innovation in 1998 was not just the search algorithm—it changed the game by using multiple variables to define which bid gets the keyword, optimizing the revenue from CPC. That is, Google redefined how CPC is calculated. (See the next section for more details on how Google defines CPC and the implications.)

Of course, as of the writing of this book in 2009, the Internet search wars are far from over, and it is too early to call the winner by knockout. In April 2009, Google had 64 percent share of searches; Yahoo!, 20 percent; and Microsoft, 8 percent. Microsoft's attempted to purchase Yahoo! in 2008, and after the unsuccessful bid revamped its search offering and launched Bing in June 2009. In August 2009, Yahoo! and Microsoft announced a partnership that gave Microsoft Yahoo!'s search business, so as of the writing of this book, search is effectively split 64 percent to 28 percent between Google and Microsoft, respectively. Google clearly has a competitive advantage, though. It will be interesting to see if history judges the advantage to be sustainable.

The CPC for Google is pretty expensive, in the range of $1 to $5, and you can burn a few hundred dollars, a few thousand dollars, or $100,000 in a day depending on the volume of search words and how broad your geography is (local, United States, or international). So how do you ensure you are getting the biggest bang for the marketing buck in SEM? For this, we need a few more metrics, and two essential ones are metric #12, transaction conversion rate (TCR), and metric #13, return on ad dollars spent (ROA).

Optimizing Sponsored Search: Metrics #12—TCR and #13—ROA

Internet search is broken out into two components: natural search, also called organic search, and sponsored search. Natural searches are the search results, in the Google case, based in part on the number of links to a page from other sites. Sponsored searches are the paid links on the top and sides of the search page.

Figure 7.1 is a heat map of where people click for an Internet search, denoted by dots. Note that the eye is drawn to the top left; the dark is the "heat" in the map. These are the top two sponsored searches and the top few natural searches. The lines on the heat map in Figure 7.1 are the folds of the page and additional pages of links—note that very few people click below the fold or on additional search pages. Hence, doing well in SEM means optimizing sponsored searches for efficiency and relevance, while optimizing your site to rank well organically.

Natural search ranking can be increased by improving your web site, incenting others to link to you, and by strategically placing tags for the search engine indexing robots.[4] I want to primarily focus on paid search, however, since, depending on your business, this can be a significant fraction of your marketing budget.

How people search is an interesting anthropological study. Say, for example, someone is interested in a wine-tasting vacation. The first series of searches tend to be very generic, nonbranded searches. These searches may contain the search words *wine* and *vacation*. As a result, tours to Napa Valley and Tuscany, Italy, may pop up. The second set of searches then is more focused, drilling into a particular geography, in this case, perhaps Napa, California. Searches produce more searches, and finally the customer starts to get brand specific—possibly searching on Expedia, Travelocity, or Orbitz for flight and hotel information to Napa. This example highlights the importance of purchasing both nonbrand generic search words (for the beginning of the search) and branded search words (for the end of the search journey) as an essential component of your SEM strategy.

To manage SEM effectively, there are a few more search marketing-specific terms to define: *bid strategy* and *match type* are the first two. Bid strategy is the placement you would like to get on the page: one to four are in the first four sponsored links, and five to six are the following two, for example. In match type, the user must type the search words in exact order ("exact" match type), or the words can be typed in any order ("broad" match type, also sometimes called "advanced"). Match type can also include phrases (phrase match) and words to be excluded (negative match).

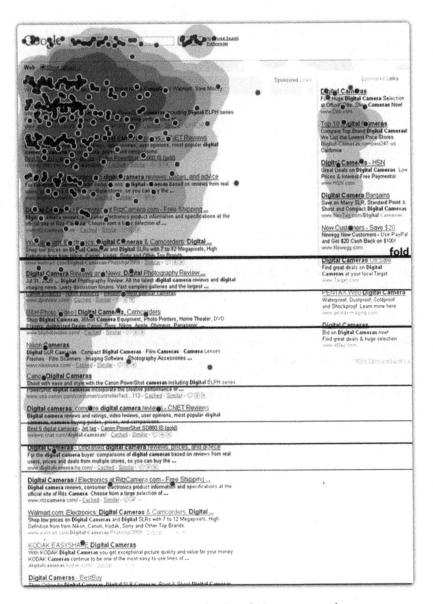

Figure 7.1 Heat map for Google Internet search.

Source: Adapted from the Enquiro Eye Tracking Report, www.enquiro.com.

As examples, keywords *VOIP* and *Vonage* can have a broad or exact match type, typed in any order or in a specific order, respectively. "VOIP calls to Turkey" is a phrase match. But searches for bourbon should be excluded, so you should specify "Wild Turkey" as a negative match. Note that the more specific the match type is, the more specific the landing page should be; for example, a broad match for "VOIP calls to Turkey" or "VOIP calls to Mexico" might point to the same page, but an exact or phrase match can go to different landing pages.

In addition to CPC, the next really useful Internet marketing metric is click-through rate (CTR). CTR is just the percentage of customers who click through on a link, and it is calculated from the number of clicks divided by the number of impressions (ads served).

The central idea of SEM marketing is that you buy keywords by bidding for keywords and placement, with specified match types. Everyone bids for specific search words and placement, such as *vacation*, *Napa Valley*, *wine*, and so on. Google ranks the sponsored link advertisement using a complex formula that includes the bid amount, CTR, the probability a customer will click, bounce rate (essential metric 14, defined later), and more. So, for example, you might bid $4 for a click for *vacation* and *wine*, with a broad match type and a bid strategy of one to four. Given other similar bids and the Google-sponsored link rank algorithm, you might get the click for $2.50, with a placement of 2. That is, the bid cleared for $2.50 and you were the second sponsored link.

Note that Google advertising rank depends on CTR, so if your sponsored link has a high historic CTR, you can get a higher placement for a lower CPC. That is, the Google advertising ranking favors high volumes and high probabilities of click-throughs—this maximizes revenue for Google (Google's revenue = CPC × number of clicks). This ranking approach also favors large brands with a history of good CTR, meaning players new to the game, with no CTR history, need a strategy for optimizing SEM to manage cost and drive performance.

For optimizing SEM, an essential metric is metric #12—transaction conversion rate (TCR).

Metric #12: The Essential Metric Connecting Internet Clicks to Dollars

TCR = Transaction conversion rate; the percentage of customers who purchase after clicking through to your web site

From the CTR and TCR, we can calculate essential metric #5, take rate, in SEM:

$$\text{Take rate} = \text{Click-through rate} \times \text{Transaction conversion rate}$$
$$= \text{CTR} \times \text{TCR}$$

So the take rate is just the percentage of customers who click through times the percentage who convert to a sale once they click through. This take rate is identical to the probability of purchase and is the percentage of customers who accept the offer given an impression of advertising.

An additional metric that helps to define the SEM effectiveness for e-commerce is net revenue:

$$\text{Net revenue} = \text{Revenue} - \text{Cost}$$

This is just the profit (essential metric #6) for Internet marketing. It does not include the cost of goods sold, just the Internet marketing cost, and measures the overall publisher contribution to the marketing campaign. The net revenue can be calculated for each click, so it is revenue per click minus CPC, or it can be added up for all the clicks.

To round out the essential SEM Internet metrics, we need the equivalent of ROI for SEM: return on ad dollars spent.

Metric #13: The Essential Return on Internet Search Marketing Metric

ROA = Return on ad dollars spent = Net revenue/cost

ROA measures the efficiency of generating net revenue from ad dollars spent when the end action is the purchase of a product or service.

The great thing about SEM is that you get lots and lots of data from the publishers. These data can be consolidated together by Double-Click, aQuantive, or an equivalent, and to get started can be analyzed in Microsoft Excel using pivot tables.[5] Figure 7.2 is a template for calculating the metrics discussed so far in this chapter for representative SEM campaign data. The first few columns of Figure 7.2(b) are the publisher (search engine), campaign name, keywords, and so on. The next columns are the bid and the actual cost per click, and the last columns of Figure 7.2(b) are the derived metrics discussed above.

(a)

	CTR (%)	TCR (%)	Total Cost per Transaction ($)	Amount ($)	Total Cost ($)	Net Revenue ($)	ROA (%)	Total Volume of Bookings	Avg. Revenue per Booking ($)	Take Rate (Booking Probability) (%)
1	9.1	900.0	0.26	8,777.95	2.31	8,775.64	379,487	9	975	81.8
2	16.7	100.0	0.63	1,574.20	0.63	1,573.58	251,772	1	1,574	16.7
3	11.1	100.0	0.39	390.15	0.39	389.76	100,584	1	390	11.1
4	2.5	12.5	2.20	935.00	2.20	932.80	42,400	1	935	0.3
5	23.1	33.3	5.21	1,685.55	5.21	1,680.34	32,237	1	1,686	7.7

(b)

	Publisher	Keyword	Match Type	Bid Strategy	Bid ($)	Clicks	Click Charges ($)	Avg. CPC ($)	Impressions	Avg. Pos.
1	Yahoo—U.S.	Fly to Florence	Advanced	Position 1-2	6.25	1	2.31	2.31	11	1.27
2	Yahoo—U.S.	Low International Airfare	Advanced	Position 1-2	6.25	1	0.63	0.63	6	1.00
3	MSN—Global	Air Discount France Ticket	Broad	Position 2-5	0.00	1	0.39	0.39	9	1.11
4	Yahoo—Global	France Online Booking	Standard	Position 1-2	0.25	8	2.20	0.28	318	2.98
5	Google—U.S.	Paris Cheap Airline	Broad	Position 5-10	6.25	3	5.21	1.74	13	1.00

Figure 7.2 Template for SEM metric calculation: (a) five example keywords with bid and CPC data and (b) related metrics. The CPC data have been disguised but are representative. The template and complete Excel data file of 7,000 records is downloadable at www.agileinsights.com/ROMI.

Given these metrics, the three steps to optimize SEM are as follows:

1. *Optimize the publisher strategy.* Figure out which publisher (Google, Yahoo!, MSN/Bing, Ask.com, or domain-specific publishers such as Kayak for travel) is getting the best results for the money you are spending.
2. *Optimize the campaign strategy.* Analyze campaigns within a publisher to determine the campaign changes needed to deliver the most value from specific campaigns.
3. *Calculate the KPI impact.* Determine the impact of campaign changes on key performance indicators (KPIs) such as net revenue and ROA. This becomes the baseline for future testing.

To get started with Step 1, I suggest allocating your SEM marketing dollars by the market share of the publishers: approximately 60 percent Google, 20 percent Yahoo!, and so on. Next, design some campaigns, buy keywords, and gather data. Figure 7.3 is a matrix for optimizing SEM for these publishers given measured click-through data. The dimensions are average CPC and take rate (CTR × TCR). The idea is to average the CPC for the specific publishers (Google U.S., Google global, Yahoo! U.S., etc.) and take rates. The publishers with low average cost per click and high take rates are clearly working (bottom right of Figure 7.3). For these publishers, we should consider increasing marketing spending. The high-CPC, low-take-rate publishers are not working. You should consider killing funding for these publishers.

The top right quadrant of Figure 7.3 corresponds to high take rate but expensive cost per click. These publisher campaigns are working, but at a high cost. The idea is to seek out high-ROA keywords and figure out what's working. For example, you can search for specific keywords where you bid for a placement of four or more but actually got the number one or two placement, because no one else bid. Higher bid placement keywords cost less than one or two placements, so you can save money and use these same keywords across other publishers.

The campaigns in the bottom left quadrant of Figure 7.3 have low take rates but the CPC is low, so they should not be discarded out of hand. The idea for these is Step 2 of the strategy framework, to optimize the individual campaigns for specific publishers. Figure 7.4 shows how to do this by looking at campaigns within a specific publisher on the dimensions of CTR and TCR.

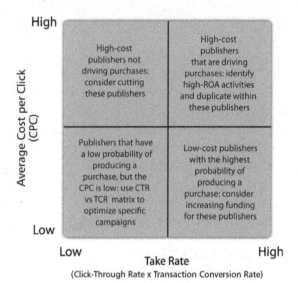

Figure 7.3 A framework for optimizing Internet search publisher strategy based on CPC and take rate (purchase probability).

In Figure 7.4, the top right quadrant denotes campaigns for a specific publisher that have a high CTR and TCR. These campaigns are doing well, and no changes are necessary. The top left quadrant, however,

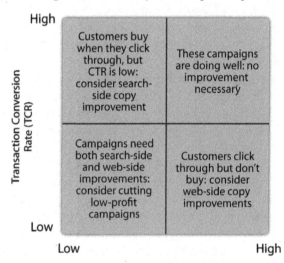

Figure 7.4 A framework for optimizing specific Internet search campaigns by analyzing TCR and CTR.

has high TCR but low CTR—this suggests that once customers click through, they buy, but they are not clicking through. For these campaigns, we need to improve the search-side copy, that is, the text under the search link. Similarly, the campaigns in the bottom right quadrant of Figure 7.4 have high CTR but low TCR—customers are clicking through, but when they get to the web site, they are not purchasing. Hence, web-side copy improvement is necessary. Finally, the lower left quadrant of Figure 7.4 has both low CTR and low TCR. These campaigns need both server-side and web-side copy improvement. You should consider killing the low-net-revenue campaigns in this quadrant.

The best way to optimize SEM is to take a rapid test-and-learn approach. The key levers are defined by the metrics CPC, CTR, and TCR—improving the copy on the publisher side can increase CTR, and improving the landing page increases TCR. Improving the copy and the landing page also has the benefit of reducing CPC, since the Google algorithm rewards high CTR and low bounce rate (essential metric #14 of the next section) in the CPC price.

The most important step of the preceding framework, Step 3, is to calculate the KPI impact. By calculating the net revenue and ROA, you calculate the value of an actual click. These data are essential for defining how much you are willing to bid for keywords in the future. The Google CPC is so high, in part, because marketers do not calculate the value of clicks. Instead, they bid up the price of keywords and end up paying more than they are worth.

ROA also enables you to answer the question, "What if I put more search marketing dollars, Y, on publisher or campaign X?" The predicted impact is just the new marketing dollars multiplied by the measured average ROA for the publisher or specific campaign. That is, the new net revenue = ROA × Y (for the same CPC). Figure 7.5 is an ROA template for a representative Google search campaign, calculating the impact of reducing the CPC by 10 percent and increasing the take rate by 10 percent. In the example in Figure 7.5, the ROA increases by 110 percent.

As an example, in 2007, Air France[6] marketers needed to improve the performance of their SEM marketing spending, driving better efficiency and higher online booking revenues. Media Contacts worked with Air France to optimize its SEM strategy following the systematic framework described in this section. For Air France, the results were impressive: CPC decreased by 19 percent, and CTR increased by 112 percent. That is, Air France was able to significantly

Assumptions								
Reduce CPC	10%	*						
Increase Take Rate	10%	*						

	Average Cost per Click ($)	Total Volume of Purchases	Average Revenue per Purchase ($)	Take Rate (Probability of Purchase) (%)	Sum of Charges ($)	Average Cost per Purchase ($)	Total Net Revenue ($)	ROA (%)
Current *	1.84	1,550	1,126	0.040	353,641	228.16	1,745,482	494
Optimized	1.66	1,705	1,126	0.044	318,277	186.67	1,920,030	603

* Input your numbers here

Figure 7.5 Template for the ROA impact of reducing CPC and increasing take rate for a representative Google campaign. Downloadable at www.agileinsights.com/ROMI.

increase overall campaign efficiency without increasing the cost per booking.

This section has provided a systematic framework and approach for optimizing SEM. As mentioned previously, this marketing is demand generation marketing, defined in Chapter 1. A weakness of the SEM approach discussed so far is that in the search to buy, the last click receives 100 percent attribution for the sale. However, there are often many clicks over time in the search journey. These multiple searches and clicks are not captured in the SEM optimization approach of this section. Later in this chapter, I discuss attribution modeling, which uses cookies to track specific customers' search journeys. As a next step, though, let's look at the essential metric for how good your web site is: bounce rate.

How Good Is Your Web Site? Metric #14—Bounce Rate

In addition to TCR, defined in the previous section, there are several metrics to measure how good your web site is. These often include time on site and number of page views. However, these metrics tend to be ambiguous. Time on site and page views are often cited to link to customer engagement. However, if your web site is designed to help customers find products and services, and quickly purchase, then time on site may not be the best metric—since you want this time to be as short as possible. In addition, if the web site is a blog, then all of the content will be on one page, so page views are not a good metric. I therefore prefer a different metric: bounce rate.[7]

Metric #14: The Essential Web Site Performance Metric

Bounce rate = Percentage of customers who leave your web site after spending less than five seconds on your site

---

I use 5 seconds, but this is a rough rule of thumb; you can use 10 seconds if you think that makes more sense for your site. Bounce rate is essentially web site churn, our essential metric #3. Why I like this metric is that in combination with the other metrics we have defined, and your other marketing activities, it helps to provide a broader picture of what's working and what's not.

As an example, Figure 7.6(a) compares various marketing campaigns—search, print, e-mail, direct mail, and impression advertising on your corporate site that point to your campaign-specific web site. If you looked just at the CTR, you would conclude that the direct mail is working the best, with e-mail second. However, when we include bounce rate as an additional metric, you see that direct mail actually has the highest bounce rate of 64.3 percent. The corporate web site has the lowest bounce rate of 43.9 percent, which suggests that it is doing well to drive relevant traffic, and e-mail is also doing well, with a bounce rate of 44.1 percent.

You can then start to look at why the bounce rate is so high for direct mail compared with e-mail. Targeting of the direct mail list is potentially an issue. As a next step, different web sites might be used to improve the bounce rate for different demographics and marketing. This is not hard to do, since it is relatively easy to have different uniform resource locators (URLs) for the different marketing channels and to measure the bounce rate for each. The insight is that by understanding who chooses not to stay on your site, you can significantly impact the acceptance to offers of those who do.

Figure 7.6(b) is a more detailed example monitoring traffic over time for a specific marketing campaign landing page and segmenting out by Google search. The table gives rich insight into how Google is performing in terms of quality of traffic and bounce rate. Simple averages of overall bounce rates, and percentage of visitors from search, define benchmarks. Given these benchmarks, you can see how the search marketing is improving over time relative to the other marketing. Specifically, in Figure 7.6(b) Google is delivering the vast majority of search visitors, the average Google bounce rate is lower than the

(a)

	Unique Visitors	Transactions	Transaction Conversion Rate (%)	Bounced	Bounce Rate (%)
Search	5,118	427	8.3	3,020	59.0
Direct Mail with URL's	2,566	850	33.1	1,651	64.3
E-mail	1,700	434	25.5	750	44.1
Corporate Web Site	758	186	24.5	333	43.9
Print Ads with URL's	568	42	7.4	329	57.9

(b)

Month	All Unique Visitors	All < 5 Sec	Total Bounce Rate (%)	Search Engine Visitors	Search % Visitors	Google Only	Google % Visitors	Google < 5 Sec	Google Bounce Rate (%)
1	2,200	1,254	57	330	15	215	65	129	60
2	1,750	1,103	63	438	25	385	88	169	44
3	2,800	1,652	59	532	19	505	95	293	58
4	1,800	936	52	468	26	370	79	129	35
5	1,795	1,041	58	305	17	269	88	110	41
6	2,150	1,097	51	473	22	454	96	145	32
Overall Trend Data Benchmark:			57		21		85		45

Figure 7.6 Bounce rate templates. (a) Bounce rates for e-mail, search, impression, and corporate web site marketing. (b) Example bounce rates over time for all search and Google-specific search marketing.

Source: Adapted from A. Kaushik, *Web Analytics an Hour a Day.* Indianapolis, Indiana: Sybex, an imprint of John Wiley & Sons, Inc., 2007, pp. 144, 358.

benchmark average, and over time the bounce rate for Google is improving—a good positive trend.

In summary, the idea is that you can segment traffic from many sources and monitor performance in terms of effectiveness of the web site to engage the customer, or equivalently, to turn-off (bounce) the customer. Measuring over time enables you to create average benchmarks for your web site performance. You can then see if the performance is improving, or not, and by exactly by how much relative to the benchmarks as a result of changing the web site.

Unless you are a content publisher, average page views and time on site are often not relevant metrics. In e-commerce, for example, high page views and time on site suggest the customer could not find the right product or service. Generic high-level metrics are also not as valuable as campaign-specific metrics segmented based on the type of marketing activity, customer segment, and so on. I therefore encourage you to think through the strategy of your web site and the clear objectives of the campaign, and then define the key metrics that define a win.

For example, the strategic objectives might be a certain number of sign-ups for a specific event and resulting leads generated with a qualified e-mail and phone number. Bounce rate from the specific marketing microsite can be monitored along with sign-ups for the event and leads generated: these three metrics are the KPIs. Segmented out on the different marketing channels, these metrics define success or failure and can be monitored for actionable improvement.

As a different example, perhaps the marketing is designed to drive potential customers to a web site to help them compare different product benefits, functionality, and specifications relative to other products or services you sell. This is "evaluation" marketing in the purchasing cycle (Figure 3.2). In this case, monitoring specific page views of product information could provide insights into which components of the web site are working and which are not. If you combine the page view data with bounce rate and downloads of specific white papers, segmented on a marketing channel, you can quickly gain a complete picture into how well the marketing is working or not working.

The theme is consistent with the other examples given in this book. First, define the strategy for your marketing campaign and then the business objectives. As you think through the execution, the web component is the easiest to measure—bounce rate in combination with specific KPIs for the campaign can enable real-time monitoring of performance. The next chapter on agile marketing gives a detailed example from Microsoft on how to do this.

Changing the Internet Search Marketing Game with Attribution Modeling

As I briefly mentioned in the first section of this chapter, the challenge with Internet search marketing is attribution. That is, the user searches, and the last click from the last search that resulted in the sale (or call-to-action click on the targeted marketing web site) is attributed with 100 percent weighting for producing the sale. Figure 7.7 shows specific search words in a representative SEM campaign based on the number of clicks they generate and the corresponding revenues that are attributed to these clicks.

In Figure 7.7, the first three keywords were branded, for example, containing keywords such as *Expedia vacation* or *Orbitz holiday*, and these three keywords produce approximately 50 percent of sales. Note that the distribution of keywords in Figure 7.7 has a long tail—these are the large number of various nonbranded search words that contribute very little to sales. This is the 80/20 rule in action—in this example, 17 percent of the keywords, the three that were branded, are 50 percent or more of the contribution to the end sale. Based on this thinking, to optimize the SEM you should stop investing in the nonbranded search

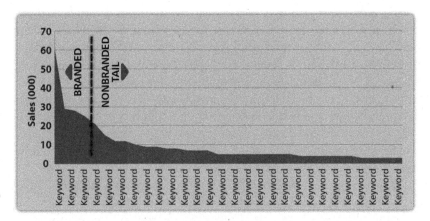

Figure 7.7 Keyword contribution to sales in Internet-sponsored search marketing.

Source: Media Contacts.

USER_ID	Search Engine Name	Keyword Name	Click Date	Product	Sales	Revenue
184	Yahoo!	Last-Minute Holidays	9/11/2007 14:22			
184	Google	Branded	9/23/2007 15:52			
184	Yahoo!	All-Inclusive Holiday	9/23/2007 16:54			
184	Yahoo!	Last-Minute Holidays	9/26/2007 15:15			
184	Yahoo!	Last-Minute Holidays	9/26/2007 15:22			
184	Google	Branded	9/26/2007 18:52	Holiday Package	2	$1,205

Figure 7.8 Actual Internet search journey of a customer shopping for a last-minute vacation.

Source: Media Contacts.

words that produce small or negligible revenue. However, this is erroneous thinking because it is based on attributing all the revenues to the last click. What is needed is a way to track the actual customer click stream search journey and figure out which nonbranded keywords are important.

Figure 7.8 is the actual search click stream for a particular customer purchasing a vacation. Note that the user used different search engines on different dates. He or she conducted six searches over a three-week period that ultimately culminated in the purchase of a holiday package for two. These data are obtained by analyzing cookie files for individual users. A cookie file is a small data file on a user's computer that can be used to store Internet activity–based information. Each time the user does a search with specific words, a cookie is updated with this information. The cookie file can be active for up to 30 days.

Media Contacts, a division of Havas, has the capability to analyze this cookie data and match specific user IDs and search campaign keywords. They are therefore able to untangle the search journey (Figure 7.8) from the other activities the user is doing. These data provide invaluable insights. In Figure 7.8, the last click, a branded search from Google, would traditionally be attributed 100 percent for the $1,205 holiday package revenues. But, clearly, the other five searches also contributed. How much? Answering this question is attribution modeling for Internet search marketing.

Media Contacts has developed a proprietary system, called Artemis, that does attribution modeling. Conceptually, the idea is to analyze all Internet campaign search words and weight the keywords by the percentage they are used in a campaign-related search and their contribution to the end sale. The weighting follows Figure 7.7, with more frequently used search words weighted more, and more accurately attributes the contribution of the search words to the final revenues. For example, Figure 7.9(a) includes click attribution for three different

	LAST CLICK				ASSIST CLICKS					
	Last click (%)	Last but 1 (%)	Last but 2 (%)	Last but 3 (%)	Last but 4 (%)	Last but 5 (%)	Last but 6 (%)	Last but 7 (%)	Last but 8 (%)	Last but 9 (%)
Campaign #1	58	18	9	6	2	2	2	1	1	1
Campaign #2	48	22	1	8	3	2	2	2	1	0
Campaign #3	42	21	1	1	5	3	2	1	1	0

(a)

USER_ID	Search Engine Name	Keyword Name	Click Date	Product	Sales	Revenue ($)	Artemis Attribution Weighting ($)
184	Yahoo!	Last-Minute Holidays	9/11/2007 14:22				36
184	Google	Branded	9/23/2007 15:52				60
184	Yahoo!	All-Inclusive Holiday	9/23/2007 16:54				84
184	Yahoo!	Last-Minute Holidays	9/26/2007 15:15				181
184	Yahoo!	Last-Minute Holidays	9/26/2007 15:22				241
184	Google	Branded	9/26/2007 18:52	Holiday Package	2	1,205	603

(b)

Figure 7.9 (a) Percentage of sales revenues attributed to clicks in a search journey for three different campaigns. (b) Actual Internet search journey of a customer shopping for a last-minute vacation with weighted revenue attribution.

Source: Media Contacts.

campaigns calculated by Artemis. The last click keywords get approximately 50 percent of the attribution; these are the 20 that give the 80 from our previous discussion. The "assist clicks" are weighted based on their attribution to the final sale for each campaign.

What does this all mean? The idea is that Internet marketing dollars should be spread proportionately across the assist click keywords, and not just be placed on the branded last click keyword. The click stream analysis enables high fidelity in terms of which search words are really contributing to the end action. Specifically, Figure 7.9(b) is the search journey (Figure 7.8) with a more accurate attribution to keywords. These data can be aggregated across all search journeys containing the campaign keywords and the average attribution calculated for each keyword. The SEM budget can then be more effectively allocated to the keywords that drive attributed revenues.

As a case example, Media Contacts conducted this type of analysis for a major travel company. Their online marketing budget was for more than 500,000 keywords, and the attribution modeling shifted 50 percent of the attribution from the last click to prior clicks in the search journey. The company therefore shifted its keyword buys to increase spending for these nonbranding keywords. The result was a 24 percent measured increase in ROA that came from better use of the keywords early in the search journey.

The discussion of Internet search marketing and attribution modeling may seem a little intimidating, but you can get started using relatively simple tools—Google, Yahoo!, and Microsoft all have free web analytics. You can easily tag the components of your web marketing campaign and start to track customers who click on your marketing, where they click and the like, and start generating actionable data.

Through DoubleClick, or the equivalent, you can get search and click-through data for specific marketing campaigns and can calculate the important metrics with the template in Figure 7.2. As a first step, the analysis can be in Excel, and you can create the 2-by-2 matrix in Figures 7.3 and 7.4. These figures enable you to do a first-cut optimization based on CPC, CTR, and take rate (CTR × TCR). The optimization is first for the search engines (the publishers), to ensure you are getting the best bang for the cost per click, and then for the specific campaign within a search engine. Finally, the ROA and net revenue analysis defines the value you are really getting for the CPC.

For SEM optimization you can get started in Excel, but as you get more experienced, you will most likely want a fast turnaround on the analysis. Tools such as Omniture or Covaro can do the analysis on large data sets and can create the maps and calculate the metrics automatically. These tools are needed for optimization of large campaigns that run for a few days or less, for example, and when you want to monitor and make on-the-fly performance improvements.

The limitation of the frameworks in Figures 7.3 and 7.4 is that they put all the weight on search words that are last click in the search journey that leads to the purchase—this is 50 percent the right answer, since the last few clicks are approximately 50 percent of the contribution to the actual purchase. To get the 100 percent answer, you need attribution modeling. Attribution modeling, discussed in this section, is not yet available as a "free" resource, and you will need help to get started. I have no doubt the major search companies will start to offer these services in the not-so-distant future; they are currently available from a few select digital agencies. Attribution modeling will enable the next level of Internet search marketing—marketers will purchase specific customers and target specific advertising at these users based on their click history.

Beyond SEM: Internet Display Advertising Impact

The discussion so far has focused exclusively on keyword-based SEM, with text ads placed as a result of the keyword search. According to eMarketer, this is more than 45 percent of the more than $24 billion spent on online marketing. What about other types of Internet advertising? Display advertising is 19 percent of online marketing spending, with video and rich media accounting for 2.5 percent and 8 percent, respectively.

However, CTRs on these display advertisements are dismally low.[8] According to DoubleClick and eMarketer, click rates on static display ads fell dramatically in recent years to average levels of only 0.2 percent in 2006, and comScore measured averages of 0.1 percent in 2008. According to research from DoubleClick, eMarketer, Eyeblaster, and IAB, rich media ads don't perform much better, with a CTR of roughly only 1 percent in 2006. One could conclude from these data that traditional impression advertising is dead on the Internet; however, this is not the case.

comScore studied 139 online display ad campaigns conducted across a variety of vertical industries and found some interesting results. They conducted controlled experiments of users exposed to impression advertising and compared them with those who were not (the control). For those exposed to impression advertising, there was:

- At least 46 percent lift in visits to the advertiser's web site over a four-week period.
- At least 38 percent lift in the percentage of consumers conducting a search query using the advertiser's branded terms.
- An average of 27 percent lift in online sales of the impression advertised brand online.
- An average lift of 17 percent in a consumer's likelihood of buying at the advertiser's retail store.

Hence, impression advertising, in spite of a lack of clicks, can have a significant impact on consumers in the online context.

In the last section, we discussed attribution modeling for SEM. In partnership with Yahoo!, Media Contacts has extended its attribution modeling to include display advertising. It uses cookies, usually over a 30-day window, to track individual consumers and look at three possible scenarios after exposure to impression advertising: (1) the customer buys

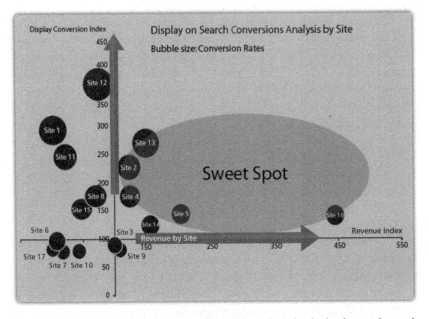

Figure 7.10 Optimizing Internet marketing based on both display and search advertising effectiveness for conversion to revenues.

Source: Media Contacts.

immediately after clicking on the impression, (2) the consumer comes back later and purchases, or (3) the consumer searches later and buys.

For scenarios 1 and 2, the impression advertising performance can be optimized using the approaches discussed earlier for SEM. Scenario 3 is particularly interesting, though—Media Contacts found that optimizing campaigns with combined impression advertising and search delivers 83 percent lift in the search conversion rate.

Figure 7.10 shows how to optimize search conversion, scenario 3, on the dimensions of display advertising effectiveness (Display Conversion Index) and normalized revenue (Revenue Index). The bubbles on the plot are specific web site publishers, and their size corresponds to conversion rates. The Y-axis is the number of sales transactions generated by the publisher, and the X-axis is the normalized total revenues from the publisher.

The bottom left quadrant of Figure 7.10 corresponds to impression advertising with publishers that deliver low transactions and low revenues. Campaigns with these publishers should be killed. The top left quadrant drives a significant number of transactions, but at low profitability—the advertising may be costing more than the revenues, and these should be selectively pruned. The "sweet spot" is the top right quadrant in Figure 7.10—these publishers are driving significant transactions and revenues. Marketing dollars should be shifted from the low performers to these publishers, the top right quadrant of Figure 7.10.

Said Rob Griffin, Media Contacts SVP, U.S. director of search, data, and analytics:

> The value of multiclick attribution modeling is in choosing which ad impressions and clicks we want to buy more of, or not buy at all. Media buying is evolving from publisher-centric buys to buying specific audiences, and moving them along the purchasing funnel.

The summary takeaway is that impression advertising should be an important component of your online marketing mix, but you have to optimize the placement of the display advertising in combination with your other marketing activities. The following section extends this important discussion into social media marketing.

Hypertargeting Display Advertising in Social Media

Broadly defined, social media includes all Internet content created by Internet users. Social networking web sites have exploded in popularity in the past few years. Compete.com reported Facebook unique users went from 30 million in April 2008 to 105 million in April 2009, and in 12 months Twitter increased from just over 1 million unique users to 20 million by April 2009. Social media has clearly emerged as a major force in the online world, but marketers are struggling to figure out how to best use the medium.

In 2009, the average CTRs on display advertising in social media were very low, approximately 0.03 percent. This has meant that the vast majority of marketers are not placing significant marketing dollars in this medium, and the corresponding CPC is very low, in the range of 5 to 8 cents, due to the large supply and little demand for advertising. The head of social media marketing in a Fortune 100 firm recently told me, "Impression advertising is dead in social media."

Why is the CTR so low for social media compared with SEM, which can be 1 percent or more? When people search, about 46 percent of the time they are there to buy a product; hence, we expect the CTR to be high. But when users are on a social media site, they are not there to shop but to be social and share. Herein lies both the challenge and the opportunity.

Marketing in social media up until 2009 had been rather generic. Targeting was based primarily on the user profile, which contains basic demographic and interest data. But the power of social media is that the users tell you about themselves. For example, here are a few representative posts from MySpace:

- "I'm dying to go to Vegas."
- "I want a new laptop."
- "I really should find a new cell phone."
- "I really, really, really want an iPod."
- "I've always wanted to see Spain."
- "I'm craving pizza."
- "I need to buy textbooks!"
- "I want some new music."
- "I need to find a birthday gift."
- "I gotta get a new car."

What if these people received advertising based on what they were actually wanting, feeling, thinking at that moment?

Figure 7.11(a) shows test data for an experiment conducted by Opinmind. It sent a friend request based on data mining of the individual posts on the user's MySpace page. Specifically, it looked for blogs about job searches, travel intent, auto purchases, and so on, and sent a MySpace friend request about this specific topic. CTRs increased by 439 percent, from 0.7 percent for the control to 3.9 percent for the test group.

Opinmind has developed a proprietary data-mining algorithm for hypertargeting impression advertising in social media. The algorithm analyzes blogs for specific users and can deliver targeted impressions based on what the users are actually posting to their page. The algorithm takes into account multiple dimensions of the user. For example, analysis of previous posts might identify a person who is passionate about the environment and who likes golf. If someone posts, "I really need a new car," this individual might be served an ad for a Toyota Prius

	Friend Requests Sent		Profile Impressions		Clicks		CTR		Lift (%)
	Control	Test	Control	Test	Control	Test	Control (%)	Test (%)	
Camera Purchase	290	290	134	174	1	7	0.75	4.02	439
Marriage	1,149	1,149	1,033	1,413	12	80	1.16	5.66	387
Auto Purchase	989	989	649	599	3	16	0.46	2.67	478
Travel Intent	460	460	365	415	1	7	0.27	1.69	516
Ambien	1,170	1,170	808	1,025	1	10	0.12	0.98	688
HotJobs	771	771	247	289	4	25	1.62	8.65	434
Total	4,289	4,289	3,236	3,915	22	145	4.4	23.7	439
Mean	805	805	539	653	4	24	0.7	3.9	

(a)

	Impressions		Clicks		CTR		Lift (%)
	Control	Test	Control	Test	Control (%)	Test (%)	
Auto	21,230	3,296	5	2	0.024	0.061	158
Camera	9,031	677	3	2	0.033	0.295	7895
Cellphone	38,810	3,968	12	7	0.031	0.176	471
Travel	28,761	8,975	6	4	0.021	0.045	114
Shoes	15,681	1,693	14	2	0.089	0.118	32
iPod	5,501	283	4	1	0.073	0.353	386
Weight Loss	50,023	8,503	18	4	0.036	0.047	31
Travel New	77,084	20,461	24	7	0.031	0.034	10
Totals	246,121	47,856	86	29	0.035	0.061	73

(b)

Figure 7.11 (a) Experiment to test targeted e-mail advertising in social media. (b) Opinmind test data for targeted impression advertising delivered through RightMedia.

Source: opinmind.com.

hybrid, which emphasizes the trunk has space that can fit two sets of golf clubs.

Figure 7.11(b) shows test data for impression adverting using social media hypertargeting. In some cases, the lift due to hypertargeting was hundreds of a percent, and on average was 73 percent. James Kim, Opinmind CEO, told me, "Traditional marketing approaches have not delivered the ROI on social media sites that marketers demand. The only way to improve ROI is to optimize the relevance of messages sent to users."

It is surprisingly easy to get started and run a marketing campaign in social media. Both Facebook and MySpace enable anyone to create and run profile-based campaigns. For MySpace, see advertise.myspace.com, and for Facebook, see www.facebook.com/advertising. At the time of writing this book, these sites do not use advanced hypertargeting. The Opinmind algorithm is available for self-serve marketing at opinmind .com. I highly recommend that you try these out. Impressions and CPC in social media are presently so cheap you can go wild for $100 of advertising spending. The low-cost, high-volume opportunity encourages rapid tests versus control experiments to figure out which campaigns actually work.

Metric #15—Word of Mouth (WOM) Social Media Marketing Engagement

Since untargeted impression advertising was falling short, more common approaches for social media marketing include creating "friends" who answer questions, creating Facebook-specific pages for products and services, and sponsoring blogs in specific areas. Navistar, for example, manufactures 18-wheel trucks and sponsors a blog called "Life on the Road" for long-haul truckers and their experiences.

What is the value of these social media marketing activities? This is a particularly difficult question to answer. Several services monitor keyword chatter across social media sites and are able to count the number of keyword occurrences in a particular time period and in different domains. They can also discern positive versus negative, so there is a score you can define of positive minus negative chatter as a result of a new product launch, for example. But this is an aggregate metric with limited value, since it discerns only that something has happened, and how big the positive (or negative) "buzz" is. What is needed is a social media marketing metric that points to future sales revenues.

In Chapters 3 and 4, we introduced essential metric #4, CSAT, measured by asking, "Would you recommend to a friend?" I called this the golden marketing metric because it links brand and awareness marketing with loyalty and is a leading indicator of future sales. Internet technology enables us to take this metric to the next level, as users frequently pass recommendations to friends and colleagues by e-mail, in blog postings, via Twitter, and so on.

I define WOM for Internet marketing as:

Metric #15: The Essential Metric for Word of Mouth on the Internet

WOM = Word of mouth

$$= \frac{\text{Number of direct clicks} + \text{Number of clicks from recommendations}}{\text{Number of direct clicks}}$$

---

where direct clicks are all clicks directly to the site, not referred, and will include clicks from impressions that can be any marketing interaction: corporate web site, display advertising, search, blog post, a product

Facebook page, and the like. "Would you recommend to a friend?" is captured in the second term of the WOM ratio—number of clicks from recommendations.

As an example of viral WOM advertising, Palm ran a campaign in December 2008 with the concept of a young hip Santa Claus who had "Gone Centro" and was using the new Palm Centro. The $12 million budget campaign had significant viral video and social media components that included content seeding and community engagement. The campaign was designed around two major components. The first was a text-messaging interface so that customers could "Text to Claus" and he would simulate a texting conversation, for example, answering questions about your Christmas wish list (see www.chacha.com or www.kgb.com for companies that offer this service). The second major component was a Santa celebrity Facebook page.

The Palm Centro campaign illustrates the three essential steps to an integrated social media marketing campaign:

- Step 1. Drive engagement online in Facebook and by texting through paid advertising such as TV, print, online, and billboard impressions.
- Step 2. Give customers content to share such as free music downloads, videos, and live content such as Santa actually talking on the site.
- Step 3. Measure the results through number of unique text messages, new friend requests for the Santa site, and WOM sharing.

Robson Grieve, managing director of Creature, whose agency coordinated the campaign, told me, "For social media marketing to work, you still need conventional impression advertising to seed the conversation, then you have to give users content that is cool to share, and finally you have to measure if it is working or not."

In this medium, how do you measure success? As a first step, the Creature marketing team looked at comparable celebrity Facebook pages and settled on one as the benchmark: George Clooney, the popular TV and movie actor. The Palm Centro conventional advertising blitzed for only one week, but at the completion of the campaign there were more than 98,000 friend requests for the Claus Facebook page, three times more than Clooney's page. There were also more than 400,000 unique texts. The texts and friend requests were measures of

Figure 7.12 Example WOM sharing in social media for the Palm Centro campaign.

Source: Creature and Meteor Solutions.

very significant consumer engagement, and ultimately the campaign delivered a measured 20 percent increase in revenue.

The WOM tracking component of the campaign is illustrated conceptually in Figure 7.12 for the Palm Santa's Gone Centro campaign. WOM sharing can be tracked internal to Facebook with its site-specific analytics, and Meteor Solutions has developed the capability to track WOM through forwarded links throughout the Internet. In Figure 7.12, Jane follows an ad to the Centro Santa Facebook page, where she sees the offer and browses content. She then sends the link to friends through multiple channels, such as posting on Facebook, e-mail, text message, or Twitter.

Meteor Solutions tags each link with a unique identifier. Her friends then follow the link and return to Facebook, where some accept the offer and some pass it on. When Jane's friends click on the links she sent external to Facebook, the unique identifier enables tracking, and when her friends pass on the links, new identifiers are given to the links, enabling tracking of how many times the pass-alongs come specifically from Jane and also from her friends.

As a different example, video gaming is a $3.8 billion industry in the United States, and Capcom's Resident Evil® games are some of the most successful in history, grossing $600 million revenues. For the Resident Evil 5 (RE5) new product launch in March 2009, Capcom made extensive use of viral marketing and WOM.

Figure 7.13 is the RE5 web site showing the viral video concept. The video on the web site consisted of professional Hollywood video of the characters in the game, and the concept was to share the video with friends to unlock exclusive content. After 100,000 people watched the

Figure 7.13 The Capcom Resident Evil 5 product launch web page.
*Source:*www.meteorsolutions.com.

first video, the next video in the series was unlocked for viewing. Individuals who brought back at least five people to watch the video also received access to special rewards, including access to exclusive content, leader boards, and more. The viral model encouraged sharing of the URL video link with friends and had a high level of engagement, since users must find clues to unlock additional content.

Figure 7.14 shows click data from various sources ranked based on direct traffic. Direct traffic are clicks directly to the RE5 web site, not from shared sources. Note that the first three are the paid impression advertising by AdLegend and DoubleClick. The column of Recommendation Clicks are clicks resulting from sharing with friends—these are resulting from WOM on the Internet.

In several instances, the recommendation clicks far exceed the paid advertising clicks. So if you include WOM sharing, the web sites should be completely reranked in importance. That is, the paid adverting would rank less than several of the sites that, from a direct traffic perspective, are near the bottom of the list. The lift from recommendations shows the percentage impact of the viral marketing—there was an overall 93 percent lift in the direct clicks due to sharing.

WOM, metric #15, is calculated in the last column of Figure 7.14. This metric clearly shows the impact of WOM sharing and which web sites generate the most direct and shared clicks. Specifically, the sites ranked 19 to 23 by direct clicks are generating the most WOM, and Fan Site (ranked 20) and Xbox 360 Achievements (ranked 21)

Rank by Direct Traffic	Site	Direct Clicks	Recommendation Clicks	Lift from Recommendations (%)	WOM
1	CAMPAIGN SITE	14,467	2,826	20	1.2
2	ad.adlegend.com (AD SERVER)	12,850	247	2	1.0
3	g.doubleclick.net (AD SERVER)	8,611	86	1	1.0
4	www.jeuxvideo.com	7,844	2,634	34	1.3
5	www.youtube.com	5,412	1,287	24	1.2
6	FAN SITE	4,455	731	16	1.2
7	forums.gametrailers.com	3,678	11,958	325	4.3
8	es.wikipedia.org	3,630	1,005	28	1.3
9	FAN SITE	3,494	13,780	394	4.9
10	www.pornbb.org	2,251	13	1	1.0
11	www.meristation.com	2,247	131	6	1.1
12	answers.yahoo.com	2,064	11	1	1.0
13	mail.live.com	1,985	219	11	1.1
14	www.giga.de	1,906	16	1	1.0
15	www2.hshare.net	1,531	48	3	1.0
16	www.spaziogames.it	1,481	63	4	1.0
17	www.akiba-online.com	1,477	2	0	1.0
18	www.joystiq.com	1,097	967	88	1.9
19	www.neogaf.com	1,045	7,112	681	7.8
20	FAN SITE	1,026	15,302	1,491	15.9
21	www.xbox360achievements.org	725	14,656	2,022	21.2
22	es.youtube.com	72	2,500	3,472	35.7
23	www.jeuxactu.com	61	2,171	3,559	36.6
	Totals	83,409	77,765	93	1.9

Figure 7.14 RE5 click data ranked by direct clicks and with WOM impact. These data have been disguised for confidentiality but are directionally correct.

Source: Ben Straley, Meteor Solutions, and Mark Jeffery, Agile Insights LLC. Downloadable at www.agileinsights.com/ROMI.

are actually the number two and three ranked sites, respectively, by overall traffic.

The WOM metric is what I call the social media multiplier. It tells the true value of an impression or click with WOM on the Internet. That is, the total clicks in social media are:

$$\text{Total clicks} = \text{WOM} \times \text{Direct clicks}$$

For example, in Figure 7.14, the value of a click from an impression on Xbox 360 Achievements is not 1 click but 21 clicks, the WOM score, and 1 click on es.youtube.com is worth 36 with sharing. Another way to think about this is in terms of CPC, essential metric 11. The actual cost per click with WOM is:

$$\text{CPC}_{\text{WOM}} = \frac{\text{CPC}}{\text{WOM}}$$

So for a campaign that incents recommendations to a friend with WOM, the CPC is less than what you actually pay based on direct clicks (traditional CPC). How much less? Divide CPC by the social media multiplier WOM. Of course, there is a WOM effect only if the marketing is designed to incent sharing and WOM recommendations. Otherwise, the WOM metric is exactly one, and what you see is what you get in terms of direct clicks and CPC.

Chapter Insights

- Traditional search engine marketing (SEM) is almost 50 percent of online marketing spending and consists of purchase search words for specific campaigns. The essential metrics are #11—cost per click (CPC), #12—transaction conversion rate (TCR), and #13—return on ad dollars spent (ROA). These four metrics combined with CTR enable SEM campaign optimization.

- Metric #13—return on ad dollars spent (ROA)—quantifies the value of a click in SEM and predicts the net revenue impact of increasing marketing dollars for specific publishers and campaigns.

- Metric #14—bounce rate—is the essential metric to understand how good your web site is. In combination with the other Internet metrics, bounce rate enables you to see how well the content of your web site holds customer attention and which marketing channels (search, e-mail, display, etc.,) are working best with your web site.

- CTRs on display advertising are very low (0.2 percent or less), but these impressions significantly impact take rate (essential metric #5), even though they are not the primary click. Attribution modeling enables tracking of search keywords and the impression advertising chain of events for specific users.

- Targeting of display advertising to specific users, based on analysis of blog and social media postings, increases CTRs in social media by 100 percent or more.

- Essential metric #15—word of mouth (WOM)—quantifies "Would you recommend to a friend?" on the Internet. WOM is the social media multiplier, increasing the value of clicks and impressions by a factor of WOM.

The Next Level

Agile Marketing

Using Near-Time Data to Improve
Performance by a Factor of Five or More

A business-to-business (B2B) Fortune 100 company undertook a major $35 million customer perception marketing campaign. The campaign involved posting independent third-party data and white papers on country-specific web sites, and a global ad buy was designed to drive traffic to these web sites. The date for the ad buy was set well in advance, but as the date drew near, the web site was not ready—the firm had trouble obtaining permissions to translate the independent third-party white papers into foreign languages. As a result, the campaign web sites in Japan and Germany pointed back to the U.S. web site in English, for example, killing the geography-specific impact of the marketing. The campaign launched on time, ran for nine months, and shortly thereafter was declared a victory.

Why was the campaign a success? Because there were no data to suggest it failed. The key business objectives (KBOs) for the campaign included a more than 5 percent customer perception change, as measured by the annual global customer survey. The campaign launched in January, and the customer survey launched in October. But the survey took three months to collect data and two months to analyze, and so with the holiday season, the data from the survey was not available until January. But the campaign ran for only nine months, so the survey data were not available until four months after the campaign ended. These data could have no impact on the performance of the campaign, and by the time the survey data were available, the marketers were busy working on other activities.

This example campaign illustrates traditional marketing measurement. If any data are collected and analyzed, it happens after the campaign runs, and by definition cannot impact the outcome of the campaign. In this chapter, I take a different approach. The idea is to collect data on campaign performance as the campaign is running and change course if it is not working. This is the essence of what I call *agile marketing*, and the approach can improve marketing performance by a factor of five or more. Furthermore, agile marketing includes event-driven marketing—delivering customized marketing offers based on analytics and trigger events. As we will see, event-driven marketing and analytics can also result in an additional factor of five or more improvement in marketing performance.

If You Are Going to Fail, Fail Fast

A few companies take agile marketing to the extreme. These organizations adjust their marketing in real time. QVC's Home Shopping Network, for example, monitors product sales as their live TV infomercials are running. If sales spike due to something an actor or actresses says, they instruct the actor through a wireless earphone to use more of the dialogue that produced the sales spike. As another example, online travel companies may spend $100 million or more in online advertising each year. They monitor Google keyword pricing and place ad buys based on optimal pricing every 15 minutes.

I argue, though, that to get started and show significant performance gains, you don't need real-time data—you need what I call near-time data. The idea of near-time data is to collect data from your marketing performance on a time scale that is smaller than the length of time the campaign is running.

The rough rule of thumb I use is to collect data at least 10 times during the running of a campaign. That is, if the campaign is 10 months, at the end of the first month, you should have actionable data on the performance of the campaign. Most important, though, you should be prepared to act on these data. If the campaign is not working, be prepared change it, or even pull the plug and stop. That is, it is much better to fail fast than to crash and burn $35 million of campaign dollars like the Hindenburg. Conversely, if you find out early that the campaign is working and you have a winner, you need to actively work to amplify the positive impact.

Agile marketing suggests flying by the seat of your pants, making snap decisions, and changing the campaign plan on an instant's notice. This is absolutely not the case. As we will see, agile marketing is a planned and structured activity. You have to plan in advance to collect the data, and you have to think through in advance what you will do with these data once you have them.

The Microsoft Security Guidance campaign is an example of agile marketing in action. In the early 2000s, Microsoft had a challenge of security issues with their products. These issues stemmed from high-profile hacker attacks, including the I Love You and Blaster viruses that infected millions of computers worldwide. But more disturbing was the Sequel Slammer virus that attacked business databases running Microsoft SQL.[1]

In November 2002, Microsoft entered the OpenHack competition sponsored by eWeek. In the competition, vendors such as Microsoft, Oracle, and IBM were invited to build a representative e-business system. Hackers were then given prizes if they could bring the system down. Jonathan Perera, senior director of marketing communications, Security Technology Unit, Microsoft Corporation told me:

> In 23 days the Microsoft system faced 82,500 attacks, yet had 100 percent uptime. But we learned something incredibly important from this experience: we had the dream team of Microsoft security—think Shaquille O'Neal, Michael Jordan, and Yoda. We realized that we needed to get the knowledge from our Microsoft security experts out to our users.

This became the genesis of a marketing campaign to change perception of a very important segment of Microsoft's B2B customers: information technology professionals (IT pros). In small tests, Microsoft marketers found that if IT pros were given free training on how to secure Microsoft products within the enterprise, then their perception toward

Microsoft products and security changed very significantly and positively after the training.

The goal of the $17 million Security Guidance campaign was therefore to get IT pros to sign up for Security Summit's in-person trainings on Microsoft security. Specifically, in one year the goal was to train approximately 50,000 IT pros in the United States, thereby covering the vast majority of large and midsized companies. The campaign was designed for measurement, with all campaign media tracked and channeled to the Internet.

In Chapter 7, we discussed web campaign optimization on the dimensions of click-through rate (CTR) and essential metric #13, transaction conversion rate (TCR), but in the context of search engine marketing (SEM), see Figure 7.4. The approach is also applicable to this example where the "transaction" in TCR is a sign-up for training. For the Security Guidance campaign, impressions were delivering significant traffic to the web site, with more than 34 million total impressions, and a respectable CTR of approximately 1 percent. But after the first week, only 439 IT pros signed up for the training. The marketing team realized by the end of the first week that they had a problem and if these results continued, they would not meet the target of the campaign.

For this campaign the overall take rate (CTR × TCR), essential metric #4, was very low because the TCR was low. From our discussion in Chapter 7, we know that if a campaign that has a reasonable CTR but a low TCR, there are likely issues with the web site landing pages. The original four calls to action on the Security Guidance landing page were:

- Register for training: three kinds of events, including in-person events, live webcasts, and on-demand webcasts.
- Get tools: Microsoft Baseline Security Analyzer (MBSA) and Software Update Services (SUS).
- Preorder the security guidance kit CD-ROM.
- Sign up for security newsletters and bulletins.

The Microsoft marketing team had to figure out what the problem was with the web site. Since the overall TCR was so low, Marketing had to understand what happened at intermediate clicks. The team, therefore, dissected the TCR, breaking it into an intermediate action rate and the final end action rate. The intermediate action rates is just the CTRs from the landing page to the end action pages with the trainings, tools,

Security Program Guide	Initial Responses	Total Intermediate Actions	Intermediate Action Rate (%)
Prime	546	125	22.9
O Call to Action Tracking			
n Security Summit		105	19.2
l Security Training		5	0.9
i Security Webcasts		15	2.7
n Security Strategies Roadshow		0	0.0
e Security Events		0	0.0
Search	58	0	0.0
A Call to Action Tracking			
d Security Summit		0	0.0
v Security Training		0	0.0
e Security Webcasts		0	0.0
r Security Strategies Roadshow		0	0.0
t Security Events		0	0.0
i **Task**	2,718	843	31.0
s Call to Action Tracking			
i Security Summit		593	21.8
n Security Training		168	6.2
g Security Webcasts		67	2.5
Security Strategies Roadshow		7	0.3
Security Events		8	0.3
SUB TOTAL	**3,322**	**968**	**29.1**

Figure 8.1 Microsoft Security Guidance campaign performance data measured after the first week.

Source: Microsoft Marketing, Note 1.

CD-ROM offer, or the newsletter sign-up. Figure 8.1 is the actual intermediate action rate data the team reviewed at the end of the first week of the campaign. (The number of impressions has been hidden for confidentiality reasons.)

In Figure 8.1, note that for the "prime" online advertising, impression advertising on the Microsoft.com home page, the Security Summit has an intermediate action rate of 19.2 percent compared with 2.7 percent for Security Web Casts and 0.9 percent for Security Training. What does this mean? IT pros are clicking from the impression advertising to the Security Guidance home page. They are then 7 to 10 times more likely to click on the Security Summits, which has the largest intermediate action. But the TCR is dismally low, so once they click through to the Summit, their attention is lost and they don't sign up.

The Microsoft marketers therefore made a decision to channel all of the impression advertising directly to the Security Summit web page, which had the highest intermediate action rate and which was exclusively for in-person trainings. That is, at the end of the second week, they fundamentally changed the campaign because they realized it was not working.

Figure 8.2 is summary click data for the first 10 weeks of the campaign. Note that all e-mail, print, and web advertising is tracked with weekly clicks. The third line from the bottom is sign-ups for security trainings. These data show how at the end of the first week only 434 people have signed up, and there are 262 sign-ups in the second week. Once the change was made, the sign-ups for the events jumped to 794 in the third week and to 1,272 and 1,528 in the fourth and fifth weeks, respectively. This example shows how the performance of the campaign was improved in a few weeks by more than 400 percent as a result of agile marketing. Over the nine-month life of the campaign, the agile marketing approach delivered a more than five–times performance gain.

What I particularly like about this case example is that the campaign was designed for measurement. All e-mail, print, and impression advertising was tracked and the results rolled up in weekly campaign data: this is near-time data. On a time scale of one week, the data gave invaluable insights into the performance of the campaign, which was designed to run for 12 months. When the early data came in, the marketing team realized the campaign was not working and applied data-driven marketing principles: they analyzed CTR versus TCR and realized what needed to be changed to increase performance.

I know that Figure 8.2 looks rather complicated and is an "eye chart." But realize the significance of this spreadsheet. Figure 8.2 shows how to track a $17 million marketing campaign in near time using a single Microsoft Excel spreadsheet. My point is that you can do this! You have the tools—the trick is to design the campaign for measurement and be prepared to act on the near-time data you collect.

In addition to the click data analysis, the Security Guidance campaign also made innovative use of the Internet to gather perception survey data. After users visited the Security Guidance web site, a survey popped up as they left and asked users to rate their agreement with statements such as:

- Microsoft provides tools and resources to help secure products.
- Microsoft is committed and responsible about security.

All Media Tracked — Totals — Weekly Click Data

Marketing Component	Start / Mail Date	Total Impressions	Delivered Impressions	21-Feb-04	28-Feb-04	6-Mar-04	13-Mar-04	20-Mar-04	27-Mar-04	3-Apr-04	10-Apr-04	17-Apr-04	24-Apr-04	Actual Clicks to Date	Actual Response Rate (%)
E-mail Tracked by FWLink															
New York (NY)	24-Mar-04								274	78	8	1	1	362	31.1
New York	24-Mar-04								186	35	14			236	1.5
Raleigh	24-Mar-04								110	35	24			169	0.6
Minneapolis	24-Mar-04								432	120	14		1	567	
Chicago	24-Mar-04								105	33	11	28		177	
Washington	24-Mar-04								344	44	15	14		417	
Denver	24-Mar-04								180	80	25	11		296	
Phoenix	24-Mar-04								255	45	14	188	25	527	0.5
E-mail Initial Response Subtotal									1,886	470	125	243	27	2,751	
Other (Direct Mail, E-mail & Misc.)															
Event Flyers- RSA in February, CTA Integrations	25-Mar-04				9	28	3	9	8	2	7	6		74	
Partner E-mail and Flyers		2	2					5	35	780	258	554	48	1,683	1.5
Generic Field Sales Template URL		75			115	186	280	215	350	150	100	156	108	1,735	0.6
Posters and Centralized URL		198	118			4,016	4,319	2,304	400	3,988	4,600	5,038	4,086	29,067	1
Keyword Searches					117					41		117	3,336	3,494	
Other Initial Response Subtotal		277	242			4,230	4,603	2,533	793	4,920	5,006	5,871	7,578	36,053	
Microsoft Web Placements															
Microsoft Web Placements (from Security Program Guide to Security Summit Page)		84,563	84,563			1,012	2,938	4,715	3,779	3,572	3,022	2,210	2,372	26,276	31.1
www.microsoft.com/exchange/		194,982	194,982					225	427	518	680	559	445	2,855	1.5
msdn.microsoft.com		2,102,526	2,102,526					316	7,987	2,364	1,519	464	4	12,655	0.6
www.microsoft.com/technet/default.mspx		1,116,312	1,116,312				4,648	5,740	5,737	10,069	6,098	8,076	8,723	42,995	3.9
www.microsoft.com		26,143,740	26,143,740				13,593	17,264	21,797	6,098	864	785	760	59,338	0.2
www.microsoft.com/windowsserver2003/default.mspx		432,680	432,680					1,545	847	2,189	864	785	752	4,583	1
www.microsoft.com/windowsserversystem/default.mspx		456,840	456,840				1,132	2,055	2,189	2,128	2,660	1,438		11,602	0.5
MS Web Placements Initial Response Subtotal		30,388,643	30,388,643			1,012	2,938	25,175	38,697	36,968	24,380	14,832	13,795	160,354	0.5
Microsoft Newsletter Placements															
Business Newsletter		115,503	115,503		0	0	0	0	0	0	25	8	258	258	0.2
Microsoft for Partners		87,220	87,220		0	0	0	0	508		25	6	6	546	0.6
Microsoft Security Newsletter		103,085	103,085		0	0	1,024	185	39	12	9	522	80	1,870	1.8
Microsoft This Week!		2,136,328	2,136,328		0	70	244	158	152	181	180	165	106	1,255	0.1
MSDN Flash		312,855	312,855		0	0	0		420		38	35	8		0.2
TechNet Flash		988,955	788,955		0	0	0	94	9	3,462	864	159	43	4,103	0.5
Windows Platform News		813,955	813,955		0	0	0		620	5,821	705	620	33	2,410	0.3
Microsoft E-newsletters Initial Response Subtotal		4,357,751	4,357,751		0	70	1,268	436	620	5,821	705	1,490	533	10,941	0.3
Initial Response Total		34,746,394	34,746,394	1,582	1,593	5,312	8,809	28,144	41,896	48,179	30,216	22,436	21,933	210,099	0.6
Security Summit Site Activity (www.microsoft.com/seminar/security/summit/default.mspx)															
Web Site - Page Views				1,344	1,158	2,608	14,048	15,400	15,928	23,738	17,718	14,392	13,828		
Actual Registrations by Week				439	262	794	1,272	1,528	1,741	3,293	1,980	1,302	940		
Cumulative Registrations by Week				439	701	1,495	2,767	4,295	6,036	9,329	11,309	12,611	13,551		
% of Total Goal Achieved				2	3	5	10	15	22	33	40	45	48		
Misc. Program Guide Tracking															
External Newsletters to Program Guide					1	3	3	310	120	22	131	7		909	
External E-mail to Program Guide														2	
Direct Mail to Program Guide				2	12	5	7	7	18	367	236	181	171	989	
Misc. Program Guide Initial Response Total					12	5	317	312	138	390	367	188	171	1,900	0.6

Sign-Ups for Training

Figure 8.2 Detailed tracking of Microsoft Security Guidance media effectiveness.

Source: Microsoft Marketing, Note 1.

- Microsoft provides information that helps you get secure and stay secure.
- Microsoft is committed to providing secure products.

Three months of survey data are shown in Figure 8.3 for two of the perception questions. Note that there is on average a more than 10 percent change between strongly disagree and strongly agree over the three-month period. Is this good data? Well, not really; the data is clearly a biased sample of only those who came to the web site; although with several hundred respondents each month, it is a good sample of these customers. But remember—it is better to be approximately right than exactly wrong. These data are trending in the right direction and suggest that the marketing campaign is working to change perception, at least for those visiting Microsoft.com.

Large firms typically undertake brand perception surveys once a year. These large sample objective surveys are important, and the web survey is by no means a replacement. But the large brand survey cannot impact the running of actual campaigns. The near-time data from the online survey enables directionally correct trend data over a few months. If the data was trending negatively, indicating that perception was getting worse, a rational marketing manager should rethink the efficacy of the customer perception changing marketing. There is an important insight here—the web survey enables near-time data collection on customer perception that early in the campaign points to success or failure.

Design for Measurement

When talking about agile marketing, I often hear, "It can't be done in my organization" or "I do brand marketing and these ideas don't work." There is no question that agile marketing requires a new approach—you have to plan in advance to be flexible based on data, and this can be very challenging for old-style marketing organizations accustomed to running only very big, monolithic marketing campaigns. Old organizations can learn new tricks, though.

As an example, E.I. du Pont de Nemours and Company was founded in 1802 as a manufacturer of gunpowder and is one of the oldest companies in the United States. As discussed in Chapter 1, DuPont sponsors Jeff Gordon in NASCAR and uses the sponsorship extensively

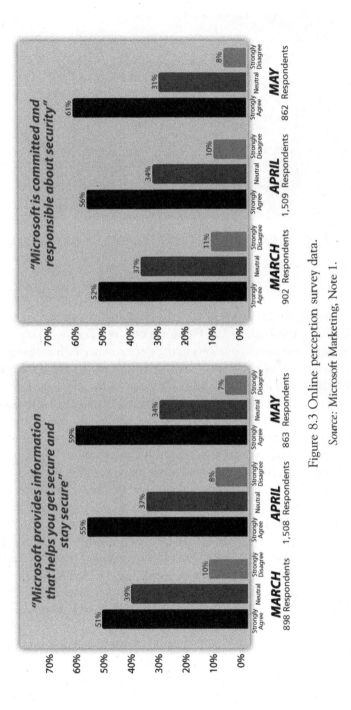

Figure 8.3 Online perception survey data.

Source: Microsoft Marketing, Note 1.

Figure 8.4 DuPont Performance Alliance URL on Jeff Gordon's
#24 NASCAR car.

Source: DuPont Marketing, Note 2.

in its marketing. In November 2007, the marketing team had the idea to put a URL on the back of Jeff Gordon's car (see Figure 8.4).[2]

The URL pointed TV viewers to the Performance Alliance web site. The marketing team knew that NASCAR fans are incredibly loyal, so the URL directed viewers to auto-body shops in the United States that exclusively used DuPont auto paint. Figure 8.5 shows click-throughs to the Performance Alliance web site shop locator when, during the race, the camera in the car behind was on Jeff Gordon's car for 1 minute, 30 seconds—there is a large spike during the TV exposure. I applaud that the marketing initiative was designed for measurement. The data informed DuPont campaigns in subsequent NASCAR races and also demonstrated the value of placing URLs in sponsorship advertising.

Note the URL in Figure 8.4, www.PA24.DuPont.com. I asked the marketers why they used this rather long and confusing URL: "That's what IT told us they could do." It turns out a redirect from one URL to another is one line of code on a web server, so it would have been very easy to redirect www.dupont.com/Performance to www.PA24.DuPont .com and track the clicks, for example. This is how the Microsoft click data in Figure 8.2 were tracked.

As Groucho Marx once said, "A child of five would understand this. Send someone to fetch a child of five." The younger generation, such as my six-year-old, has an innate grasp of technology. As you venture into agile marketing, there is an increased reliance on technology and

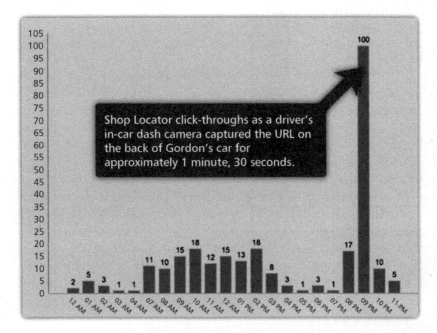

Figure 8.5 Shop locator click-throughs.
Source: DuPont Marketing, Note 2.

analysis for decision making. The need to learn tech speak and new
analysis skills may feel intimidating. My perspective, though, is that you
just need to know enough to be dangerous.

In the next chapter, I introduce the three essential data-driven
marketing analysis techniques so that you know what the major
approaches are, how they are used to radically improve marketing
performance, and what you need to get started and make these methods
work in your organization. Chapter 10 gives strategies and approaches
for you to work collaboratively with IT and deliver on the promise of
data-driven marketing. Chapter 10 will also arm you with the right
questions to ask when working with technologists.

For now, the insight is that campaigns and marketing activities must
be designed for agility, with near-time data collection on a time scale
shorter than the length of the campaign. The network (Internet or cell
phone) is a tool that can facilitate this near-time data collection. But
before the campaign runs, the marketing team should think through what
they will do with the data once it is collected. Before you start, ask: What

are the possible outcomes? What criteria will we use to decide to kill the campaign? How will we reallocate resources if the campaign is really working?

It is not hard to apply the agile marketing approach to your campaigns. If you have a nine-month campaign, design the campaign for stage-gate review sessions at a minimum of once per month; if the campaign is 10 weeks, then do a review each week. You have to plan in advance to collect the key success metrics. You should also think through the criteria to continue at each stage and the criteria to stop or kill the campaign.

For example, if you planned a 12-week campaign to deliver 1,000 qualified leads per week to the sales force and it delivers only 100, you can ask whether these leads are worth the cost of the campaign. If not, then review how you might improve performance. Maybe you try changing the campaign in the second week, but if it still does not deliver, then drop the hammer—put the campaign out of its misery and reallocate the remaining 75 percent of funding.

Chapter Insights

- Campaigns should be designed for agile execution by collecting near-time data. That is, collect data on campaigns on a time scale less than the length of time the campaign will run, and be prepared to change the campaign based on this data.
- Fail fast and in a small way by killing campaigns early that do not produce results.
- Win big by increasing funding for campaigns with early demonstrated results.
- Define both success and failure criteria before starting a marketing campaign.
- Design decision points into the campaign execution plan—be prepared to act at these stage gates.
- The agile marketing approach can deliver more than five times campaign performance improvements.

CHAPTER 9

Wow, That Product Is Exactly What I Need!

The Three Essential Approaches to Analytic Marketing

A few years ago, I received a small box in the mail from my friends at Procter & Gamble (P&G). I didn't know I had any friends at P&G. On the cover of the box was a baby boy about one year old and the slogan, "Now that you're standing you can't stand to sit down." Inside the box was a sample pull-up diaper. I am guessing that this diaper marketing is not relevant for the vast majority of people reading this book. After all, even if you have children, they wear diapers for only a few years. What is intriguing about this marketing is that it came to my house a few weeks after my son started walking, so in that brief window of time the marketing was highly relevant to my family.

This is an example of what I call the "Wow, that's exactly what I need!" effect. You give the right offer to the right person at the right time. Children start walking at about one year old, and prospective parents often sign up for the free parenting magazine soon after they find they are having a baby—this is my guess where P&G got our address. The trigger event was the baby starting to walk and the marketing offer was a sample pull-up diaper (and they were right, one-year-old kids don't sit still). There is a high probability that the customer will accept the offer because it occurs when there is a specific need.

As another example, Lowe's is a $48 billion revenue home improvement company with big-box stores throughout the United States. Lowe's started as a small hardware store business in North Carolina. As they grew into a chain of 1,640 superstores, Lowe's kept the corporate philosophy of customer service. As an example, there are representatives in stores who help customers design decks for their houses and help select the appropriate materials.

Lowe's analysis of product purchases found that someone who builds a deck for their house has a high probability of purchasing a new barbecue grill shortly after building the deck. The basic ingredients of a deck are low-margin commodity products: lumber, bolts, and nails. A grill is a potentially high-margin product, but there is no guarantee the customer will return to Lowe's to buy the grill. The customer could go to Lowe's direct competitor, Home Depot, or he or she could go to Sears, Wal-Mart, or a similar store.

The idea is to send targeted print advertising shortly after the customer leaves Lowe's. The flyer is all about grills and, depending on the demographic, the flyer may have the $600 stainless steel grill on the front or a lower-cost alternative. The reaction of the customer is "Wow, that's exactly what I need!" and there is a high probability the customer will return to Lowe's to purchase the grill.

Creating the "Wow, that's exactly what I need!" effect requires analytics to target the customer and the marketing. There are three essential approaches that are used depending on the type of marketing activity: (1) propensity models, (2) market basket analysis, and (3) decision trees. Let's take a look at each of these with detailed examples from Meredith and EarthLink.

The First Essential Approach to Analytic Marketing: Propensity Modeling

With $1.6 billion in annual revenues, Meredith Corporation is the leading media and marketing company serving American women.

Meredith combines well-known national brands—including *Better Homes and Gardens, Parents, Ladies' Home Journal, Family Circle, American Baby*, and *Fitness*—with local television brands in fast-growing markets. Meredith also provides clients and their agencies access to their vast portfolio of media products through Meredith 360°, a strategic marketing unit.

Meredith had a 25+-year history of data-driven marketing in direct mail for magazine subscriptions, and it wanted to extend this knowledge into e-mail marketing. Meredith's early e-mail marketing consisted of one-shot generic e-mail blasts, and the company knew it could do better. E-mail marketing is different from direct mail in one important way. In the latter, the customer does not mind if you send three or four different messages by mail, as different postcards, for example. But, for e-mail, there needs to be just one concise offer to maximize the impact and minimize e-mail inbox clutter. The Meredith e-marketing team therefore started by answering the question: "For our existing customers, what is the best product to offer via e-mail?" Answering this question requires something called a propensity, or next-best product, model.

Meredith created 20 different propensity models (using logistic regression[1]), one for each magazine product. It took the "everything and the kitchen sink" approach to modeling, including all possible variables they could capture. The model was run based on 1,000 existing data points, and all the variables that were kept were statistically significant. Variables included the Meredith web site on which the customers registered, customer age, hobby/interest score (passion points), age of children, other magazine subscription information, the type of neighborhood in which they lived, and the like. The model then scored each individual customer on the propensity to purchase a particular product, and the highest score determined which product was "best" for the week.

Figure 9.1 shows the different Meredith products and the number of customers that the model predicts have a highest probability (score) of purchasing the product that particular week. That is, individual customers are scored using the models to figure out which particular product they are likely to purchase, and Figure 9.1 is the summary of this scoring. This figure is part of the executive dashboard Meredith uses to monitor success.

The models are updated (rebuilt) every 9 to 12 months and are tested weekly to ensure the predicted performance matches the actual

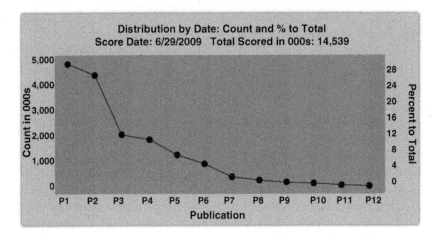

Figure 9.1 Propensity to buy model selection for different products (P1–P12).

Source: Meredith Corporation.

performance. Customer data change daily in some cases, so weekly scoring of 14 million customers is necessary for the best results. E-mails are sent to individual customers not more than once a week, where the frequency of touches are based on past campaign response: if the customer opened or clicked, he or she may get an e-mail in one week; if no response, Meredith may wait four weeks to send the next e-mail offer.

Figure 9.2 is an example e-mail advertisement customized and targeted given the modeling analysis. The offer is for *Better Homes and Gardens* magazine and has a free *Sensational Grilling* cookbook offer. Similar targeted marketing with the analytic modeling resulted in a 29 to 50 percent increase in order take rates, and overall there were 20 to 40 percent more e-mail-generated subscriptions compared with the previous year's rate, without modeling and targeting.

For the example (Figure 9.2), Meredith also used interest scores to further define segments. That is, the propensity models picked the product, and a composite interest code was used to determine which free gift to offer. For example, if the customer had a high food interest, they got the grilling premium offer; a high decorating interest, they got a decorating-related gift; and the same with gardening. Meredith measured a 15 percent lift by segmenting the gift offers based on known interest in addition to the 40 percent average increased conversion from the propensity models.

Figure 9.2 Targeted e-mail advertisement for *Better Homes and Gardens* with a *Sensational Grilling* cookbook offer.

Source: Meredith Corporation.

Erin Hoskins, Meredith's Director of e-Commerce and Online Marketing, provided insight into how to get started and the importance of having a good analyst on the team. Said Hoskins,

> I'm a marketer and knew we could improve upon our existing mass e-mail campaigns. When I started, there was very little dedicated budget, database, or tools for e-marketing. My first step was to make friends with Kelly [Tagtow] our lead analyst at the time. When we started to work together, I didn't understand what he was talking about, but I knew if we applied analysis to our e-mail marketing, good things would happen.

The challenge for Hoskins was to do more fine-grained segmentation and targeting of more products, but with the same number of resources: one marketing person and half a production head count. Meredith did have a sound data infrastructure foundation, though. It had previously outsourced its marketing database, but the senior executive team realized the strategic importance of the data and brought it back inside the firm, consolidating the data into a new customer data warehouse. Meredith was capturing e-mail addresses but did not have the tools for e-mail-specific direct marketing.

Kelly Tagtow, Meredith's director of business intelligence, told me, "We did a lot of manual and time-consuming pulling of data for the early e-mail targeting campaigns. It was painful at the beginning. But we proved that the propensity model approach worked and this became the business case for an investment in more automated e-mail marketing tools." This investment paid off many times over with the increase in take rates and the more than 20 percent increase in e-mail order subscriptions.

The Second Essential Approach to Analytic Marketing: Market Basket Analysis

Meredith's e-mail marketing is an example of using regression to predict what specific customers are most likely to buy next given their prior purchases and demographics; this is called a propensity or next-best product model. Another common analysis approach is called market basket analysis, which is particularly relevant to retail.

The concept is to figure out what bundles of products (or services) customers purchase together when they shop. For example, Amazon .com uses the approach extensively on its web site and in e-mail marketing. When you log in to Amazon, for example, it says, "You looked at this [book or DVD]. You might also consider [this book or DVD]" at the bottom of the screen.

Cluster analysis is the data-mining technique most often used for market basket analysis. The insight is not in the technical details,[2] however, but that the analysis can be done and the results are actionable recommendations. These recommendations are called association rules, such as "customers who buy a new personal computer also buy a new power cord." This real association rule is immediately actionable and can be used to influence in-store or online product and marketing mixes, for example. Said Hoskins, "Don't be afraid of the data. Marketers often get hung up on what they think is intuitively correct. But the analytics may tell a different story." You therefore have to be prepared to rethink your intuition and act on the analysis results.

The Third Essential Approach to Analytic Marketing: Decision Trees

So how do you do event-driven marketing? The trick is accomplished with analytics to figure out which events or purchases are connected, and then by designing targeted marketing that is activated upon a trigger event by specific customers. That is, you need predictive models to understand customer behavior and purchasing characteristics and a marketing plan to act on these predictions. With these models, essential metrics like take rate, profit, and/or churn are measured to quantify the marketing impact. A detailed example will help illustrate how to get started and actually do this type of analysis.

EarthLink is a midsized Internet service provider based in Atlanta, Georgia, with 2008 revenues of $956 million. The company provides Internet connections to millions of consumers and small to medium business subscribers. EarthLink provides high-speed Internet access to about one quarter of those customers and offers other services such as web hosting and online advertising. The company provides high-speed

Internet access through agreements with companies such as Time Warner Cable and Comcast Cable, and digital subscriber line (DSL) access through BellSouth, Covad, AT&T, and others.

EarthLink makes extensive use of data, analytics, and event-driven marketing, but its journey had a challenging beginning. Stuart Roesel, EarthLink's director of customer insights, analytics and strategy, told me:

> For data-driven marketing to work, the analytics team has to engage product managers and marketers. But the early work based on regression modeling was hard for them to understand. Many marketers were uncomfortable with the analysis, and so it never got used. You have to keep it simple to get widespread adoption.

Sam McPhaul, senior manager, business intelligence for EarthLink, added:

> The old predictive models were based on logistic regression, and they never gained traction in the organization because the results were difficult for the marketers and product managers to visualize, so the insight did not seem meaningful or actionable. When we started to model using decision trees, the insights were easier to understand and, after some internal education and pilot programs, the models really caught on.

A decision tree is one of the three core methods of data mining. The other two are cluster analysis and neural networks.[3] The details of these algorithms are fascinating to a nerd like me, but to most marketers the reaction is one of "you lost me at hello." Don't worry, though—you just need to know enough to be dangerous.

So what is a decision tree in data mining? The idea is to sequentially split a data set into subgroups that are more "pure," or have more clearly defined characteristics, than the original population. In effect, the idea is to pour the data through a sieve that filters the data into two groups[4]— the one that goes through and the one that does not.

As an example, think about a data set where the customers are either blue or green, but all mixed together, so you have a random assortment of blue and green. If the sieve is set to filter on these two colors, then, after sieving, all the green customers will be on one side and the blue on the other; the resulting components are more "pure" than the original data. The process is then repeated on a different variable, then another, and so on, so that the data set is decomposed into a tree containing "leaves" (the subpopulations of blue and green) connected together by "branches" (the connections).

To really get this idea, we need a concrete example. Figure 9.3 (on the following page) is an example from EarthLink showing the first two splits of the decision tree from SAS Enterprise Miner.[5] The total population are dial-up customers, and the first split (branching) of the data is between customers who contacted EarthLink and asked, "Am I serviceable for broadband?"; the left branch of Figure 9.3 includes the customers who called to ask if they are serviceable, and the right branch shows those who did not. Note that the trigger event is the call to the service center to ask, "Am I serviceable?"

In the top box of the decision tree in Figure 9.3, 5.2 percent of the total population of dial-up customers churn in 60 days, and 94.9 percent do not. But among those who do call (see the left branch first split), there is big difference in churn rate: 12.8 percent churn for those who call versus 4.2 percent for those who do not call (see the churn in the second layer of boxes in Figure 9.3). That is, those customers who call to ask if they are prequalified for broadband are 246 percent more likely to churn than the general population (calculated from 12.8 percent/5.2 percent)—this is the "high-churn" branch. The right branch is the "low-churn" branch—customers who had no broadband prequalification requests are about 20 percent (4.2 percent/5.2 percent) less likely to churn than the general population.

Another way to think about the decision tree (Figure 9.3) is as a way to do very detailed segmentation of your customers based on a very complex set of variables, including events. The important marketing question is, "Why is there a difference in churn between these two groups?" That is, what makes the churn so much higher on the left than on the right of the tree? The answer is that customers who are curious about their broadband serviceability may be considering an upgrade from dial-up to high-speed. They are most likely actively looking for upgraded service.

The third layer of the tree splits the "Am I serviceable for broadband?" groups into additional subsets; the node on the right (no serviceability inquiries) is split on a variable indicating WebMail usage: the number of WebMail boxes they use. The node on the left (more than one serviceability inquiry) is split on a variable closely related to engagement: number of sessions per month. WebMail boxes were

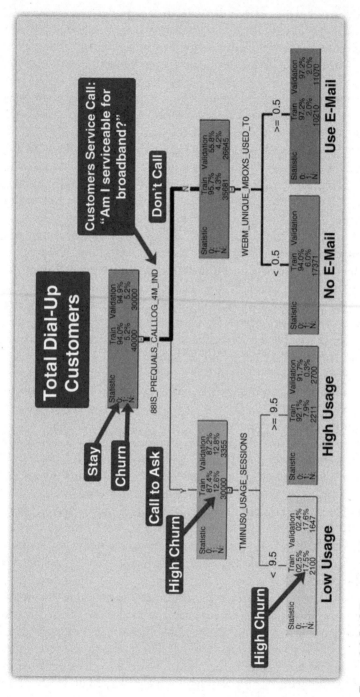

Figure 9.3 SAS Enterprise Miner decision tree for EarthLink. The statistics in each box are the percentage of customers who do not churn (0) and those do churn (1) in 60 days, and N is the number of customers at each branch.

Source: Sam McPhaul, EarthLink.

determined by the tree algorithm to be the best splitting variable for customers who are relatively satisfied with their dial-up service, whereas number of sessions is the best splitting variable for customers who are considering an upgrade to broadband.

The second split provides important insights to the customer behavior linked to churn. For the left branch, customers who had a prequalification call but are low users, with fewer than 9.5 sessions in a month, are 338 percent (17.6 percent/5.2 percent) more likely to churn than the general population. These customers are shopping around and are relatively disengaged with their dial-up service; these are the ones to target with an engagement, adoption, or loyalty marketing campaign. Customers in this same branch (who had a prequalification call) but are relatively high users, with more than 9.5 sessions in a month, are only 160 percent (8.3 percent/5.2 percent) more likely to churn than the general population.

For customers who did not have a broadband prequalification (the right branch in Figure 9.3), the most important splitting variable is the number of mailboxes they used to access WebMail. Customers who used zero mailboxes (0.5 is interpreted as < 1 or zero mailboxes) have a slightly higher likelihood to churn than the general population (5.7 percent compared with 5.2 percent). The effect of disengagement is higher churn. Customers who have one or more mailboxes for WebMail have the lowest likelihood of churn of 2.8 percent compared with 5.2 percent, which is only 54 percent of the churn in the general population. These customers are not shopping around for broadband and are still engaged in e-mail.

The insight is on which customers to focus the customer retention marketing: customers who called to ask if they are prequalified and who have low usage (measured by the number of monthly sessions) have the highest customer churn. Said Stuart Roesel, "You can't expect customers to stop considering a move to broadband, but you can lower churn by targeted marketing to encouraging them to use EarthLink and e-mail more."

Every few weeks, EarthLink runs the tree and identifies the specific set of customers who are at a high risk of churn, based on important characteristics identified by the model. Specific marketing EarthLink uses for these customers includes a surprise and delight: a $5 or $10 "have a Starbucks coffee on us" since you are a valued customer gift card, a priority support telephone number, or an offer for broadband Internet service. Figure 9.4 shows the impact of these marketing initiatives on churn for one program specific to dial-up customers:

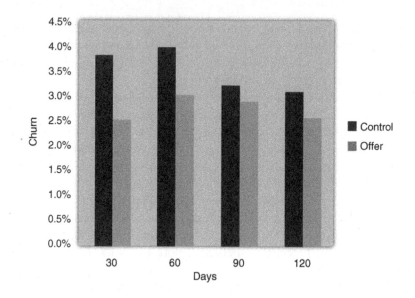

Figure 9.4 EarthLink churn data for targeted retention marketing of one segment of dial-up customers 30 to 120 days after treatment.

Source: Adapted from EarthLink dial-up retention data.

there is a 44 percent 30-day reduction and almost 20 percent 120-day reduction in churn relative to the control group who do not receive the marketing message.

EarthLink also quantifies the financial impact of churn reduction from a current profit (see Chapter 5 for how to do this) and from a customer lifetime value (CLTV) perspective (see Chapter 6). In the short term, the impact of reducing churn by approximately 30 percent is relatively small, but over time and across all segments, the retained customers deliver a 20 times improvement in profitability. The marketing impact is therefore very significant over time, delivering millions of dollars to the bottom line each month, and much more in terms of goodwill generated for future loyalty.

Today, EarthLink's very time-consuming regression modeling process has been replaced with a much more intuitive decision tree approach. New iterations of the dozens of different models take days instead of weeks. This means more time is spent in interpreting data, innovating new target marketing, and developing strategy and execution with cross-functional teams.

There are some things to watch out for, though. Roesel told me:

A pitfall I see a lot of marketers fall into with this analysis is that they compare the impact of the marketing to the whole sample as a control. This control may be very different from the treated group and when you do this, the measured impact is often small. To see the real impact, you have to compare customers who received the offer to a set of similar customers who did not get the offer. This is where you see the huge impact due to the marketing.

How did EarthLink get started? "Four years ago, we had basic metrics but few marketing programs were really measured. We were definitely not a data-driven marketing culture, and instead of conducting analysis and generating insight, were just creating a bunch of reports that marketers did not use. So we started over again from scratch and took a more sophisticated approach," said Roesel. Earthlink branded the new initiative as TIAD internal to the organization: Today Is Another Day. It reached out to the business and worked to understand what the real needs were, recruited talented analysts to fill the skill gap, and put in place tools and infrastructure to support the analytic marketing effort.

By using the new tools, slicing and dicing the data, the EarthLink analytic marketing team demonstrated some big wins. The customer retention marketing reduced churn by more than 30 percent relative to a control group. Profitability analysis also identified telemarketing as a very high-cost, low-effectiveness channel, so EarthLink switched to e-mail to communicate with customers, which was much lower cost. Furthermore, the take rate to offers (essential metric #5, Chapter 4) dramatically improved because Earthlink was targeting the right offer to the right customer at the right time. Taken together, the impact was a 60 percent decrease in the marketing operational expense, with significantly improved marketing performance.

These wins drove a real shift in attitude within the marketing organization. The result was to move from asking data questions such as "What percentile of customers churned?" to asking business questions like "Why did this type of customer churn?" "What can we do to reduce churn?" and "What is the financial impact of the marketing efforts?"

A key component for how EarthLink drove the data-driven marketing culture change was to create a Customer Experience Council. The council has an executive leadership steering committee, consisting of Roesel and other senior marketers and product managers, and a broader group of about 40 marketers across the organization. The Customer Experience Council meets monthly to share results of previous activities, best practices, and new models. "The continual iterative pilot test, run the campaign, measure and learn cycle is reinforced through the Customer Experience Council," said Roesel.

In summary, the decision tree approach is a great way to segment customers for actionable insight. The approach is broadly applicable and enables you to answer questions such as "Customers who buy this product or service also buy what other products or services?" and "Which events should I look for that are indicators the customer will buy new products or services?" or "What are the events and behaviors that suggest the customer will churn?" You then run the models and, based on the insights from the analytics, deliver targeted marketing at customers triggered by events or characteristics suggested by the models. Models can be run daily, weekly, or monthly, or as in the examples in the next section, they can be executed in real time for each interaction of a customer with your firm.

But most marketers don't have the skill set to do data mining and design SAS queries. So, most likely, you will need to recruit someone who does. What is important is to understand the power of the techniques and how to interpret the data, and take action. Although it sounds very complex, the output of data mining is actually pretty straightforward and relatively easy to interpret. I'm an opportunist: the economy is down right now—what a great time to hire an analyst!

Timing Is Everything: Event-Driven Marketing Case Examples

Providing the right marketing offer to the right customer can have a huge performance impact. Propensity modeling, market basket analysis, and decision trees, discussed in the previous section, are tools to enable hypersegmentation and targeting. But the real bang happens when you combine this analytic targeting with timing: A person whose washing machine just broke will be much more receptive (as measured by a higher take rate and profitability) to marketing for a new washing machine than someone who has just purchased a new washer. A few case examples (starting on pg. 216) illustrate the performance improvements possible with true event-driven marketing.

Sidebar: Regression versus Decision Trees

Regression analysis is the main focus of all core MBA decision science courses, so why the secondary focus in this book? The idea of regression is to fit a line (linear model) to data to predict sales, for example, as a function of marketing and other inputs. Regression is great if you have lots of clean data and are comfortable interpreting the log of variables. But missing data or extreme outliers are death to regression: you have to throw out entire records of data. Decision trees are more forgiving—missing and extreme outliers are allowable. Regression also assumes a simple linear model where the elements are uncorrelated. Trees are "nonparametric," having no preassumed distribution to the data, so they can automatically detect variable interactions and select the best input variables—overcoming two major headaches associated with predictive modeling such as regression.

Trees are not without limitations, though. A big challenge is that a decision tree can "overfit" the data. That is, you can sometimes fit a model so well to a test data set that the model will not work well when applied to a new set of data. To overcome this, you need to test small and big before finalizing a model—a process handled automatically by many algorithms. Another challenge is that the tree output is a step function—yes or no, high or low splits—and this can compromise the predictive power. Regression is continuous, which is an advantage, but large trees approximate linear functions well. That is, a tree allowed to split many times will approximate a continuous function, which is one reason decision trees perform well on large data sets.

I am not saying that regression is bad. Indeed, regression worked well for Meredith's e-mail marketing propensity modeling and, in this case, worked better than decision trees. But tree analysis has some advantages, most importantly that you don't need perfectly clean data and the results are much easier to visualize by marketers.

DIRECTV

With $17 billion in annual revenues, DIRECTV is a provider of satellite-based television services, founded in 1994 by Hughes Electronics. The company has 7,500 employees and delivers service to about 18 million U.S. and over 5 million Latin American customers. Its challenge was similar to the EarthLink example of the previous section: to retain at-risk customers.

The analysis follows the previous section, but DIRECTV took its marketing and customer service to the next level with an automated system that enabled near real-time data collection and analysis. The system loads 60 million transactions per day, and, as one example, the company uses the system to identify customers who call to cancel service. DIRECTV runs "save" models every 15 minutes. These models generate "leads" to the Save Team to recontact potentially defecting customers within three hours with special retention packages/incentives.

The results are impressive: DIRECTV saves 25 percent of these at-risk subscribers from discontinuing service, and the overall churn rate dropped in 2008 from 19 percent per year to 16 percent per year, the lowest in the industry. A 3 percent annual churn reduction may not seem like a lot, but realize that for a $17 billion annual revenues company, this is more than $500 million that is saved each year.

National Australia Bank

Traditionally, banks run mass marketing campaigns that are untargeted and often not relevant to customers. A better approach is to use technology to watch for relevant opportunities. For example, a major bank began analyzing customer accounts and noticed a deposit of $160,000 in a non-interest-bearing account, which was an unusually large transaction for the customer. A personal banker called the customer within 24 hours and found that the deposit was startup money from family and friends for a new business. The phone call resulted in the sale of a small business checking account, credit card, and line of credit.

National Australia Bank (NAB) is a leader in event-driven marketing in the financial services industry. With $14 billion in annual revenues, the bank is the number one retail bank in Australia, and in 2008 NAB won a National Center for Database Marketing Platinum Award for its event-driven analytic marketing. NAB scans 2.7 million customer events every single day using "event detectives" in its database, and that drives more than 3 million annual opportunities that are identified to personal bankers. From these leads, approximately 500,000 outbound calls with marketing offers are made each year and the take rate to these offers is more than 40 percent.

Most interesting is the impact of NAB applying these principles at newly acquired banks such as National Australia Bank Group Europe, which includes Yorkshire Bank and Clydesdale Bank in the United Kingdom. In these banks, prior to the NAB acquisition, the marketing process and customer management processes were not well coordinated and, compounding the challenge, ownership of customers was also not well defined—different groups competed for the same customers with different offers. All of this duplicate marketing created a lot of wasted effort as well as confusion by the customer.

NAB used its experience to consolidate the European banks' customer data into a centralized enterprise data warehouse, and then use data mining and analytics for targeting and event-driven marketing. Messaging was coordinated across channels for better consistency and to stop duplication. Campaign objectives were transformed to focus on customer needs, behavior, and CLTV. Outbound offers were more timely, the customers were contacted within 24 hours after inbound requests, and marketing was much more relevant and personalized.

The results were pretty amazing. Response rates to marketing offers improved immediately by 30 times (3,000 percent!) and continued to improve at 15 percent per year as they tuned and adjusted their analytics using a rapid test-and-learn agile marketing approach. Customer churn declined by 17 percent, and coordinating outbound marketing with inbound increased take rates by an additional 20 percent. Furthermore, lead volumes decreased 22 percent overall but had an increased conversion of 15 percent, as more qualified leads were followed up.

Ping Golf

As a last example, the real-time enterprise has benefits beyond just marketing performance. Ping is a midsize privately held custom golf club manufacturer. Ping's clubs are made to player's exact specifications and shipped within 48 hours—the product is customized by club colors, lengths, shaft flexibility, and grip size. The challenge involves 3,000 orders per day, 10,000 active retail accounts, 20 active distributors, and just-in-time assembly to order. This challenge is compounded by 3- to

12-week component lead times, and lumpy annual sales—more than 40 percent of Ping's total sales are in the second quarter of the year.

The trick is accomplished using a real-time data warehouse and analytics. Its call center has 15 to 20 reps and handles 1,000 to 3,000 calls per day, resulting in an average of 2,000 orders per day. The system stores over 12 million equipment serial numbers, so customers can instantly order their exact club replacement—via the call center or over the Web. Real-time response enables best-in-class call center performance, resulting in high customer satisfaction (CSAT). The point is that the analytics and data-warehousing infrastructure for radically improving marketing performance through event-driven marketing can also dramatically improve other parts of the business.

The Business Case for Analytic Marketing

Analytic marketing is most often used for cross-sell, up-sell, or retention (churn reduction). These marketing activities all result in either measurable new sales or, in the case of churn reduction, the realization of revenues that would have otherwise been lost by customer attrition. Since the marketing activities directly result in sales revenues, financial return on marketing investment (ROMI) of Chapter 5 works great.

Figure 9.5 is an example of how to calculate ROMI for analytic marketing and justify an investment. This template is for up-sell marketing for a firm with 400,000 customers. The idea in this example is that there are three value-based tiers of customers: silver, gold, and platinum. The marketing is designed to up-sell and move customers from silver to gold, and gold to platinum. The assumptions are given in Figure 9.5(a) and are easily changed for your firm using the online template. The top of the ROMI template in Figure 9.5(b) is the base case—this is the estimated impact of the marketing with business as usual. The bottom part of the template is with analytic marketing; this is the upside with the analytic segmentation and targeted marketing.

The impact of analytics is to (1) increase the take rate of the marketing offers (in this case assumed to be 5 percent lift) and (2) increase the share of wallet by up-sell of a percentage of customers to the next value segment. The cost of the data warehousing and analytics, estimated to be $7 million, is on the bottom. These assumptions are just estimates, and you can plug your company-specific numbers into the template in Figure 9.5. You can also change the segments (silver, gold,

Assumptions	
Customer Base	400,000
Percent Platinum	5%
Percent Gold	10%
Percent Silver	85%
Annual Growth Target for Platinum Customer Base	5%
Annual Growth Target for Gold Customer Base	12%
Take Rate for New Offers	2%
Projected Lift in Take Rate	5%
Cost to Contact One Potential Customer	$ 0.50
Average Quarterly Spending per Platinum Customer	$ 23,750
Average Quarterly Spending per Gold Customer	$ 13,500
Average Quarterly Spending per Silver Customer	$ 1,650
Projected Lift in Average Quarterly Spending	5%
Gross Margin Platinum	70%
Gross Margin Gold	50%
Gross Margin Silver	2%
Tax Rate	38%
WACC (Discount rate r)	14%
Campaign Frequency	quarterly

System Costs	
Hardware	$1,500,000
Software	$2,500,000
Professional Services	$3,000,000
Investment Cost = Depreciable Basis	$7,000,000

(a)

Base Case

	Year 0	Year 1 ($)	Year 2 ($)	Year 3 ($)
New Sales Platinum		35,625,000	96,781,250	101,620,313
New Sales Gold		97,200,000	270,864,000	303,367,680
Less: New COGS Platinum		(10,687,500)	(29,034,375)	(30,486,094)
Less: New COGS Gold		(48,600,000)	(135,432,000)	(151,683,840)
Less: Contact Cost Gold		(25,000)	(26,250)	(27,563)
Less: Contact Cost Silver		(120,000)	(134,400)	(150,528)
EBIT		73,392,500	203,018,225	222,639,968
Less: Taxes		(27,889,150)	(77,146,926)	(84,603,188)
Old Cash Flow		45,503,350	125,871,300	138,036,780

Upside with Analytic Marketing

	Year 0 ($)	Year 1 ($)	Year 2 ($)	Year 3 ($)
New Sales Platinum		37,406,250	101,620,313	106,701,328
New Sales Gold		102,060,000	284,407,200	318,536,064
Less: New COGS Platinum		(11,221,875)	(30,486,094)	(32,010,398)
Less: New COGS Gold		(51,030,000)	(142,203,600)	(159,268,032)
Less: Contact Cost Gold		(23,810)	(25,000)	(26,250)
Less: Contact Cost Silver		(114,286)	(128,000)	(143,360)
Less: Maintenance		(1,166,667)	(1,166,667)	(1,166,667)
Less: Depreciation		(2,333,333)	(2,333,333)	(2,333,333)
EBIT		73,576,280	209,684,819	230,289,352
Less: Taxes		(27,958,986)	(79,680,231)	(87,509,954)
Net Profit		45,617,293	130,004,588	142,779,398
Plus: Depreciation		2,333,333	2,333,333	2,333,333
New Cash Flow	(7,000,000)	47,950,627	132,337,921	145,112,731
Incremental Cash Flow	(7,000,000)	2,447,277	6,466,621	7,075,951

Net Present Value (NPV)	4,898,655

Internal Rate of Return (IRR)	45.8%

(b)

Figure 9.5 ROMI template for analytic marketing: (a) assumptions in the model and (b) ROMI analysis. Downloadable at www.agileinsights.com/ROMI.

and platinum) and relatively easily focus on cross-sell, up-sell, or churn reduction for your specific business.

The take-rate lift and revenue as a result of the analytic marketing are best obtained from industry-specific benchmarking data. The assumptions in the template are rather conservative, although the costs and revenue number may be large compared with those of your firm. The cost of the infrastructure will depend on the size of the customer base and the complexity of requirements specific to your business (see Chapter 10).

Realize that you can use the template in Figure 9.5 for any scale of investment. So, for example, as a first step, the initiative might be a few hundred thousand dollars on a subset of customer data. Just scale the numbers down to the size of your initiative. There should be a real measurable impact from applying analytics to a small customer base. Starting small has the advantage that it will enable you to validate the assumptions as you gain experience and will give you credibility when presenting future ROMI analyses. For a more detailed example of financial ROMI for analytical marketing, see the case *ROI for a Customer Relationship Management Initiative at GST*.[6]

In the example (Figure 9.5), the IRR is 45.8 percent, the NPV is $4.9 million, and the payback period is less than two years. The ROMI metrics suggest that this is a good initiative for investment (NPV > 0, IRR > r, and payback < 2 years). However, following Chapter 5, you should also conduct sensitivity analysis to test the best, worst, and expected case, where the key risk factors are take rate and spending lift, and possibly the cost of the technology project. The next chapter answers the question "What's it going to take?" from a technology infrastructure perspective. I give you strategies for working in collaboration with IT to deliver on the promise of agile marketing and to actively manage the risks.

Chapter Insights

- Event-driven marketing takes agile marketing to the next level. Use analytics to target the right offer to the right customer at the right time and deliver more than five times improvement in take rates (essential metric #5).

- There are three essential approaches for analytic marketing: (1) propensity models predict likelihood to purchase, (2) market basket analysis provides actionable association rules (answering questions such as customers who buy this product also buy what else?), and (3) decision trees enable hypersegmentation based on events and other customer characteristics.

- The analytic marketing business case is straightforward to quantify using the essential financial ROMI metrics—#7, NPV; #8, IRR; and #9, payback—where the key drivers are increased take rates (essential metric #5) to offers and increased profit (essential metric #6) from the resulting orders.

CHAPTER
10

What's It Going to Take?
Infrastructure for Data-Driven Marketing

Throughout this book, I have emphasized that you don't need millions of dollars of data-driven marketing infrastructure to get started and that you can use Microsoft Excel as the tool of choice as a first step. I stand by this statement, but I want to manage expectations. The answer to "What's it going to take?" from an infrastructure perspective is very much the business school answer: *It depends*.

If, for example, your data-driven marketing goal is to get a handle on the customer life cycle discussed in Chapter 3, with balanced scorecards of brand awareness, customer satisfaction (CSAT), test-drive, take rate metrics of Chapter 4, the ROMI metrics of Chapter 5, and the new-age Internet metrics of Chapter 7, then you can absolutely get started with Excel and some 3″ by 5″ index cards.[1] However, if you want to actively manage churn (Chapters 4 and 6), do value-based marketing based on customer lifetime value (CLTV; Chapter 6), and/or do event-driven marketing (Chapter 9), then you are going to need data warehousing and analytics infrastructure. How much infrastructure and at what cost?

Well, that depends. Let's take a look at how to figure it out from a marketer's perspective.

Which Data Do You Really Need?

One of the first questions I often get asked by marketers when we start talking about marketing databases and technology is, "What data do I need to put in the data warehouse?" It turns out this is the wrong first question. A better question to ask is, "What are the business requirements?" That is, what business questions are you trying to answer and for how many customers? The data you need (data requirements) are defined by the business questions you want to ask and answer.

Put in the context of an airline, the business questions might be how many frequent flyers aged 30 to 49 stopped flying between Chicago and Washington, D.C., last month? Why did they stop flying? What similar customers are likely to churn that are high value? What will be the impact of marketing to reduce churn of these high-value customers? To answer these questions requires data obtained by specific searches of all accounts to find the target customers. Follow-on questions require even more data. Specifically, in addition to flight and demographic information, you need to define the value of the customer (CLTV; Chapter 6), which requires data from across the enterprise.

Note that each business question often leads to a cascade of follow-on questions; see Figure 10.1. For example, if the discussion starts with a question such as, "How many customers canceled their account last month?" this leads to an answer: 0.5 percent. Note that at the first step of Figure 10.1 we are looking to find out what has happened. The next step is to understand why the event happened: Why did they cancel? At the third step of the question and answer train of thought we try to predict what will happen in the future by answering the question, "How many more customers are likely to cancel for the same reason?" This question leads to a cascade of follow-on steps to obtain the data required to answer the question, and ultimately take action based on this information.

Figuring out CLTV from Chapter 6 requires cost and revenue data from all the touch points of the customer. For retail these touch points and related data include store, Web, catalog, reseller, and so on. For the cost side of the equation you need to get the costs such as manufacturing cost, warranty cost, service cost, returns, customer

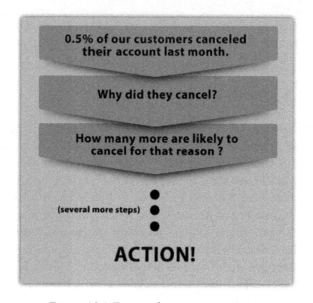

Figure 10.1 From information to action.

acquisition cost, customer retention cost, discounts, and the like, and marketing costs to individual customers such as direct mail, e-mail, Web, and so on. These data are most likely scattered across the enterprise in isolated databases, called data marts. So to answer the marketing questions you need to pull the data from the isolated databases and put it into a central database, the enterprise data warehouse (EDW), where it can be analyzed.

Figure 10.2 is a schematic of the data in an enterprise needed for CLTV analysis. The picture shows how essential data for customer profitability are contained in all the different functional areas of the business: these data are from multiple and different sources. The analysis therefore requires access and integration of these data, which can be a highly complex challenge.

Most important, though, is the flow of the thought process: understand the marketing business problem you are trying to solve and the questions you want to answer to solve this problem. These questions will define the infrastructure and the data you need. There are several additional factors that significantly impact the data management requirements, including the number of customers, the need for detailed data, the complexity of the queries and analysis, and the need for unpredicted analysis.

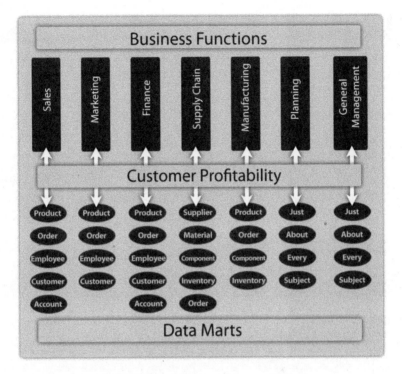

Figure 10.2 CLTV requires data from multiple functions.
Source: Richard Winter, www.wintercorp.com.

Do You Need to Build a Ranch House or Empire State Building Infrastructure?

The amount of data warehousing infrastructure you need for data-driven marketing depends on two important dimensions: (1) the number of customers and (2) the complexity of requirements. The first, the number of customers, is directly related to the size of the EDW—since each customer interaction (purchase, call to the call center, product return, etc.) creates data for the customer. These data need to be retained for three to five years for CLTV analysis, which means data volumes can get big fast if you have a large customer base. The second dimension, complexity of requirements, acts as a multiplier of infrastructure cost and complexity. I explain requirement complexity in more detail in the following section.

	Small	Medium	Large
Metaphor	Residential Home	Office Building	Empire State Bldg.
Floor Space (sqft)	2277 (Median U.S. new residential home)	26,300 (Average U.S. three-floor office building)	2,158,000
Scale Multiplier (X)	1X	12X	948X
Customer Data Warehouse	Local Retailer 10 Stores	Regional Chain 400 Stores	Largest Retail Businesses 5,000 Stores
Customers	100,000	1,000,000	100,000,000
Data Volume (TB)	1	10	1000
Estimated System Acquisition Price (List)	$50k -$250k	$500k - $2.5M	$50M - $250M

Figure 10.3 Ranch house versus Empire State data-warehousing infrastructure.

Source: Richard Winter, www.wintercorp.com, and Mark Jeffery, www.agileinsights.com.

Figure 10.3 is a conceptual table comparing three different-sized organizations, each with an increasing level of complexity. The example is for retail but can be generalized to any business. To put the scale of the challenge in context, it is useful to use an analogy of different-sized buildings to compare the scale and complexity of the different problems. In Figure 10.3, the building metaphor is on the top of the figure; the data-driven marketing infrastructures for small, medium, and large companies correspond to a ranch house, midsized office building, and the Empire State Building, respectively.

The lowest level is a regional retailer with about 10 stores and 100,000 customers. How much data-warehousing infrastructure is it going to take for this scale of business? This is analogous to a ranch house, and according to the U.S. census, the average U.S. home is 2,277 square feet. The ranch house analogy, the small regional retailer with 100,000 customers, will have a data volume of 1 TB (terabyte). This assumes average data for each customer of 10 MB (1,012 bytes/ 10^5 customers $= 10^7$ bytes per customer $= 10$ megabytes per customer), which is a realistic average.[2] To acquire a system that could store and analyze this volume of data, assuming average complexity of analysis, will require data-warehousing infrastructure hardware and software that cost in the range of $50,000 to $250,000. Note that these costs are very approximate and are presented to provide just an order-of-magnitude rough estimate for your reference.

Let's take this example to the next level of a midsized retailer, which corresponds to infrastructure on the scale of a midsized office building. The average office building is about 26,300 square feet, which is 12 times bigger than the ranch house. In this analogy, an equivalent retailer would be a regional chain with 400 stores and 1 million customers. The corresponding data volume for this midsized example is approximately 10 TB. That is, there is 10 times more data for a midsized retailer compared with a small one! For these date volumes you need more horsepower, more infrastructure, at a cost of between $500,000 and $2.5 million depending upon the complexity of the data analysis. Again these are only approximate cost numbers.

At the third level is a national retailer with 5,000 stores and 100 million customers. This is at the extreme and is analogous to the Empire State Building with 2,158,000 square feet of space. The Empire State is nearly 1,000 times bigger than a ranch house. The national retailer will have upwards of 1,000 TB data, which is 1,000 times more than a local retailer! To handle these massive data volumes and queries requires industrial strength data warehousing infrastructure, at a cost of $50 million to $250 million (this is an order-of-magnitude cost estimate).

The takeaway is that the difference in requirements driven by the business questions can have massive implications; the ranch house compared with the Empire State Building infrastructure is a few hundred thousand dollars versus many tens of millions of dollars. Said Richard Winter, chief executive officer (CEO) of WinterCorp, and an expert in large-scale data warehousing design and architecture:

> Business stakeholders need to have a feel for the scale and complexity of the data warehouse being created for them, just as they would if sponsoring a building. They should know whether the project was to create a residential home or the Sears Tower; and, their oversight of design, engineering and construction would vary accordingly. Unfortunately, because data warehouses are invisible, executives sometimes undertake a project with the scale and complexity of the Sears Tower, while imagining they are just building another residential home, and the seeds of a disaster are planted.

The pitfall happens when the information technology (IT) team in your organization has only ever built a ranch house. There is an old saying that when all you have is a hammer, everything looks like a nail. The same goes for IT—if all you know is how to build ranch houses, then all marketing IT systems will look like a ranch house. The problem is scalability: As you add more customers, will the system scale? That is, if the system works with a few customers, will it work with lots and lots of customers?

This lack of scalability mistake happens surprisingly often and with rather public consequences. In 2001, AT&T initiated a new branding campaign for mLife, a bundle of AT&T mobile wireless services. The campaign launched during the 2001 Super Bowl at a cost of more than $20 million. The TV ads featured very simple www.mLife.com text on a white background. But the more than 100 million Super Bowl viewers were disappointed—overwhelmed by the number of clicks on the web site, the site crashed and no one got to find out what mLife was about, or that it had anything to do with AT&T. What a way to kill a brand before it even got out of the gate! This is the classic example of the marketing guys and gals not talking to IT guys and gals.

As another example, a specialty grocery chain consisting of several hundred stores, and with more than $10 billion revenues, decided to put in place a new system with the goal of reducing stockouts. The retailer sold organic fresh produce and from a market research study found that reducing stockouts would significantly increase profits and customer satisfaction. The idea was to analyze point-of-sale (POS) data in each store and figure out which products needed to be replenished each day, such as fresh fruit, yogurt, fish, beef, and the like. Every day stores closed at 9:00 PM, and between midnight and 5:00 AM trucks were loaded at the distribution center warehouse so that the goods could be at stores by 6:00 AM.

The IT team built the EDW and found that instead of being able to analyze hundreds of stores, the solution it built took the capacity of the entire system for one store, and took all night to calculate; but the team needed the solution for hundreds of stores in three hours, from 9:00 PM to midnight. The management team had not understood the requirements correctly. The system was logically correct but would not perform, since no one had thought through the capacity needed to handle the vast amounts of data. Winter told me:

> Data warehouse scalability problems surface at the worst possible time. They are created during the design, engineering and construction of the database—often because the requirements have been left vague or

the wrong platform has been adopted—but no one knows until the system has gone into large-scale production. Scalability problems caught early are readily corrected, but scalability problems that surface late sink projects, careers, and companies.

As a marketing executive, there can be considerable uneasiness when dealing with IT, since most likely this is not your area of expertise. In a way, if you are the data-driven marketing business owner, your position is similar to the owner of a football team. You don't get to train the players or call the plays, you just get to pay the bills but really need results to sell tickets and keep the stadium full.

So, if you are a marketer, how do you manage this challenge? I suggest changing the context to something you know. What if someone in your firm presented you with a marketing plan that you felt had an unrealistic sales target? Most likely, you would ask probing questions to validate if indeed the team could get there from here: What are the assumptions, market research data, execution steps, and the like? The idea is the same for data-driven marketing infrastructure.

If you have a feeling of uneasiness with respect to the IT team's ability to deliver, you can ask the team members to present a plan for how they will meet the scalability issues. For the stockout retail example described, some business questions to ask would be: Can you get all the POS data from 500 stores into the EDW and analyzed by midnight to have food in trucks by 5:00 AM? Show me the engineering argument that this will work. You can also have an independent expert evaluate the plan.

Like a football team owner, you need to know that the goal posts are in the right place on the field, that the team is solving the correct problem, and that there is a reasonable plan for moving the ball down the field and scoring touchdowns. The takeaway is that you need to get a handle on the scale of the business problem you are solving so that you can figure out if you need a ranch house or the Empire State Building for data-driven marketing infrastructure. In summary, the technology for data-driven marketing is way too important to leave to the technologists.

Requirement Complexity

The size of your customer base drives the size of the data warehouse for data-driven marketing. The second important dimension is the complexity of requirements. Figure 10.4 is a framework for thinking through

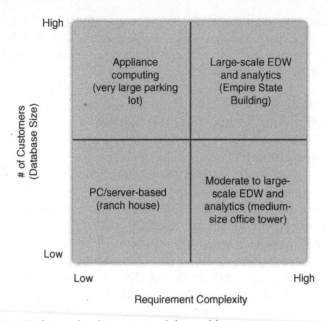

Figure 10.4 Defining the dimensions of the problem—size versus requirement complexity.

how much data-warehousing infrastructure you need given these two dimensions. As I discussed in the previous section, complexity of data requirements derives from what business questions you plan to ask and answer.

So for a retail example, low complexity corresponds to the data model of Figure 10.5. In this example, there is a simple set of business questions to answer: What, where, and when are products selling in my stores? There is just one set of facts, the sales transactions, and four analytical dimensions: products, customer, store, and date. The analysis is very straightforward and could run overnight. If this is all you need to know, then for a small customer base, the system is inexpensive; you have a ranch house. For a very large customer base, you can easily scale the infrastructure to very large data volumes with the simple data model in Figure 10.5. In this case, there could be a massive transaction volume but because the analysis is simple, on a single data table, it can be accomplished using appliance data marts.

What is an appliance? The idea is a low-cost IT system, like a microwave in your kitchen, that just does one thing—heat food, for example. An appliance for marketing is a data mart that handles

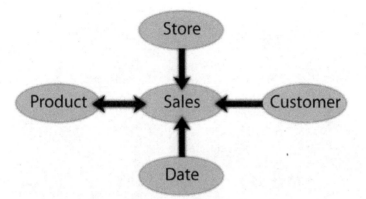

Figure 10.5 Low-complexity retail sales data relationships.
Source: Richard Winter, www.wintercorp.com.

relatively simple data models, that typically look like Figure 10.5, but that can operate on large volumes of data. This low-complexity, high-data-volume example is the top left quadrant of Figure 10.4. In this case, instead of building a ranch house, you are building a structure with not much complexity that is very, very big; think of a parking lot a mile square, where you are just duplicating parking spaces to add capacity.

Complexity of requirements arises when the business questions require data from lots of different places and you have complicated queries of these data. Figure 10.6 is an example data model for CLTV in retail. In this case, there are multiple analytical problems, multiple related sets of facts, and a complex web of relationships. It is not uncommon for real high-complexity data models to have thousands of data records and relationships.

The complexity-of-requirements dimension can be even more important than the number of customers for driving the scale of the infrastructure needed. The bottom right quadrant of Figure 10.4 has a relatively small number of customers but high complexity. An example is a major Fortune 500 manufacturing company with 1 million business-to-business (B2B) customers. There was only 1 TB of data associated with these customers, which would be a ranch house–level infrastructure if there were low complexity.

However, the B2B company had 10,000 direct salespeople and a philosophy of the salespeople following specific managers in the client firms when they transition to a new job, often in a different firm.

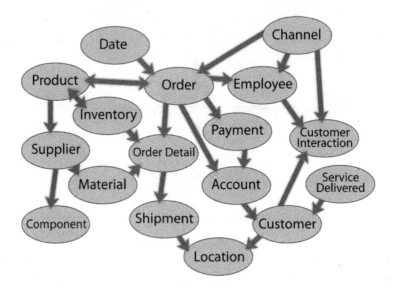

Figure 10.6 Complex data relationships for customer lifetime value.

Source: Richard Winter, www.wintercorp.com.

Salespeople following executives has the advantage that sales repre-
sentatives develop very deep long-term relationships over time, but this
creates a very complex web of relationships, since salespeople manage
multiple products and customers in accounts.

In this example, the million customers created 1 TB of direct
customer data, but there was 10 TB of derived data from the complex
relationships. So the data volume was actually 11 TB due to the
complexity. Where did the complexity come from? The permutation
of 1 million customers, 10,000 salespeople, 100,000-plus special relationships, 10,000 plus products, and so on. So if you ask, "How much
sales volume do we expect this quarter in district X from products Y?"
this question involving territories, products, and customers is usually a
simple question, but in this case is nightmarishly complex because of the
vast number of permutations.

A final thought on complexity: complexity is compounded by a
factor of approximately 10 times if a business requirement is "real-time"
response. That is, if you want to do on-the-fly CLTV analysis and use
this to drive a real-time interaction in the call center, as is done by Royal
Bank of Canada (see Figure 6.7). The top right quadrant of Figure 10.4 is
the Empire State Building of infrastructure: large numbers of customers

and highly complex requirements. This is $50 million to $250 million of data-driven marketing infrastructure.

This discussion of bits, bytes, feeds, and speeds potentially involving millions of dollars may seem intimidating, but there is a clear winning strategy: think through the data model up front; this is the big picture of what you need based on the business questions you want to answer. These business requirements define the end-state infrastructure you will need; the ranch house or the Empire State Building. But you don't need to build the Empire State out of the gate. The most successful firms I have seen started small—they understood the end-state data model up front, but built it out one table at a time. That is, they started small, applying the 80/20 rule, putting in the system first the 20 percent of data that constitutes 80 percent of value. So the first iteration of the data model can be simple, such as Figure 10.4. Then show the win and continue the build out to populate the complex model (see Figure 10.5).

The insight is that you need to plan ahead if the true complexity is something like Figure 10.5. Amazon.com, for example, started by selling books over the Internet because there was a very large number of different scannable units (stock-keeping units [SKUs]), and they were relatively easy to warehouse and ship. But as Amazon grew to become the global purveyor of everything, it did not have to rearchitect all of its systems—the company planned ahead.

Should You Forklift or Rearchitect Data in the Enterprise Data Warehouse?

In 1995, Continental Airlines had 45 different databases, or data marts, and when these were ultimately consolidated into a single EDW, the airline realized a cost saving of $5 million per year. The cost savings come from multiple sources, including fewer contracts to negotiate with database vendors and less physical space for the systems (overhead), but, most importantly, fewer people to feed the beast—you don't need as many database administrators. Combining all of the different databases into a single EDW is called data mart consolidation, and the cost-saving business case is straightforward.[3] Yet, this business case is at the heart of a major pitfall to be avoided: forklifting versus rearchitecting the data in the new system.

Forklifting the data means that you take the existing data in the small databases and you lift it, as is, into the big EDW. If you have 50 independent data marts, then inside the EDW there will be 50 independent databases—they will be in one consolidated system, so the maintenance and personnel costs will be significantly reduced, but the data will still be the same. This means you will not be able to answer complex business questions.

Why, as a marketer, do you need to know this? I can't tell you how many very senior marketing executives have voiced their frustration to me at being unable to answer basic marketing questions with new EDW. What happened? IT got sold on the cost savings of consolidating into a large EDW but did not tackle the real business problem due to the increased cost: you need to rearchitect the data to get the enterprise view.

Conceptually, rearchitecting is thinking through the complex queries and web of relationships, and optimizing the data model so as to answer the important marketing questions across the enterprise. The cost of rearchitecting can be significant but the benefit can be immense. I once calculated the difference between forklifting and rearchitecting for a major financial institution.[4] The rearchitected solution had 300 percent more NPV benefit compared with that of the forklifted system!

What We Know Can and Will Go Wrong (If You Don't Watch Out!)

The road is littered with failed large-scale IT projects, and EDW for data-driven marketing is no exception. The Standish Group, which tracks thousands of IT projects every year, estimates that 72 percent of IT projects are not on time or on budget as originally planned. This means that you have only a 28 percent chance out of the gate that the system will work as planned. EDW is actually worse, though: Barbara Wixom and Hugh Watson[5] found that 55 percent of executives reported that the new data-warehousing system failed to deliver business results.

Given these rather dismal statistics, you might be inclined to run the other way before getting into an EDW project for marketing. The patterns of failure are well documented, however. Here are the key risk factors identified by Wixom and Watson:

- Lack of focus and vision—the overall objectives of the EDW effort are not well defined.

- Lack of senior management support and sponsorship.
- Lack of a champion to promote the project and provide information, material resources, and political support.
- Organizational politics and cultural issues.
- Lack of resources—funding, time, and/or personnel.
- Scalability of the solution—they built the ranch house but needed the Empire State Building.
- Development technology—the system may be new technology, or the wrong technology solution is chosen.
- Lack of skills—the implementation team lacks the skills and training to deliver the system. You need very good project managers and an experienced technology team to pull big EDW projects off.
- Quality of existing databases—this is a surprisingly major challenge, discussed below.
- Reliance on external IT help—often an external contractor is used and the IT team may by default accept what they are given, which may not be what marketers need, and/or IT is not able to maintain the system after the contractor leaves.
- Changes in job skills and personnel displacement—key people on big projects often leave. For contractors, this can be managed in the consulting contract.
- No end-user participation—this can be due to poor communication of the needs. If there is no marketing involvement, the IT project to build the data-driven marketing EDW is dead out of the gate.
- Lack of training—the system is built but there is no instruction on how to use it.

You can use this list as a checklist for your organization. Although all are important, the really major risks to watch out for are lack of vision and senior executive support, politics, lack of resources, scalability, and quality of databases. The lack-of-vision problem is astounding to me, but it happens surprisingly often. I once met with executives in a Fortune 500 company who had spent more than $30 million creating an EDW, but they had not thought through what to do with the data once they had it. The result was that the system was not meeting the business needs. This is why starting small and learning by doing is so important. You should formulate the data-driven marketing strategy of Chapter 1 before building a skyscraper.

Data quality can be a particularly thorny challenge. If you have a large organization with lots of data marts, most likely the data are stored in all kinds of different formats in each database. This means you have multiple and different records, and different data and descriptions for each customer. The challenge is compounded by different names for the same things. Taken together, cleaning the data and getting them extracted and loaded into the EDW can be very difficult and time consuming. One company, for example, analyzed its 70 systems with customer data: For its 20 million customers, the company found it had 200 million customer IDs!

As another example, marketers at Continental Airlines had the idea to send a thank-you letter to high-value customers on their birthday and highlight the number of years of dedicated loyalty to Continental. Cleaning the data for this campaign was no trivial task: the format of dates, day and month, are transposed in Europe and the United States, and they found they had been tracking customer acquisition dates only since the late 1990s, so there were significant data gaps.

The point of this chapter is not to scare you to death, but rather to ensure that you go into a large-scale data-driven marketing infrastructure effort with your eyes wide open. You should not try to solve the whole problem at once. Rather, for the data-cleaning challenge, if there are 150 subject areas, then map them out, know what they are, and define what you want to do with these data. You can guarantee there are going to be problems with duplicate data, missing data, wrong data, units, and so on. Do the analysis up front to define the problem, then focus on integrating a small number of subject areas, say three subject areas in six months. The theme is consistent throughout this book—deliver value incrementally, but have a clear road map of where you want to go.

Technologists by training will often integrate data in a very logical and sequential manner; they are engineers, after all. The problem is that the logical and best technical order may not be the best for the business. For example, if you are hemorrhaging customers in Wisconsin, then the Wisconsin data mart should be integrated first and analyzed. Again, data models and data management are too important to be left to the technologist.

Politics is an inevitable challenge, given the nature of the beast—an EDW is a system that spans across the enterprise and requires key divisional stakeholders to relinquish power over their siloed data. The result can be turf battles and resistance that translates to low user acceptance, difficult integration of data, and lack of resources to get the job done. This is why senior executive sponsorship and leadership are so important.

Chapter 2 discussed the five barriers to data-driven marketing, and provided strategies to overcome politics and to get executive support. In summary, the theme was to get the quick win, show substantive results using data-driven marketing principles, and use this as a springboard to gain senior executive sponsorship and support for the broader initiative. In Chapters 2 and 6, I gave detailed examples of how managers at Royal Bank of Canada and Continental Airlines accomplished this. The following section is a detailed example of how Harrah's Entertainment incrementally built the Empire State Building of infrastructure for the casino gaming industry.

Harrah's Entertainment: Creating the Data-Driven Marketing Infrastructure Portfolio

Casino gaming is entertainment for many millions of Americans, and Harrah's Entertainment is the world's largest gaming company. Harrah's owns, operates, and/or manages about 50 casinos (under such names as Bally's, Caesars, Harrah's, Horseshoe, and Rio), primarily in the United States and the United Kingdom. Operations include casino hotels, dockside and riverboat casinos, and Native American gaming establishments. In 2005, Harrah's acquired rival Caesar's Entertainment for $9.4 billion in cash, stock, and debt. The deal cemented Harrah's as the world's number one gaming company, larger than the merged MGM Mirage/Mandalay combination. Harrah's was acquired by affiliates of TPG Capital and Apollo Global Management, which took the company private in a leveraged buyout that closed in 2008.

In the years preceding the Apollo/TPG buyout, when Harrah's was a public company, it accomplished an extraordinary feat. Harrah's created a data-driven marketing infrastructure that was globally recognized as second to none, across industries. I would like to focus on this journey and the infrastructure story at Harrah's up to 2004, since there are important lessons to be learned.

In the early 1990s, Harrah's rapidly expanded as a few states liberalized its gaming standards, but by the mid-1990s most of Harrah's markets were under increasing competition and the company began to struggle. The executive team therefore started to formulate a new strategy based on data-driven marketing and customer loyalty.[6]

In the U.S. casino gaming industry, Harrah's had a potential competitive advantage—it was, and still is today, the most geographically diverse gaming company in the United States. Returning to Michel Porter from Chapter 1, sustainable competitive advantage is created by the coordination of activities that are not easily duplicated. In Harrah's case, one potential sustainable competitive advantage was geographic presence. But the question remained as to how to capitalize on this advantage.

In the mid-1990s Phil Satre, Harrah's CEO, and John Boushy, Harrah's Senior Vice President of marketing services and chief information officer (CIO), realized that there was a significant opportunity to increase cross-market play. That is, the demographics of the United States are such that approximately one in four adults gamble in a casino once or more a year, and one in four of these gamble multiple times a year in multiple geographic locations. Say, for example, a customer lives in Philadelphia, Pennsylvania, and a couple of times a year he goes to Atlantic City, New Jersey, and plays at a Harrah's property. In addition, he is a frequent gamer and also goes once a year to Las Vegas and once or twice a year to New Orleans to see old friends and family. During these trips, he enjoys time at a casino.

Just because the customer visits a Harrah's property in Atlantic City does not mean he will "shop" at Harrah's in the other cities. Las Vegas, in particular, has many distractions and properties, such as the Bellagio, with the impressive water fountain; the Mirage, with an erupting volcano outside; and the Luxor, shaped like an Egyptian pyramid, as examples. Harrah's Las Vegas, in contrast, is much less impressive—there is no spectacular pirate ships show out front to entice visitors to come in.

In Chapter 9, I gave the Lowe's example. After building a deck, there is a high probability the customer will purchase a grill. The Harrah's example is similar. Just because you bought the deck materials from Lowe's does not mean you will return and purchase the grill from Lowe's—there are a lot of other retailers who sell grills. The trick was to send targeted marketing to these customers shortly after they purchased the deck materials.

This same idea is the essence of Harrah's original business case for investing in data-driven marketing infrastructure. If Harrah's knew the value of each and every customer, and knew who gambled in multiple geographies, it could target marketing to incent cross-market play. With customer value data, Harrah's could also do targeted retention marketing. The importance of data to drive its strategy was articulated in the 1996 board of directors meeting of the vision for Harrah's in 2000: "Harrah's dominates the casino industry! We have the most competitive systems and processes in the business. This starts with the best customer database information allowing us to treat customers as individuals."

Harrah's created the first "frequent flyer card" for the gaming industry, today called Total Rewards. The first $20 million infrastructure investment consisted of networking all of the casino slot machines and POS systems, and tagging these transactional data with each customer's Total Rewards number. CLTV was then calculated for each customer, based not only on what the customer actually won or lost, but, more importantly, on the theoretical value of gaming revenue given the "house advantage" and how much the customer played.

It turns out that the actual winnings or losses in gaming are not an accurate predictor of CLTV in casinos, due to the random chance of gaming. However, the house has an "advantage" in slot machines, for example, so there is a "theoretical win" for the house. This theoretical win corresponds to the expected value of gaming revenue from a customer given the house advantage for the games the customer plays. One of Harrah's innovations during this time was that they used the theoretical win to calculate CLTV rather than the actual win or loss of the customer, which is more random.

Shortly after a visit to a Harrah's, customers who exceeded a minimum CLTV received targeted marketing offers to incent cross-market play, and the higher the CLTV, the greater the value of the offer. The results were impressive: cross-market play increased by more than 68 percent over five years, and the data-driven marketing investment had a measured return on investment (ROI) (including the marketing offer's cost) of 24 percent. This was the first big win that started to build momentum for the data-driven marketing initiative.

By 1998, Harrah's had a consolidated customer database and three years of longitudinal transactional data on customers; it had demonstrated a substantial increase in cross-market visitation capture. Gary Loveman, who had been a consultant, became chief operating officer (COO) of Harrah's in 1998 (he was appointed CEO in 2003). Satre, Boushy, and Loveman saw the incredible opportunity to use the rich customer data and take Harrah's to the next level.

Given the cross-market play win, Harrah's next focused on a tiered loyalty program. That is, in 1999, Harrah's created gold, platinum, and diamond gaming levels for Total Rewards with highly differentiated service in the actual casino. Customers noticed the different check-in lines and "free" perks at different levels, and as a result there was a structural change in the spectrum of customer value—customers were incented to consolidate their play at Harrah's to get to the next level. Given the existing infrastructure, the new investment was $1.4 million with a measured ROI of 35 percent.

The next step was to link in the web site www.Harrahs.com. The original business case was to enable customers to book their hotel online, thus providing a lower cost of service and a significant cost saving over call center reservations. In addition, customers could manage their Total Reward points online and see offers, and Harrah's could also add e-mail "Play for Fun" marketing. This required a $9.9 million investment, with a primary business objective of customer acquisition and self-service booking. New infrastructure was required to integrate the casinos and slot machine network with the hotels and Internet. The result was a measured ROI of 18 percent. These first three data-driven marketing activities (cross-market play, tiered Total Rewards, and Web) were the low-hanging fruit for Harrah's and had a significant measured payoff. As a next step, Harrah's worked to optimize the revenue from its hotel rooms.

Instead of pricing all of the hotel rooms at the casino the same, the idea was to price the room based on a revenue management model. This model included customer profitability from all sources of revenue, market condition, room availability, and so on (see Figure 10.7). For room price, there is an efficient frontier: the best room rate versus predicted gaming revenue for a customer. Sometimes, the highest expected profitability came from "giving away" the hotel room to the "right" customer.

Adding this yield management capability required a new room revenue management system, integrated with both the CLTV capability and the hotel system. The system was designed to give the right room to the right customer at the right price, and a requirement was the ability for "real-time" pricing, analysis of the model Figure 10.7, with a pricing decision for each unique customer delivered in no more than four seconds. Again, the results were impressive: from 2000 to 2003, total revenue per room increased 30 percent from $172 to $224 per customer, adding more than $40 million in revenues. The additional infrastructure

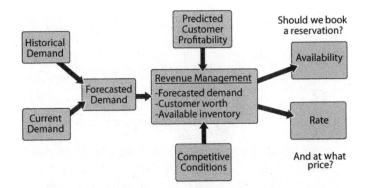

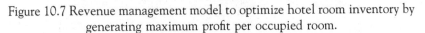

Figure 10.7 Revenue management model to optimize hotel room inventory by generating maximum profit per occupied room.

Source: Harrah's Entertainment.

for the room revenue management capability was an $8 million investment and had an 18 percent measured ROI.

The infrastructure capably reached critical mass and now began to create additional self-reinforcing opportunities. The rich transactional data that Harrah's was capturing on all of its customers opened up new possibilities. For example, Harrah's added the capability to correlate longitudinal CSAT survey data with longitudinal customer profitability. In 2001, Harrah's received 51,000 CSAT surveys, and measuring CSAT as in Chapter 4, found that customers who would "definitely recommend" compared with those who would not generated 6 percent more in gaming revenues. The company, therefore, undertook specific CSAT marketing activities in the casino properties and were able to measure the typically elusive financial impact of customer satisfaction initiatives!

John Boushy, who at this time was the Harrah's Senior Vice President Operations and CIO overseeing the improvement in guest experience as well as the infrastructure development, told me, "Given the information and technology infrastructure we had already built, for a $50,000 investment, the ROI was priceless. It gave operating management the hard, unshakable facts about the growing profitability driven by our customer satisfaction initiatives." Boushy later went on to become the chief integration officer at Harrah's, responsible for the successful integration of Caesars with Harrah's, and then CEO of Ameristar Casinos, Inc.

Figure 10.8(a) is particularly intriguing. The heat map is gaming revenue transacted on a Harrah's casino floor: dark (red) is a lot of

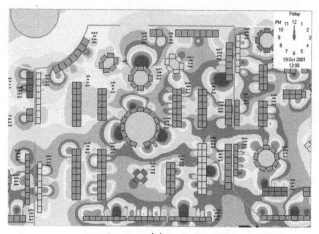

(a)

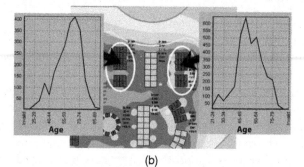

(b)

Figure 10.8 (a) Dynamic heat map of slot machine revenues; dark colors are high revenues, and white is zero. (b) Overlay with player age demographics.

Source: Harrah's Entertainment.

money, and light (white) is no money. It created a video of real-time revenue generation on the casino floor. How do you use this? The casino was laid out by an expert in the gaming industry, with more than 20 years of experience. He looked at the video and gained immediate insights—some of the slots on the bottom and on the top left were always cold. They needed to be changed out to a different game that customers would play.

But the story gets even better. Figure 10.8(b) illustrates the respective ages of the players on two different banks of slot machines; one is a 10-cent slot machine and the other 50 cents. The players on the right,

"The Price Is Right" slots, average 50 years old. The players on the left bank, the dime slots, are nearly 70 years old.

The Harrah's product experience is entertainment, so Harrah's product design should be fundamentally different from a grocery store. In a grocery store, the milk is always in the back so that customers walk through the store to get the milk, and on the way out hopefully purchase other products. But a casino is different—from a product design perspective you can start to ask questions such as, "Should the 50-year-olds be playing next to the 70-year–olds?"—probably not. A better product design would be taken from Disney theme parks: cluster games for specific demographics, and use the data analysis to figure out what games the demographics like. Interestingly, Harrah's found that there was a key requirement for where those over 75 years old liked to play: proximity to the bathrooms.

I once gave a keynote speech at an executive event at the NCR Senior Open golf championship in Dayton, Ohio. There is not a whole lot in Dayton, except for NCR (National Cash Register corporation), founded in 1884 by John Patterson. But Dayton is also the birthplace of aviation. The Wright brothers had their bicycle shop and invented the first airplane in Dayton in the early 1900s.[7] Today, Dayton is the home to Wright Paterson Air Force Base.

After my session, a man came up to me. He was in his late 50s, had silver hair, and was extremely fit. On his shoulder were four stars—he was the general in command of the U.S. Air Force. The general exclaimed: "That is exactly what we need!" referring to the Harrah's infrastructure story and heat map analysis. My point is that these principles are not limited to Harrah's Entertainment.

The Harrah's dynamic heat map capability required a $3.5 million investment and delivered immediate value by informing selection and placement decisions of different slot machines on its casino floors—the result was a 104 percent measured ROI. The theme of the Harrah's case example is to add self-reinforcing and integrated capabilities step by step, where at each phase there is a well-defined business case, with an ROI that can be measured. The result is to incrementally build data-driven marketing infrastructure over time. From an architecture perspective, this approach has some challenges, though.

Figure 10.9(a) is a schematic of the Harrah's infrastructure from 1997 to 2001. The approach of incrementally adding value works well for quick wins, but if built on a shaky infrastructure foundation, over

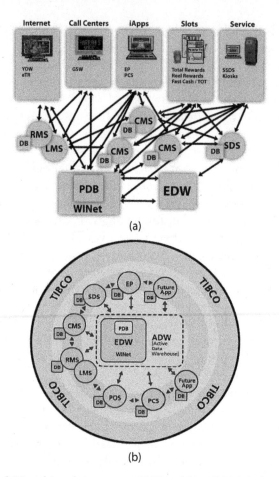

Figure 10.9 (a) Harrah's infrastructure, 1997 to 2001; (b) Harrah's architecture and infrastructure transformation, 2002 to 2003.

Source: Harrah's Entertainment.

time it becomes unmanageable. By 2001, the mess of systems pictured in Figure 10.9(a) had incredible complexity, and, as a result, maintenance and scalability increasingly became a headache.

Boushy told me, "Our strength and focus on building capabilities based upon business outcomes, while very successful, led to several unintended consequences: greater complexity, longer project timelines, and ever-increasing maintenance costs." So, in 2002, Harrah's began to completely rebuild its infrastructure (see Figure 10.9 (b)), at a cost of $100 million: it built the Empire State Building.

The $100 million investment in infrastructure was accompanied by a business case, however. The business case was to upgrade Total Rewards to further drive cross-marketing play, to reduce churn, and to optimize marketing spending. The measured ROI of the 2002 Harrah's infrastructure upgrade was more than 60 percent. This IT infrastructure, combined with Harrah's national presence and cross-market play strategy, is a source of sustainable competitive advantage, since it is not easily duplicated by competitors.

The summary takeaways have important implications for your data-driven marketing infrastructure capability. To get started, the infrastructure investment needs a business case with a solid financial return. Chapters 5 and 9 of this book gave detailed examples of how to create this ROMI business case. You then have to measure the return after the investment, that is, keep score. In Harrah's case, it began measuring ROI of its marketing capabilities in 1995 and have periodically done so ever since.

Follow-on investments should also have business cases and measured returns. There is a note of caution, however—Harrah's was so focused on creating new business value that it lost sight of the ever-increasing complexities and costs of its IT infrastructure, so Harrah's ultimately had to blow up the systems and "rearchitect." Commented Boushy, "If we had the luxury to do it over again, the architecture would be a key component of every project."

Previously in this chapter, I discussed that a major risk for all data-driven marketing infrastructure projects is senior executive support and project sponsorship. "If we did not have a business sponsor for the project, we did not do the project. We always required a business case, even for an infrastructure project, and a business sponsor," Boushy told me. The Harrah's case exemplifies the four critical success factors for delivering successful data-driven marketing infrastructure: (1) a quantifiable and measurable business case, (2) a willing business sponsor to partner with IT, (3) a commitment from both the business sponsor and IT to an ROI, and (4) an IT architecture and road map.

Again, a theme of this book is to think big, start small, and scale fast. You cannot scale fast, though, without infrastructure and a road map for success. Knowledge is power, and this chapter provides insights into data-driven marketing infrastructure so that you can ask the right questions, dramatically increasing your odds of success: you know enough to be dangerous!

Chapter Insights

- Getting started with balanced scorecarding, ROMI analysis, and Internet data analysis can be accomplished with simple tools, such as Microsoft Excel. But churn management, value-based marketing (CLTV), and event-driven marketing require infrastructure.

- Marketers need to understand the scale of their data-driven marketing challenge so that they clearly understand what they are getting into and what they are asking the technology team to build.

- The infrastructure you need to support data-driven marketing depends on the size of the customer base and the complexity of requirements; these are the business questions to answer.

- The difference between small and large customer bases, and simple and complex data requirements, is the difference between building a ranch house or the Empire State Building: you need a few hundred thousand dollars for the former and hundreds of millions of dollars of infrastructure for the latter.

- The risks for data-driven marketing infrastructure projects are well known and documented. The major pitfalls are lack of vision, lack of senior executive sponsorship, politics, lack of resources, scalability, and quality of databases.

- Thinking big, starting small, and scaling fast requires a scalable infrastructure and a road map. Know where you want to go first, then build the road by incrementally adding valuable capabilities and measuring the ROMI results at each step.

- Data-driven marketing technology is too important to leave to the technologists.

Marketing Budgets, Technology, and Core Processes

Key Differences between the Leaders and the Laggards

In life, subtleties often make the difference between good and great: a good wine and a great wine, prime and choice steak, hundredths of a second in the Olympic 100-meter sprint, and the cut of an Armani suit, for example. Yet the difference in good and great for marketing is less subtle. As we will see in this chapter, there are a few repeatable processes that separate the great marketing organizations from the average.

After writing this, I hear someone exclaiming: "But wait, what about the creative?" I have already discussed that the vast majority of organizations (72 percent) outsource the creative component of their marketing. I argue that creative is becoming a commodity, and since all organizations have access to similar creative, it cannot be the source of a sustainable competitive advantage (if you work in an agency, please see the last section before throwing this book across the room). I argue that a big difference between good and great marketing organizations is their internal processes for selecting, executing, and measuring campaign performance, and how they use technology to support these processes.

This chapter shares insights from my research on essential marketing processes, the difference between the leaders and the laggards, and the role of technology, and it provides a phased approach to upgrading your marketing campaign management processes. I do not want to discount the impact of creative out of hand, though, and the last section is about the Creative X-factor—how brilliant creative combined with data-driven marketing can be a 100× multiplier for campaign performance.

Sidebar: Research Methodology

HYPOTHESES

The formal research objective was to test four specific hypotheses:

1. A maturity model exists for marketing campaign management (MCM).
2. Firms at the highest level of maturity experience tangible performance gains.
3. Firms at the highest level leverage centralized customer data and analytics to realize these gains—that is, there is a link between advanced marketing management and using an enterprise data warehouse (EDW) to keep score.
4. Firms are held back from maximizing value by a recurring set of hurdles; focusing on these hurdles first will enable firms to unlock value from marketing.

In parallel, the team wanted to find out if there were any broadly applicable stages of MCM effectiveness. By comparing

MCM application data with responses regarding implementation hurdles, a general MCM adoption trajectory was identified and, along with it, best practices to help organizations accelerate along that path.

SURVEY AND INTERVIEWS

The data needed to test the five hypotheses were gathered through a mass survey and targeted interviews. A survey called "Strategic Marketing ROI: Myth versus Reality" was mailed to and made available on the Web to top marketing executives at U.S.-based Fortune 1,000 companies. Prior to sending the survey, the research team interviewed 10 senior marketing executives from a representative sample of organizations to gather more detailed examples of implementation hurdles and best practices.

SAMPLE: RESPONDENT DEMOGRAPHICS

The team received completed surveys from over 250 respondents. More than 92 percent of the respondents identified themselves as chief marketing officer (CMO), Director, Vice President of marketing, or their direct reports. The average respondent has 12 years of marketing management experience. The average respondent's organization generated $5 billion in revenues and spent 8 percent of those revenues on marketing. In total, the survey responses were responsible for approximately $53 billion in annual marketing spending.

RESEARCH TEAM

The original interviews, hypothesis formulation, and survey research were conducted by Mark Jeffery and Saurabh Mishrah at the Kellogg School of Management. Alex Krasnikov later joined the team and, with Dr. Mishrah, validated the link between MCM capability and firm performance.

Marketing Campaign Management: The State of the Industry

The focus of this chapter is on marketing budgets and processes for marketing management. These processes are an essential component of effective data-driven marketing since, as we will see, just collecting metrics or buying technology tools is not enough to produce results. The insights in this chapter come from research of 252 firms capturing $53 billion of annual marketing spending. (See the sidebar on the research methodology.)

The survey results and interviews show that senior marketing executives are committed to making marketing more transparent to the rest of the organization. They recognize the need to speak the language of finance and strategy, and they are willing to go the extra mile to ensure that the marketing department is well integrated with the business strategy and goals. However, they are also struggling to optimize marketing management in their organizations.

The MCM cycle starts with campaign selection and the decision to invest in the campaign, then continues with campaign execution, and ends with value capture and measurement. However, a differentiator of advanced MCM is learning and feedback when the campaign is complete (see Figure 11.1). Here are some sobering survey statistics on the state of marketing management for the campaign management cycle.

Campaign Selection

- Seventy-three percent do not use scorecards rating each campaign relative to key business objectives prior to a funding decision.
- Sixty-eight percent do not use experiments, contrasting the impact of pilot marketing campaigns with a control group, to guided campaign selection.
- Sixty-one percent do not have a defined and documented process to screen, evaluate, and prioritize marketing campaigns.
- Fifty-seven percent do not use business cases to evaluate marketing campaigns for funding.

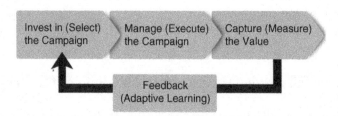

Figure 11.1 Closed-loop marketing campaign management (MCM).

- Fifty-three percent report that marketing campaign selection is not guided by forecasts of campaign return on investment (ROI), customer lifetime value (CLTV), and/or other performance metrics such as customer satisfaction (CSAT).
- Forty-four percent do not consider intercampaign synergies at the time of marketing campaign selection.

Execution

- Sixty-three percent report that they do not break down each marketing campaign in stages and do not use metrics to review the campaigns at each stage.
- Fifty-three percent say they do not actively modify or terminate underperforming campaigns at any stage of implementation based on ongoing campaign evaluation.

Measurement and Value Capture

- Forty-three percent indicate that they do not actively track and monitor realized benefits (versus targets) after completion of marketing campaigns.
- Forty percent report that campaigns are often not designed to be measured and specific metrics for success are not defined.

Learning and Feedback

- Forty-three percent say they do not use metrics to guide future marketing campaign selection and management.
- Thirty-six percent of organizations do not conduct postimplementation reviews to solicit campaign team opinions and intuitions regarding successes and mistakes of past campaigns to guide future marketing campaign selection and management.
- Thirty-four percent do not use insights gained from analysis of data from past campaigns to guide innovations in future.

These data suggest that the majority of organizations are not optimizing their marketing campaign management. Don't worry if your organization is one of them; as we will see, there are a few repeatable processes that differentiate the leaders.

Research: Marketing Processes, Technology, and the Link to Firm Performance

So what are the essential marketing management processes, and do firms that have these processes get better firm performance? The original interviews provided insights into what these processes should be. Here are a few representative quotes from marketing executives:

"You have to have a good marketing and business strategy, but this is not enough. You need sound work processes that monitor all marketing efforts against their objectives to ensure that these strategies work."

"There is a need of alignment across all marketing campaigns. What I mean by alignment is to avoid, as much as possible, the situation where multiple campaign leaders plan execution targeted more or less at the same region or area of the world against the same set of customers with the same script. However, this requires a great deal of portfolio approach and a great deal of human coordination."

"In our organization, projects are looked at as a worldwide portfolio. We centralize the view and then we manage cross-divisionally everything to ensure optimal customer experience."

"We have a formal process that focuses on continuous improvement. We earmark budget dollars to go do certain things and then as we work we make sure that those things still make sense. This is needed because no one in our business is clairvoyant on the new customer opportunity that will become apparent to us in nine months. This involves a fairly sophisticated assessment of activities. And what we are always striving to do is figure out, based on where we invested our marketing dollars last year, or the years before, based on the current strategy, based on the field input, what stays, what changes, what we are missing that we need to add to the process."

From our interviews we therefore identified four marketing management capabilities that comprise the MCM capability of a firm: (1) selection, (2) portfolio view, (3) monitoring, and (4) adaptive learning.

Marketing Campaign Management (MCM) Capability, a Working Definition

·MCM is the combination of processes, methods, and tools used to develop, monitor, measure, and control marketing campaigns and programs to increase the return on both individual and aggregate marketing investments. Marketing campaigns are defined to include all direct and indirect organizational marketing endeavors such as promotions, advertising, analyst relations, customer relationship management initiatives, and so on.

The four MCM capability processes are as follows:

1. *Selection.* A documented process guiding the selection and funding of marketing campaigns. It includes business cases for campaigns and scorecards to align with the business strategy.
2. *Portfolio view.* A holistic portfolio view used for the selection of marketing campaigns for execution. The idea is that Campaign A on its own may have more value than when combined with Campaign B. This synergy value is taken into account in the selection process and is the "portfolio view" at selection.
3. *Monitoring.* Measuring and evaluating progress of marketing campaigns; put simply, this is the capability to "keep score" using the metrics defined in this book.
4. *Adaptive learning.* This is the ability to learn from past campaigns and initiatives and use these insights to guide future marketing campaigns.

These are the essential processes, MCM capability, needed to effectively manage marketing. There is one additional support capability:

5. *Technology.* Technology capabilities and infrastructure such as EDW, marketing resource management (MRM), and analytic tools for marketing decision making.

The research investigated how these capabilities are connected, and Figure. 11.2 is a summary of the analysis. The picture is a structural equation model—think of it as a regression equation on steroids; the

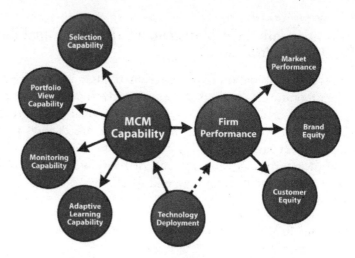

Figure 11.2 Marketing process capabilities and the link to performance. All block arrows are statistically significant ($p < 0.05$). The dashed line is not significant.

model shows how the capabilities are connected through MCM capability to firm performance. Figure 11.2 may look a little complicated, but the insights are important to grasp.

The four capabilities on the left in Figure 11.2 (selection, portfolio view, monitoring, and adaptive learning) are the components of a higher-order capability, the MCM capability. MCM is then connected to firm performance (market performance, brand equity, and customer equity) on the right.

What does this mean? It means that there is a statistical link to firm performance through the MCM component capabilities of selection, portfolio view, monitoring, and adaptive learning. That is, firms that have these processes in place have better market performance, brand equity, and customer equity relative to the market average.

The analysis in Figure 11.2 is based on primary data; this is data collected from the survey. We also did the analysis using secondary data, from the COMPUSTAT database of financial performance metrics for publicly traded firms. This analysis also showed a statistical link between the MCM capability and firm performance. In this case, the performance metrics were sales growth, firm ROI, and long-term shareholder equity. The significant finding is that organizations that have the four MCM capabilities have better firm performance relative to competitors. And a key insight is that metrics and keeping score (monitoring) are one of the critical capabilities.

The astute reader will notice that I have not so far mentioned technology, which enables data-driven marketing. Notice something interesting in Figure 11.2—there is a dashed line from the technology capability to firm performance, and this link is zero. That is, technology for marketing is not directly connected to firm performance. Instead, the connection is through MCM capability.

There is an important implication here: just investing in technology for marketing does not lead to firm performance. Instead, technology supports the management processes. That is, to drive performance from marketing technology investments, an organization must also have the four essential MCM process capabilities in place: selection, portfolio view, monitoring, and adaptive learning. Interestingly, these results are independent of industry or firm strategy and go to market channel. That is, MCM capability is a universal capability that all organizations should implement to improve the performance of their marketing.

The research shows that there is a broad spectrum of marketing process maturity in firms. Figure 11.3 is the distribution of MCM capability, where high capability on the right means that firms have completely adopted the four MCM capabilities, and low performers are in the beginning stages with minimal elements of the capabilities. We have shown that the high performers have significantly better financial

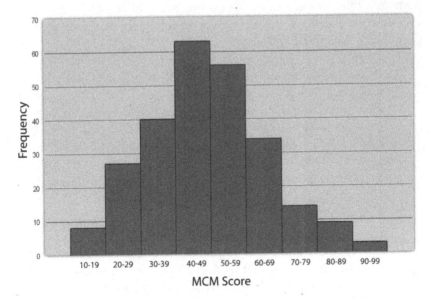

Figure 11.3 MCM capability distribution for the surveyed firms.

performance, brand and customer equity, and long-term shareholder equity than do the low performers.

The research has highlighted the need for four major processes (selection, portfolio view, monitoring, and adaptive learning) and investment in technology infrastructure to support these marketing capabilities. These research results are independent of industry; that is, the four core MCM process capabilities are universal for marketing across all firms and industries. Furthermore, by focusing on the essential 15 metrics throughout this book, I have shown how you can radically improve marketing performance across the spectrum of MCM activities: metrics are essential to "select" the best marketing campaigns, "monitor" if they are working, and "adaptively learn" from your trials and errors.

B2B versus B2C Investment Portfolio Mixes: Leaders versus Laggards

The research results are industry independent for MCM processes and the link to firm performance. However, there is a difference in how business-to-business (B2B) and business-to-consumer (B2C) firms invest their marketing dollars. Think of the marketing budget as a portfolio, like an investment portfolio, with different categories of investments. I defined the five major components of the marketing portfolio in Chapter 1 as follows:

1. *Branding.* Marketing to create brand equity and designed to make a product or service top of mind for the customer. Examples include advertising focusing on a feeling or experience such as associating the product with being cool, hip, relaxed, and the like, or association with another positive brand, such as Nike's sponsorship of top athletes. The impact is quantified using essential metric #1—brand awareness of Chapter 4.

2. *Customer equity.* Relationship marketing to build customer equity. Examples include exclusive offers for loyal customers, executive events in B2B, reward cards, and so on. The impact is measured using essential metrics #3—churn and #4—CSAT of Chapter 4, and metric #10—CLTV of Chapter 6.

3. *Demand generation.* Marketing to drive sales in the short term. Think coupons, sales, limited time offers, etc. The impact is quantified using essential metrics #6—profit, #7—net present value (NPV), #8—internal rate of return (IRR), and #9—payback of Chapter 5. Internet search engine marketing (SEM) for e-commerce is also demand generation marketing, quantified by essential metrics #11—cost per click (CPC), #12— transaction conversion rate (TCR), and #13—return on ad dollars spent (ROA).

4. *Shaping markets.* Marketing to shift customer perception toward the need for a product or service and/or to influence groups of customers toward a product using third-party recommendations. Examples include social media marketing such as sponsored community building with influential blog postings and analyst relations in B2B. The essential metrics for measurement are closely related to branding, #1—brand awareness, but also include #2—test-drive metrics from Chapter 5, and 15—word of mouth (WOM) from Chapter 7.

5. *Infrastructure and capabilities.* This last category of the marketing portfolio is investments in technology infrastructure such as EDW, analytics, and MRM—these capabilities support broader marketing activities. Developing the business case for infrastructure investments was discussed in Chapter 9. This category also includes training of the sales and marketing teams to improve skills.

In Chapter 1, I discussed how there is a marketing divide between how the leaders and laggards invest their marketing budget portfolios (see Figure 1.6). The laggards spend more on demand generation marketing, whereas the leaders spend more on branding, customer relationships, and infrastructure to support data-driven marketing.

Figure 11.4 is the leader and the laggard marketing budget breakdown for firms that were distinctly either B2B or B2C in the research. The leaders and laggards were defined by the top and bottom 20 percent of firms based on MCM score (see Figure 11.3). For both groups, B2B and B2C, there is a marketing divide—the laggards spend more on demand generation marketing, and in both cases the leaders spend more on branding, customer equity, and infrastructure and capabilities.

The leaders spend significantly more on marketing overall, 14 to 25 percent more than the average. The difference between B2B and

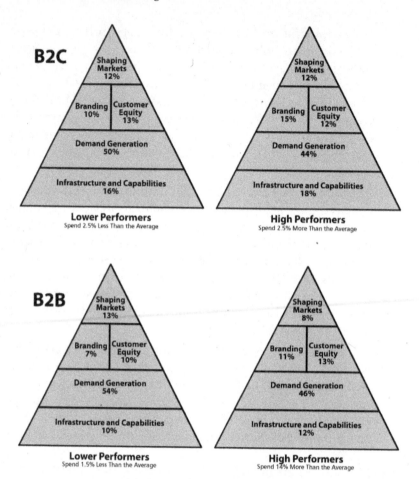

Figure 11.4 Leader versus laggard marketing portfolio budget mixes for (a) B2C and (b) B2B companies. Both B2B and B2C firms reported spending an average of 6 percent of revenues on marketing.

B2C is in the percent allocation of marketing budgets within the portfolio. For the B2C portfolio, the leaders and laggards are different in that the leaders spend less on demand generation marketing and more on branding and infrastructure. For B2B, the demand generation marketing is allocated toward branding, customer equity, and infrastructure—that is, the B2B leaders invest the most in customer relationships, with a secondary focus on branding.

Shaping markets is an interesting category of the marketing portfolio. This component was suggested by one of my colleagues, Mohan

Sawhney. The fun thing about research is that the answer is not known in advance, and we thought that shaping markets would be more important to the leaders. It turns out the opposite is true, especially in B2B. For B2C, shaping market percentages is the same, although the leaders spend 25 percent more on overall marketing, so more is spent proportionately in each category. But for B2B, shaping markets is clearly less of the portfolio for the leaders than the laggards—this is an interesting insight.

Shaping markets for B2B is primarily based on analyst relationships and thought leader influencers to positively portray a product or service. In the technology industry, for example, the Gartner magic quadrant ranks different firms' products on the dimensions of "ability to execute" and "completeness of vision." For technology vendors, the Holy Grail is to be in the top right of the Gartner magic quadrant, with a complete vision and high ability to execute. Some firms spend considerable effort to influence analysts to get the top rating.

The research in Figure 11.4(b) suggests that shaping markets for B2B through analyst relations may be overrated. That is, the leading firms spend less on shaping markets than do the laggards, even though they spend 14 percent more than the average. Instead, they focus their effort on branding and customer equity. It may be that a good brand and customer equity are enough to shape the market and influence analysts.

In summary, the leaders compared with the laggards have similar marketing portfolio spending, for both B2B and B2C. Both sets of leaders spend less on demand generation and more on branding and infrastructure. There were some differences, however, between B2B and B2C leaders in the major categories of customer equity and shaping markets.

I want to add a word of caution about the data in Figure 11.4, since the data are based on qualitative survey research. That is, the senior marketing executives were asked to give the approximate percentage allocation of their budgets in the five categories. These data are not from in-depth audits of marketing budgets. However, the 250 responses are a statistically significant sample and are directionally correct.

I am not suggesting that your marketing budget should exactly follow the percentages of Figure 11.4. Rather, they should be used as a guide. For example, if your firm spends only a few percent on branding or infrastructure, ask whether that makes sense. Similarly, a portfolio significantly overweighted toward any category is probably out of balance.

Overcoming the Four Barriers to Professionalizing Marketing Processes

One of the most revealing insights from the study is that despite the impact of MCM capability on performance, very few organizations appear to have implemented optimized MCM. What is holding them back? The survey respondents point to four specific challenges: (1) lack of top management support, (2) lack of respect, (3) lack of cross-functional alignment, and (4) lack of employee skills.

1. Lack of top management support:
   a. Sixty-nine percent said that senior managers primarily make funding decisions for individual marketing campaigns based on their gut feel and intuition.
   b. Sixty-nine percent say that business leaders do not understand that ROI is not always applicable to marketing campaigns.
   c. Fifty percent report that the top management in their organizations does not provide specific strategic goals based on metrics such as ROI to guide marketing campaigns.
   d. Forty-nine percent indicate that marketing is not perceived by the CEO as the main driver of strategic advantage.
2. Lack of respect:
   a. Fifty-six percent claim that in their organization most senior managers perceive marketing as a "necessary evil."
   b. Fifty-four percent claim that in their organization there is a lack of mutual respect between marketing and other business executives.
   c. Thirty-two percent say that their business and strategy decision makers do not have a good knowledge of marketing.
3. Lack of cross-functional alignment:
   a. Forty-eight percent do not solicit a cross-functional senior executive input to allocate their marketing campaign funds.
   b. Twenty-five percent say that within their organization marketing is not an essential component of business activities.
   c. Finally, 21 percent report that marketing is not an important integrated function within their organizations.

4. Lack of employee skills:
   a. Sixty-four percent report that they do not have enough employees who have the skill to track and analyze complex marketing data.
   b. Forty-seven percent said that overall their marketing staff does not have sufficient working knowledge of financial concepts such as ROI, NPV, and CLTV.

How do you overcome the first barrier and gain senior executive support? Senior executive support is built upon a foundation of trust and understanding. Trust is developed by a proven track record of delivering on promises. Chapter 2 gave strategies for getting senior executive support based upon delivering results: start small, get the quick win, show results, and get senior executive sponsorship. Marketers must take the lead communicating the value of the results in a way that senior executives understand—use the language of business, finance, and data where appropriate. The data-driven marketing approach of this book will help you build both trust and respect within the organization, overcoming the first two barriers. Later in this chapter, I discuss how the four MCM processes create a governance process for marketing that overcomes the alignment barrier.

The last personnel skills gap barrier was echoed in interviews. The theme here is that to bring up the game of the overall marketing organization requires training. You need to give your people the new approaches, tools, techniques, and skills to optimize marketing management and deliver best-in-class MCM. In addition to top management support and marketing personnel skills, our analyses underscore the importance of using advanced tools and techniques to manage, design, and execute marketing campaigns. For example, one of the essential requirements of optimized MCM is the extensive use of data across all marketing campaigns to develop a sound investment process. However, 83 percent of the survey respondents indicated that estimating marketing campaigns benefits is often a major challenge for them.

Our observations indicate that the way to minimize this problem is through the use of new technological tools that enable the complex data collection and analysis required for optimizing MCM. These include centralized database, customer relationship management (CRM), and MRM. Our survey results show that there is a statistically significant positive link between the use of advanced tools and return on marketing investment (ROMI). Specifically, organizations that are using an EDW to track marketing campaigns, assets, and customer interactions with the firm (along with deploying automated software such as MRM and using active data warehousing to guide event-driven marketing campaigns) report higher sales growth, increased market shares, and enhanced brand equity.

However, we again observed that very few organizations appear to actually use some of the advanced tools available today. A few data points to illustrate this:

- Fifty-seven percent of respondents do not use a centralized marketing database to track and analyze their marketing campaigns.
- Seventy percent do not use an EDW to track customer interactions with the firm and with marketing campaigns.
- Seventy-one percent of respondents do not use EDW and analytics to guide marketing campaign selection.
- Seventy-nine percent do not use an integrated data source to guide automated event-driven marketing.
- Eighty-two percent never track and monitor marketing campaigns and assets using automated software such as MRM.

Clearly, there is a pressing need to address these gaps by promoting the deployment and use of advanced tools in organizations. However, it is important to note that the buck doesn't stop at just deploying advanced tools and techniques. Even after deployment, organizations differ greatly in their ability to use these tools. Therefore, it is important to take a phased approach to the adoption and use of these tools and new processes. Establishing a phased time line with clear milestones will enable successful alignment of these tools with the existing organizational structure. A phased approach is critical for a smooth transition from the routine way of managing marketing to a more optimized MCM process.

Upgrading Marketing Campaign Management Processes: A Three-Phased Approach

The primary conclusion drawn from the discussions about implementation hurdles is that successfully optimizing MCM is not a matter of a "big-bang" initiative but instead involves a deliberate step-by-step process. A phased approach will help keep implementation momentum

Maturity Level

Defined	Intermediate	Advanced
-General objectives	-Specific objectives	-Scorecards to align marketing with strategy
-Centralized campaign oversight	-Defined process for selecting campaign investments	-Portfolio view at selection
-Marketing database	-Metrics to measure success	-Active campaign management
	-Measurement of business benefits once campaign is complete	-Agile marketing—tracking of business benefits while campaigns are running
	-Data warehouse	-Adaptive learning and feedback of result to inform future campaign selection
		-Analytic marketing and CLTV measurement
		-Event-driven marketing
		-Infrastructure—marketing resource management (MRM), enterprise data warehouse (EDW), and analytics

(Capabilities)

Figure 11.5 Three stages of marketing campaign management capability.

up; foster senior executive confidence, which will increase their buy-in; warrant a planned and manageable increase in cross-functional alignment; and give employees enough time to develop their skills and comfort levels with the use of these tools.

Our analysis identified three broad categories of MCM adoption competency: defined, intermediate, and advanced (see Figure 11.5). We mapped survey questions into criteria that characterized each category. An MCM "level score" in the range of 0 to 100 was computed for each respondent. The score was based on an average of the total affirmative responses to questions across all categories. The distribution of those scores was used to determine the general category groupings of respondents. A chart of the distribution of MCM scores for all respondents is shown in Figure 11.6. Note that only 11 percent of organizations are at the advanced sage of MCM capability and that the vast majority of organizations (nearly 90 percent) are either defined or intermediate.

Stage One: Defined

The average organization in the "defined" level focuses on developing processes and procedures that provide general objectives and goals to

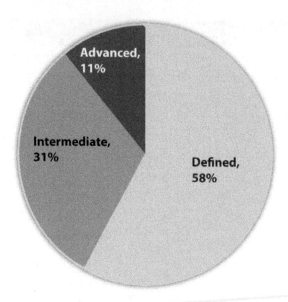

Figure 11.6 Percentage breakdown of marketing organization MCM maturity.

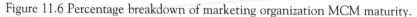

guide marketing campaign selection and management. Organizations at this level have put in place a centralized database that tracks the performance of all marketing campaigns and assets. Finally, a learning culture, albeit weak, is in place where campaign team opinions and intuition regarding mistakes and successes of past campaigns is used to guide future campaign selection and management.

In short, a "defined" process is established to manage all marketing activities for the organization. The benefits of these processes are straightforward, since decision making is simplified by a single comprehensive view of all marketing assets, investments, and resources. Unmonitored marketing spending is eliminated and resource utilization is improved, and general objectives and goals reduce planning and management rework. Finally, the marketing manager is better equipped to learn from past mistakes and therefore improve marketing management over time.

Stage Two: Intermediate

The average organization in the intermediate level has already achieved a centralized view of marketing assets, investments, and resources.

Intermediate organizations have also adopted the practice of providing specific objectives and goals to guide marketing campaign selection and management and also learn from past mistakes. MCM efforts at this level are focused more on rigorous provision of objectives and goals regarding final deliverables of marketing investments and application of advanced metrics for planning, managing, and reviewing marketing investments. Intermediate-level organizations have adopted the use of a data warehouse to track customer interactions with the firm and marketing campaigns. Finally, along with opinions of campaign team members, analysis of data is also used to guide future campaign selection. In short, an intermediate repeatable process is established to control all marketing activities.

The benefits of achieving competency at this level include improved alignment of marketing spending with corporate strategy to reduce or eliminate stranded marketing investments, better communication with a corporation's finance department and corporate leadership through the common language of financial metrics, and easier comparison of results with peer companies. Frequent review cycles also help address deviations from plans in scope, budget, and strategic alignment, allowing for corrective actions earlier rather than later.

Stage Three: Advanced

The most savvy marketing management teams distinguish themselves by their ability to track and monitor marketing campaigns and assets using automated software such as MRM. At campaign selection, they utilize scorecards rating each campaign relative to key business objectives and take a holistic view of all their campaigns, applying portfolio management techniques to fund the overall best set of campaigns. Advanced-level organizations also use event-driven marketing and agile marketing (see Chapters 8 and 9) for flexible campaign execution while continually monitoring realized benefits and business value (ROMI) for marketing campaigns during campaign execution. In these organizations, there is an institutionalized learning culture with disciplined feedback of measured results to inform future campaigns.

The benefits observed by these organizations include improved valuation of marketing investments and an ability to maximize the value of the marketing campaign portfolio while ensuring alignment with corporate strategy. Taken together, the advanced infrastructure, process, and personnel of the advanced MCM organization deliver a true agile marketing capability (see Chapter 8).

The three stages of MCM sophistication are approximations based on the survey responses and personal experiences shared in interviews. As one would expect, few companies fit perfectly in any one of the three stages. A typical organization combines elements from two or three stages, but nevertheless has one stage it primarily resembles. One can look at the three stages as target outcomes or target capabilities. But how does one actually get from one stage to the next? The key is to first prepare a scorecard of the progress of an organization across the various dimensions of MCM. Once the key problem areas have been established, road maps to address them should be developed.

The best road maps include these elements: clear description of the goals and time line regarding the phased rollout of advanced tools and techniques, and training programs for the empowerment of employees to deal with the change. The road map should also include a fair assessment and allocation of resources needed to reach the goal. The overarching best practice is to focus, get early wins to build trust, and build momentum based on these wins.

Lessons Learned from the Research: Complexity Requires Governance

Senior marketing managers are struggling with great complexity in their organizations. Large marketing budgets may have hundreds or even thousands of campaigns running in a year. Without a structured and methodical approach to management, there is a natural tendency for marketing to run in an ad hoc way with a hugely inefficient duplication of effort.

What is needed is a simple set of rules to govern how senior managers get information and how decisions are made. For marketing, this "governance" is the MCM capability: selection, portfolio view, monitoring, and adaptive learning processes. The survey and research interviews yielded clear insights into the best practices for how to develop the MCM governance capability.

Start with common integrating processes that use scorecards and foster business unit involvement. Successful MCM enables alignment with business strategy and direction. It provides rigor and establishes the right balance of priorities. Successful MCM also entails working collectively to define common metrics, such the 15 defined in this book that help measure and plan campaign success.

The use of advanced tools and capabilities is no longer a matter of choice but a necessity. EDW and analytics enable keeping score. MRM helps to digitize and professionalize the process of marketing. Taken together, the deployment of infrastructure makes marketing more agile. But don't start with the infrastructure—the leaders defined the process first, showed results, and then invested in the infrastructure to standardize and automate the process.

Although MCM should be a joint responsibility of the senior executive team, the marketing leaders must take the lead to establish the process and metrics. Successful CMOs make efforts to develop a synergistic partnership with other members of the senior executive team. Further, these leaders promote and encourage their employees to facilitate change that is often accompanied in implementing new process and techniques.

Last but not least, it is critical to build a team of trusted people to manage the MCM process. Also, successful CMOs ensure that they provide adequate resource for personnel training in the process, financial skills, and campaign management. Encouragement in the form of appropriate reward systems is essential to align incentives and retain good people.

In Chapter 5, we briefly touched on the challenge of capital rationing—that funding for marketing is limited, or rationed, and there are always more good marketing initiatives than funding. Many organizations fund campaigns for the executives that "shout the loudest." The governance process discussed in this chapter is the key to ensuring that marketing dollars are optimally allocated and that you get the greatest proverbial "bang for the buck." Successfully implementing marketing governance and MCM processes can transform your executive marketing funding meetings to productive data-driven discussions.

I have worked with many organizations to help them implement or improve the MCM and data-driven marketing capabilities. One of the first things I ask for in an engagement is to see the process documentation: I ask to see everything the marketing organization has written down that defines its MCM process. There are usually two different responses to the request. The first is the organization tells me it needs to hunt down Joe or Sue for the PowerPoint. There is a big hint here—if the process is not well known to the marketing organization, then it is not a standard. How do you know if you have an MCM capability?

Effective and standardized governance requires that the process be written down and widely disseminated to the organization.

The second response is to give my team a thick set of binders with marketing processes in them. Most often, the thick set of binders were a gift from a consulting engagement. In follow-up interviews, I most often find that for organizations with the thick binders, few, if any, marketers follow these processes and/or know they exist. The marketing management processes should be created collaboratively by your organization and communicated in simple, easy-to-understand documents.

There is therefore an artifact that exists in intermediate and advanced MCM capability organizations—a process document that clearly articulates how campaigns are screened and prioritized and how selection decisions are made. Furthermore, there is documentation of the scorecards and essential metrics the organization uses to measure success, and templates for ROMI business cases. I therefore suggest that as you start the data-driven marketing journey, in parallel, you should develop living process documents. These documents must be highly readable and accessible, though. I suggest short 10- to 15-page reviews of the essential processes that are easily read and followed by the marketing team, and I suggest standardized ROMI templates for campaign business cases that are straightforward to fill out.

In summary, it is not enough to buy technology for data-driven marketing. You have to upgrade both processes for MCM capability and the skill level of the marketing organization. Yet the process has four manageable components (selection, portfolio view, monitoring, and adaptive learning), and there are 15 essential metrics given in this book to measure success. The research shows that organizations with more advanced data-driven marketing and MCM process capabilities have better market performance, customer equity, and long-term shareholder value compared with their competitors. The trick is to take a phased approach to gradually build the capability in your organization, realizing results at each stage and developing an actionable process that is easy to follow by employees.

The Creative X-Factor

This book has been entirely about metrics, data, and processes to drive quantum-leap improvements in marketing performance. Many of the strategies and approaches I have discussed for marketing can be applied to other parts of the business and can generate similar performance gains. But what makes marketing fundamentally different from many of the other functional areas is the creativity of marketing media.

Shortly after completing the research, I had a meeting with Betsy Holden, former CEO of Kraft Foods and an expert in marketing. I shared my data-driven marketing and processes for driving performance, and she suggested there was another dimension: the Creative X-factor. There are patterns everywhere, and once Betsy said this, I immediately realized how many amazing marketing campaigns have a Creative X-factor component.

As an example, if you haven't already, you have to see the YouTube videos "Will It Blend?"[1] Blendtec is a small, privately held blender company in Utah. Founder Tom Dickson got his start by applying large horsepower motors to the food grinding and blending process. While originally for commercial restaurants, Blendtec also makes blenders for home use. The entry-level model has 1.8 horsepower and about 10 amps, and their blenders go all the way up to 20 amps—which is the most powerful blending machine in the industry.

Dickson created a viral marketing campaign by seeing what objects he could put in the blender and then asked, "Will it blend?" The resulting videos were posted on YouTube. It turns out that golf balls, marbles, full-sized rakes, cell phones, and cubic zirconium will blend, but coins and crowbars do not. My personal favorite is when Dickson blends an iPhone. This is an example of the Creative X-factor at work—there are more than 7 million views of the iPhone blending video on YouTube, for example, and the cost of the marketing was only a few thousand dollars.

Said Dickson:

The videos were placed on the internet in early November [2006]. Within just a few short days, we had millions of views. The campaign took off almost instantly. We have definitely felt an impact in sales. "Will it blend?" has had an amazing impact to our commercial and our retail products. The campaign is all about brand awareness helping us to build top-of-mind awareness and establish Blendtec as the premier blender manufacturer.[2]

The Blendtec example is Creative X-factor marketing but is pretty straightforward in execution—quirky videos posted to YouTube with a logo and URL in the background. A more sophisticated example of the

Creative X-factor combined with data-driven marketing is the Nissan Qashqai new product launch. Through market research, Nissan realized an opportunity for a small four-wheel-drive sport utility vehicle in Europe. It targeted the new sport utility at the younger demographic with a product launch marketing campaign concept of an "urban-proof" vehicle that dominates the urban landscape. The Qashqai was built in England for sale in Europe, Australia, and Japan, but not in the United States. The product launch TV advertisements featured a large foot riding on top of the Qashqai like a skateboard.[3]

This new product launch marketing started with a press reveal on September 6, 2006. It was attended by 450 journalists from 22 countries, and the event created rave reviews from the media with headlines such as "Nissan Reinvents the Hatch." The official reveal to the public occurred at the September 29, 2006, Paris Auto Show. The 1.4 million visitors made 22,000 Bluetooth downloads of the Qashqai motor show video. The prelaunch direct mailer resulted in 39,444 hand raisers across Europe and the prelaunch web site traffic exceeded expectations by 200 percent.

Clearly, Nissan applied data-driven marketing principles tracking prelaunch marketing exposure, but what sets this campaign apart is the Creative X-factor component. Nissan invented a new urban sport that it called the Qashqai Games. The games consisted of "amateur" videos of the Qashqai doing amazing skateboard-like stunts with names like the "ramp mount," "aerial banana," and the "axel 360 flip." The stunts were made to appear real using special effects.[4] Quirky teams with names like Team Andromeda were made part of the videos, and the campaign also had a fan web site where customers could purchase T-shirts and other Qashqai Games paraphernalia. Finally, Nissan had a Qashqai Games convoy and did BMX bicycle stunt events in selected cities.

The viral films were taken and spread by more than 2,200 web sites, and the videos had more than 11 million views. The Qashqai launched in March 2007 and in six weeks sold 70,000 units—Nissan was unable to meet the demand driven by the marketing. As of June 2009, the Qashqai had sold 330,000 units in Europe, making it one of Nissan's most successful models globally.

This Nissan Qashqai new product launch exemplifies the Creative X-factor combined with data-driven marketing. What I really like about this campaign is how integrated all of the components were and how they targeted a clear generation X and Y demographic. The web viral component was combined with offline and in-person events, and PR and media buys accelerated the WOM impact. This example shows the potential of brilliant creative and data-driven marketing to deliver a 100× performance gain at a low cost point—the Qashqai product launch marketing cost was approximately 1 percent of the cost of designing and manufacturing the car.

For your marketing campaigns, I suggest challenging the creative teams to go beyond the standard statics ads and reach for the Creative X-factor. The real bang happens when you combine new and old media together in an integrated way using data-driven marketing principles, and with killer creative concepts.

Tying It All Together

In summary, in this book I have defined the 15 essential metrics for marketing (Chapters 1 and 3 through 7). These metrics consist of 10 classical metrics and 5 new-age Internet metrics and are used to quantify the vast majority of marketing initiatives. How do you use these metrics to drive performance from your marketing? Start with scorecards to measure performance—the act of measurement enables you to get control of your marketing. Then take an agile marketing approach: build flexibility into your campaigns so that if you are going to fail, you fail fast, and you can amplify the performance of good campaigns (Chapter 8). Designing for measurement combined with agility can increase campaign performance by a factor of five or more.

Then, beyond measurement and flexibility, analytics enables hyper-targeting and segmentation (Chapters 6, 8, and 9). Value-based segmentation combined with event-driven marketing, to give customers the right product marketing at the right time, can increase performance by another five times or more. Analytics requires infrastructure, and whether you need a ranch house or the Empire State Building of infrastructure depends on the size of your customer base and the complexity of requirements (Chapter 10).

However, it is not enough to buy infrastructure and tools; you have to also upgrade the campaign management processes in your organization. This last chapter has discussed the four processes: (1) selection, (2) portfolio view, (3) monitoring, and (4) adaptive learning, which are essential for governing the marketing portfolio. The technology should support the data-driven marketing processes of the firm.

The processes are marketing governance that is essential to control and manage an environment of great complexity. But to make this all work, you also have to train the marketing team to equip it with the new skills and approaches.

Finally, use the Creative X-factor to your advantage—integrate your marketing with the network (Internet and cell phone) to collect customer data, and combine data-driven marketing with killer creative to deliver another 5 to 100× performance gain (Chapters 7 through 9). Taken together, these data-driven marketing approaches are a true quantum leap in marketing performance, and as we have seen, the few organizations that follow these principles are on the other side of the marketing divide—they realize a sustainable competitive advantage from marketing and have better firm performance than do their competitors.

The winning strategy may seem daunting, but throughout this book I have provided examples, frameworks, and a road map of how to get started (Chapters 1 through 3 and 8 through 10). You should start small and get the quick win, show results, and gain executive support to expand the initiative. The power of the data-driven marketing approach is that the 15 essential metrics define the ROMI, which justifies future marketing investments (Chapter 5 and 9).

Chapter Insights

- MCM capability is a key process capability of the leaders to gain a competitive advantage from marketing.
- MCM capability consists of four essential processes: (1) campaign selection, (2) portfolio view, (3) monitoring, and (4) adaptive learning, and these processes are supported by technology tools and infrastructure.
- Organizations with MCM capability have better firm performance.
- Marketing technology tools and infrastructure are not directly linked to firm performance, but they support MCM capability. This means that just investing in technology does not produce marketing performance; you also have to have the four essential processes.

- There is a difference in how the leaders and the laggards spend their marketing dollars. The leaders spend more on branding and infrastructure and less on demand generation marketing. Leading B2B firms spend more on customer relationships.

- A winning strategy is to take a phased approach to developing MCM capability, starting with defined, then intermediate, before adding advanced capabilities.

- There is a magical relationship between creativity and data-driven marketing. The Creative X-factor is the 100× multiplier of brilliant creative combined with data-driven marketing.

Appendix for Instructors: How to Use This Book to Teach Data-Driven Marketing

This book is not a textbook; however, it can be effectively used as a supplement in an MBA, executive, or undergraduate course on marketing metrics and/or data-driven marketing. I teach this course at the Kellogg School of Management in the MBA program as a 10-week class, as an executive MBA five-session class, and as an open-enrollment three-day program. For the various syllabi, supplemental teaching materials, and additional readings, see www.agileinsights.com/instructor.

The courses have major modules corresponding to chapters in this book. The chapters serve as a supplement to the lectures. My pedagogical approach is constructivist, with the goal of creating a community of learners. That is, I want students to learn the concepts through intellectually challenging team case exercises that encourage complex integration of knowledge and application of the principles to real business scenarios. In order to accomplish this, I have developed a case library, distributed through Harvard Business School Publishing

(HBSP). (Just search HBSP for author "Jeffery" to find the cases.) In my courses, these cases are complemented by a few other HBSP cases.

In the course, for almost every class there is a case discussion. Specifically, the MBA class is divided into teams of four to six students and all are expected to complete the case assignment. The graded deliverable is a two-page write-up on the case, with up to three pages of exhibits. Two or three teams are selected in advance to present the case in the class, from the perspectives of real managers presenting to an executive team. The data-mining and segmentation sessions are taught by my colleague, Dr. Russell Walker at Kellogg. Dr. Walker uses SAS JMP, the PC version of SAS, for multiple hands-on exercises.

In summary, the modules of the course mapped into the book chapters, and with corresponding case exercises, are:

1. Introduction to data-driven marketing and marketing metrics (Chapters 1 through 3).
2. Nonfinancial metrics for marketing campaign performance (Chapter 4).
   a. *DuPont-NASCAR Marketing*, Mark Jeffery and Justin Williams, 2007. HBSP Case: 5-107-014.
   b. *SONY-FIFA Partnership Program: The Value of Sponsorship*, Mark Jeffery and Saurabh Mishra, 2006. HBSP Case: 5-206-250.
3. Financial return on marketing investment (ROMI) (Chapter 5).
   a. *B&K Distributors: Calculating ROI for a Web-Based Customer Portal*, Mark Jeffery with Tim Ritters and Jim Anfield, 2006. HBSP Case: 5-404-764.
   b. *ROI for a Customer Relationship Management Initiative at GST*, Mark Jeffery, Robert Sweeney, and Robert Davis, 2006. HBSP Case: 5-404-766.
4. Value-based marketing (Chapter 6).
   a. *Customer Profitability and Customer Relationship Management at RBC Financial Group*, V. G. Narayanan, 2002. HBSP Case 9-102-072.
5. Internet marketing: metrics and optimization (Chapter 7).
   a. *Air France Internet Marketing: Optimizing Google, Yahoo!, MSN, and Kayak Sponsored Search*, Mark Jeffery, Lisa Egli, Andy Gieraltowski, Jessica Lambert, Jason Miller; Liz Neely, Rakesh Sharma, 2009, HBSP Case: 5-407-753.

b. *Meteor Solutions: Word of Mouth in Social Media Marketing*, Mark Jeffery, Zev Kleinhaus, Twinkle Ling, Itaru Matsuyama, Thien Nguyen-Trung, and Keita Suzuki, Kellogg Case, 2010. [In preparation for HBSP.]

6. Agile marketing (Chapter 8).
   a. *Marketing @ Microsoft: The Value of Customer Perception*, Mark Jeffery, Ichiro Aoyagi, and Ed Kalletta, 2006. HBSP Case: 5-106-004.

7. Analytic marketing—data-mining and segmentation (Chapter 9).
   a. *First Bank USA One—An Analytical View of Market Segmentation*, Russell Walker and Mark Jeffery, Kellogg Case, 2010. [In preparation for HBSP.]
   b. Also see the EarthLink SAS data set and decision tree segmentation at www.agileinsights.com/ROMI.

8. Infrastructure for data-driven marketing (Chapter 10).
   a. *Teradata: Data Mart Consolidation Return on Investment at GST Inc.*, Mark Jeffery, Robert Sweeney, and Robert Davis, 2006. HBSP Case: 5-404-774.
   b. *The Value of Flexibility at Global Airlines: Real Options for EDW and CRM*, Mark Jeffery with Chris Rzymski, Sandeep Shah, and Robert Sweeney, 2004. HBSP Case: 5-404-768.

9. Data-driven marketing strategy (Chapters 1, 10, and 11).
   a. *Carnival Cruise Lines*, Lynda M. Applegate, Robert J. Kwortnik, and Gabriele Piccoli, 2006. HBSP Case: 10.1225/806015.
   b. *Netflix vs. Blockbuster—The Emergence of Data-Driven Video*, Russell Walker and Mark Jeffery, Kellogg Case, 2010. [In preparation for HBSP.]
   c. *DuPont Tyvek®—Commercializing a Disruptive Innovation*, Mark Jeffery, Robert A. Cooper, and Scott Buchanan, 2007, HBSP Case: 5-306-510.

The vast majority of these cases are accompanied by detailed solution files and PowerPoint debrief slides. A few of the cases (dated 2010) are in the publication and posting process at HBSP—these cases can be obtained directly from Kellogg Case Publishing by e-mailing: cases@kellogg.northwestern.edu.

NOTES

Chapter 1

1. Mark Jeffery and Justin Williams, *DuPont-NASCAR Marketing* (Harvard Business School Press, Prod. #: KEL166-HCB-ENG, 2007).
2. This Sears example is from 2001, prior to the acquisition by Kmart, and may or may not be representative of Sears marketing in 2009.
3. Philip Kotler and Kevin Keller, *Marketing Management*, 13th ed. (Upper Saddle River, NJ: Prentice Hall, 2008).
4. Michael Porter, *Competitive Strategy: Techniques for Analyzing Industries and Competitors* (New York: Free Press, 1998).
5. The astute reader will note that "Shaping Markets" is trending in the opposite direction, comparing high and low performers. We will see that this is dependent on direct versus indirect sales model for the firm, and we will look at the breakout of B2B versus B2C firms' marketing investment portfolio mix in more detail in Chapter 11.
6. McGraw-Hill Research, *Laboratory of Advertising Performance Report 5262* (New York: McGraw-Hill, 1986).
7. Recession Study, Penton Research Services, Coopers & Lybrand, and Business Science International, 2003.
8. Matt Kinsmann, "Defying downturn, Hanley Wood continues to invest," *Folio B2B*, November 6, 2007.

Chapter 2

1. Mark Jeffery, "Return on investment analysis for e-business projects." In Hossein Bidgoli (ed.), *The Internet Encyclopedia*, 1st ed., vol. 3 (Hoboken, NJ: John Wiley & Sons, 2004), 211–236.
2. Mark Jeffery and Ingmar Leliveld, "Best practices in IT portfolio management," *Sloan Management Review*, 45(3) (Spring 2004, Reprint 45309): 41–49.

3. Gordon Bethune, *From Worst to First: Behind the Scenes of Continental's Remarkable Comeback* (New York: John Wiley & Sons, 1999).
4. For every rule there is an exception. Chapter 4 discusses how to approximate the value of a brand using financial metrics.
5. In Excel 2010 there is no official limit to the number of rows in a spreadsheet—the limitation is set by the amount of RAM in your PC. However, I want to caution the reader that Excel alone is not designed to be a marketing database.
6. John Kotter, "Leading change: Why transformation efforts fail," *Harvard Business Review*, March–April 1995.

Chapter 3

1. Robert Kaplan and David Norton, *The Balanced Score Card: Translating Strategy into Action* (Cambridge, MA: Harvard Business School Press, 1996).
2. This example is adapted from Arnold and Lane, *MasterCard International: World Championship Soccer Sponsorship* (HBS Case 500036, 1999).

Chapter 4

1. To hear the radio ad, visit www.agileinsights.com/ROMI.
2. This example is for illustrative purposes, assumes a static market, and makes high-level assumptions. The details of your business and customer base will drive the specific churn reduction impact for your firm.
3. Lasik is not for everyone. I highly recommend thoroughly checking it out with your doctor if you are considering the procedure.
4. Frederick F. Reichheld, "The one number you need to grow," *Harvard Business Review*, December 1, 2003.
5. Customer lifetime value (CLTV) includes the customer acquisition cost and is the best metric for figuring out if a customer is profitable and if/how that customer should be marketed to; see Chapter 6.

Chapter 5

1. See, for example: Morris Engleson, *Pricing Strategy: An Interdisciplinary Approach* (Portland, OR: Joint Management Strategy, 1995); and Thomas Nagle and John Hogan, *The Strategy and Tactics of Pricing: A Guide to Growing More Profitably*, 4th ed. (Upper Saddle River, NJ: Prentice Hall, 2005).
2. Students often say that they will take the $520K today and invest it, since this could be more than $614K. However, when making financial decisions, one should assume the investing and discount rate are the

same. If the rates are the same, then the relative value in the future will always be the same, and the $614K will be worth more than the $520K in 10 years if you invest at $r = 10\%$.

3. This is the textbook answer. In reality, funding is always limited or rationed. We discuss capital rationing and the importance of a marketing portfolio view in Chapter 11.

4. Richard Brealey, Stuart Meyers, and Franklin Allen, *Principles of Corporate Finance*, 9th ed. (New York: McGraw-Hill, 2009).

5. If the firm has debt, to calculate the share price subtract the debt from the value of the firm before dividing by the number of shares outstanding.

6. This example is completely hypothetical and the numbers were chosen for illustrative purposes only.

7. For the interested reader, multiply both sides of the NPV = 0 equation by $(1 + \text{IRR})^n$ and you will see that indeed the IRR is the rate the profit, $B_n - C_n$, in each time period is compounding.

8. To be rigorously correct $r_{\text{monthly}} = \sqrt[12]{(1 + r)} - 1$, where r is the annual return. I want to keep things simple, though, and for decision making, $r_{\text{monthly}} = r/12$ is close enough. A similar argument applies to IRR calculated on an annual versus monthly basis.

9. See, for example, Mark Jeffery and Saurabh Mishra, *Sony-FIFA Partnership Marketing Program: The Value of Sponsorship* (Harvard Business School Press, Prod. #: KEL195-PDF-ENG, 2006); and Mark Jeffery and Justin Williams, *DuPont-NASCAR Marketing* (Harvard Business School Press, Prod. #: KEL166-PDF-ENG, 2007).

10. For the detailed case study, see Mark Jeffery, James Anfield, and Tim Ritters, *B&K Distributors: ROI for a Web Based Customer Portal* (Harvard Business School Press, Prod. #: KEL149-PDF-ENG, 2006).

11. Clyde Stickney, Roman Weil, Jennifer Francis, and Katherine Schipper, *Financial Accounting: Introduction to Concepts, Methods and Uses* (Florence, KY: Cengage Learning, 2009).

12. If the CFO wants to see the financial ROMI of a branding campaign, then some education is necessary to explain that nonfinancial metrics don't work (see Chapter 4).

13. For detailed instructions, see Mark Jeffery and Chris Rzymski, *How to Perform Sensitivity Analysis with a Data Table* (Harvard Business School Press, Prod. #: KEL151-PDF-ENG, 2006).

Chapter 6

1. Traditionally, this topic falls under customer relationship management (CRM). However, CRM has fallen out of vogue in the last few years, and I believe value-based marketing is a more accurate description.

Chapter 7

1. As we will see later in the chapter, for rapid test and response SEM campaigns, you will most likely need to automate the analysis process with tools such as Omniture or Covario.
2. Today, the Google page rank algorithm includes multiple variables, such as bounce rate, essential metric 14, discussed later in this chapter.
3. Overture was originally named GoTo and was purchased by Yahoo! in 2003.
4. For natural search optimization, see *The Professional's Guide to PageRank Optimization*, available at www.seomoz.org.
5. For a detailed example of SEM click data analysis and optimization in Excel, see Mark Jeffery, Lisa Egli, Andy Gieraltowski, et al., *Optimizing Google, Yahoo!, MSN, and Kayak Sponsored Search* (Harvard Business School Press, Prod. #: KEL319-PDF-ENG, March 06, 2009). The click data set is available at www.agileinsights.com/ROMI, and you can actually do the analysis described in this section in Excel.
6. Ibid.
7. This discussion of bounce rate is adapted from Avinash Kaushik, *Web Analytics an Hour a Day* (Indiapolis, Indiana: Sybex, an imprint of John Wiley & Sons, Inc., 2007).
8. Gian M. Fulgoni and Marie Pauline Mörn, *How Online Advertising Works: Whither the Click?* Empirical Generalizations in Advertising Conference for Industry and Academia, Philadelphia: The Wharton School, December 4–5, 2008.

Chapter 8

1. Adapted from Mark Jeffery, Ichiro Aoyagi, and Ed Kalletta, *Marketing @ Microsoft: The Value of Customer Perception* (Harvard Business School Press, Prod. #: KEL189-PDF-ENG, 2006).
2. Mark Jeffery and Justin Williams, *DuPont-NASCAR Marketing* (Harvard Business School Press, Prod. #: KEL166-HCB-ENG, 2007).

Chapter 9

1. For details on how to build logistic regression models for direct marketing, see Bruce Ratner, *Statistical Modeling and Analysis for Database Marketing: Effective Techniques for Mining Big Data* (Boca Raton, FL: Chapman and Hall/CRC 2003), 32–86.
2. For the details, see Michael J. A. Berry and Gordon Linoff, *Data Mining Techniques*, 2nd ed. (Hoboken, NJ: John Wiley & Sons, 2004), 287–320.
3. Ibid., pp. 165–209.
4. Tree data mining algorithms are more sophisticated than a simple filter (a sieve), since they split the data in all possible ways and then figure out the best order to split to give the purest components.

5. A sample data set for this analysis is available online, and you can play with the analysis in SAS JMP on a PC. For the data and instructions, see www.agileinsights.com/ROMI.
6. Mark Jeffery, Robert J. Sweeney, Robert J. Davis, *ROI for a Customer Relationship Management Initiative at GST* (Harvard Business School Press, Prod. #: KEL232-PDF-ENG, January 1, 2006).

Chapter 10

1. Large organizations will most likely need to automate this process of campaign tracking and execution monitoring. The software to do this is called Marketing Resource Management (MRM), discussed in the next chapter on key marketing processes. Internet search engine marketing (SEM) will require more advanced tools also, such as Omniture or Covaro, but you can absolutely get started with Excel.
2. Data are stored in ones and zeros, the on and off of transistors. A single "1" or a "0" is called a bit; 8 bits are a byte, so 1 terabyte = 1 TB = 1,000,000,000,000 bytes = 8,000,000,000,000 bits of data.
3. See, for example, Mark Jeffery, Robert J. Sweeney, and Robert J. Davis, *Teradata Data Mart Consolidation Return on Investment at GST* (Harvard Business School Press, Prod. #: KEL196-PDF-ENG, 2006).
4. Michel Benaroch, Mark Jeffery, Robert Kauffman, and Sandeep Shah, "Option-based risk management: A field study of sequential information technology investment decisions," *Journal of Management Information Systems* 24 (2) (2007): 103–140.
5. Barbara Wixom and Hugh Watson, "An empirical investigation of the factors affecting data warehousing success, *MIS Quarterly* 25(1) (March 2001): 17–41.
6. Gary Loveman, "Diamonds in the data-mine," *Harvard Business Review*, May 1, 2003.
7. The Wright brothers' first flight was at Kitty Hawk, North Carolina, on December 17, 1903, on the sand dunes, selected because of the good winds and potential for a soft crash landing.

Chapter 11

1. "Will It Blend" videos: www.youtube.com/watch?v=qg1ckCkm8YI; accessed August 7, 2009.
2. Kate Klonick, "Will it blend?" *Esquire*, May 3, 2007.
3. The Qashqai TV ad: www.youtube.com/watch?v=El6OVFhipwM; accessed August 7, 2009.
4. Qashqai games videos: www.youtube.com/watch?v=xuVB_dLNu3k& feature=fvw; accessed August 7, 2009.

INDEX